Durkheim

Morality and Milieu

Durkheim

Morality and Milieu

Ernest Wallwork

Harvard University Press
Cambridge, Massachusetts
1972

© Copyright 1972 by the President and Fellows of Harvard College
All rights reserved
Library of Congress Catalog Card Number 70-188346
SBN 674-21865-5
Printed in the United States of America

The following publishers have granted permission to quote from works to which
they have rights: The Macmillan Company and Routledge and Kegan Paul, Ltd.,
for Jean Piaget's *Moral Judgment of the Child* and Emile Durkheim's *Professional
Ethics and Civic Morals, Sociology & Philosophy,* and *Suicide*; the Macmillan
Company for Emile Durkheim's *Moral Education* and *Education and Sociology*;
Presses Universitaires de France for Georges Davy's *Sociologues d'hier et
d'aujourd'hui* and Emile Durkheim's *L'Evolution pédagogique en France*; Prentice-
Hall, Inc., for Richard B. Brandt's *Ethical Theory*.

*To my mother, Irene Baldwin Wallwork,
and to my father, Ernest Edward Wallwork*

*Si vous voulez mûrir votre pensée,
attachez-vous à l'étude scrupuleuse
d'un grand maître, démontez un
système dans ses rouages les plus
secrets.*

Emile Durkheim

Preface

Emile Durkheim's stature as one of the principal architects of modern social science cannot be gainsaid. His work is used as an authoritative body of brilliant hypotheses and lucid empirical insights. Even those who have criticized him severely praise his perspicacity and draw more than they frequently acknowledge from his writings. Yet, despite widespread acquaintance with his fundamental ideas and high appreciation of his contributions, much of Durkheim's work relating to his moral philosophy has been ignored by American sociologists.

Realization of this striking lacuna in Durkheimian scholarship initially prompted an essay on previously neglected aspects of the French scholar's moral thought. As my study of the unacknowledged Durkheim progressed, I became increasingly convinced that he stood solidly in the classical tradition of moral philosophy that stemmed from Plato and Aristotle. All of the traditional issues of classical moral philosophy were at or near the center of Durkheim's thought, and it was this insight that eventually gave rise to the thesis of this book: namely, that many of the distinguishing characteristics of Durkheimian sociology derive from his interest in moral philosophy. This is true to such an extent that it is not an exaggeration to say that Durkheimian sociology is inseparable from, even a by-product of, his moral philosophy.

Inevitably, investigation of Durkheim's moral thought generated a fresh interpretation of his entire work. By concentrating upon less widely known essays and lectures, especially his early journal articles, hitherto unsuspected aspects of his thought were uncovered. The principal discoveries included new views vis-à-vis Durkheim's methodology, philosophy, social psychology, sociology, pedagogy, and ethical theory.

To those familiar with Durkheim, it is hoped that this book will provide new perspectives; to those unacquainted with Durkheim, it is hoped that this study will prove a useful introduction to an important dimension of his thought. Other legitimate intellectual portraits are possible, but none is apt to sound the depths of Durkheim's thought more profoundly than one devoted to his moral philosophy and its relationship to his sociology.

This book was originally presented as a doctoral dissertation at Harvard University and entitled "The Moral Philosophy of Emile Durkheim." It reflects the interdisciplinary nature of my doctoral training in theological ethics, philosophy, sociology, and psychology. I have interpreted Durkheim as an interdisciplinary figure partly because he was a moral philosopher as well as a social scientist, but also because I am convinced that there is a current need for responsible interdisciplinary work, especially in the human sciences and ethics. Thus, Durkheim is important not only as the French father of contemporary sociology, but also as a significant representative of the type of interdisciplinary study needed today.

I have interpreted Durkheim as a philosophical naturalist for similar reasons. Philosophical naturalism is not only the underlying perspective that gives unity to Durkheim's philosophy and sociology; it is also the source of his principal contributions to these fields. For the reasons expressed in the critical sections of this analysis and joined in the conclusion, I feel that a naturalistic moral philosophy provides the best means of integrating Durkheim's work with recent developments in psychology, sociology, and ethical theory.

Many individuals have directly and indirectly contributed to the preparation of this book and I express with pleasure my appreciation to them. To my thesis adviser, Professor Arthur Dyck, who read several drafts of the entire manuscript, I owe a special debt of gratitude for important substantive comments and editorial suggestions. Few graduate students have had as fortunate a relationship with their dissertation adviser as I have enjoyed. To Professor James Luther Adams and Professor Robert Bellah I owe the special thanks due stimulating teachers who initially kindled my interest in Durkheim and encouraged me along the way. I also wish to express my gratitude to several esteemed teachers who provided me with the intellectual background reflected on the pages of this manuscript, especially Professors Gordon Allport, James Dittes, Joseph Fichter, James Gustafson, David Little, H. Richard Niebuhr, Richard R. Niebuhr, Talcott Parsons, Herbert Richardson, and Robert W. White. My appreciation also goes to the Fund for Theological Education which provided me with a Rockefeller Doctoral Fellowship while working on this study and to Wellesley College for financial assistance in preparing the manuscript for publication. Finally, I wish to express my profound thanks to Doctors Gregor Goethals, Clifford Green, Roger Johnson, and Linda Miller for their supportive friendship and stimulating fellowship during the period in which this book was written.

Contents

Durkheim

Morality and Milieu

Abbreviations

AS	*L'Année sociologique*
RB	*Revue bleue*
RIE	*Revue internationale de l'enseignement*
RMM	*Revue de métaphysique et de morale*
RP	*Revue philosophique*

Introduction

Social philosophers wax and wane through intellectual history, most leaving but faint imprints on the sands of time. Occasionally, however, there is a seminal figure, usually at the outset of a new era of thought, who proposes views so manifestly original and penetrating that he seems, in retrospect, to have inaugurated a veritable intellectual revolution. Emile Durkheim was such a social philosopher. His career, even his severest critics acknowledge, was one of incredible achievement.

Only the briefest review of Durkheim's cultural impact is attempted here. The story of his manifold contributions to twentieth-century scholarship has been told many times.[1] For our purposes, it is sufficient to note that Durkheim not only helped launch critical re-examination and resulting disparagement of many nineteenth-century assumptions regarding human behavior, but he is also responsible, along with two or three other major scholars of his generation, for several of the basic presuppositions concerning the nature of man and society that characterize contemporary scholarship and popular thought.

Among these reformative presuppositions, Durkheim's fundamental concept of man as a "being-in-society" is especially important. Rarely has a concept in intellectual history had a wider cultural impact than the general notion that man is morally and spiritually "society's child," as a recent song puts it. In the social sciences and in such diverse fields as political science, education, philosophy, and theology, the concept of the "social self," which Durkheim helped introduce into modern thought, has largely supplanted, in the course of the twentieth century, the "rational self" of the Enlightenment and the "economic self" of the early nineteenth century. This is true to such an extent, in fact, that "sociological man" now clearly vies with Freud's "psychological man"

1. See Harry Alpert, *Emile Durkheim and His Sociology* (New York: Columbia University Press, 1939); Robert Bierstedt, *Emile Durkheim* (London: Weidenfeld and Nicolson, 1966); Robert Nisbet, *Emile Durkheim* (Englewood Cliffs, N.J.: Prentice-Hall, 1965); Talcott Parsons, *The Structure of Social Action* (Glencoe, Ill.: Free Press, 1949), pp. 301-450; Edward A. Tiryakian, *Sociologism and Existentialism* (Englewood Cliffs, N.J.: Prentice-Hall, 1962), pp. 11-68.

1

and Kierkegaard's "existential self," as "the dominant moral type of contemporary Western culture."[2]

No less significant with respect to its subsequent impact upon Western thought is Durkheim's cultural conception of society, a conception which entails viewing society as an interrelated system of shared beliefs and values.[3] Within the humanities, as well as the sciences of man, this conception of society has so thoroughly supplanted the organic and atomistic views dominant throughout most of Western history that pre-Durkheimian writers now seem strangely anachronistic to most modern readers.

No analysis of the impact of Durkheim's work would be complete without mention of the widespread influence of the numerous specific concepts, hypotheses, and empirical insights that he introduced into sociology and anthropology. As the works of Talcott Parsons, Robert Nisbet, Peter Berger, Robert Bellah, and many other scholars clearly demonstrate, Durkheim's writings have provided sociologists with a veritable gold mine of new ideas and fresh perspectives. His influence is so great, in fact, that it is safe to say that contemporary sociology would be very different indeed if it did not continue to benefit from the French scholar's treatment of structural functionalism, institutional differentiation, anomie, religion, and the like.

Yet, despite these several achievements and the high esteem in which he is generally held, Durkheim's qualities as a moral philosopher have seldom been given the attention they are due. Even his disciples and admirers invariably regard his lifelong quest for enlightenment vis-à-vis the classical problems of moral philosophy as ill-conceived and poorly executed. Or, to use the words of Melvin Richter: "Today even Durkheim's admirers consider as misguided his lifelong quest for a scientific ethic. It is his empirical insights, the problems he posed on that level, and the brilliant hypotheses he suggested which have made much of his work classic. Indeed, his efforts to derive normative prescriptions from social facts have come to appear increasingly curious, a question for the sociology of knowledge."[4] In short, students of Durkheim have perpetuated the legend of a man so lacking in philosophical acumen that it

2. Philip Reiff, *Freud: The Mind of the Moralist* (London: Victor Gollancz, Ltd., 1959), p. 4.

3. For a brief analysis of Durkheim's cultural sociology, see Werner Stark, *The Fundamental Forms of Social Thought* (New York: Fordham University Press, 1963), pp. 234-243.

4. Melvin Richter, "Durkheim's Politics and Political Theory," in *Emile Durkheim, 1858-1917*, ed. Kurt H. Wolff (Columbus: Ohio State University Press, 1960), p. 171.

is hard to understand why his conclusions regarding moral issues were ever seriously entertained—the legend of a perspicacious sociologist, who, like Columbus, failed to realize his lifelong quest.[5]

What can be said of this negative representation of Durkheim's moral thought? In seeking to answer this question, it is necessary to recall that classical moral philosophy, as understoood by Durkheim, was considerably broader than contemporary metaethics. From Plato to Durkheim, at least, Western moralists have considered five distinct, but related, questions: What is the nature of moral experience, and how is it to be explained? What factors account for the existence of conflicting ethical standards in different societies? How do we come to be moral both developmentally and pedagogically? What constitutes an adequate defense of moral standards, and which ethical standards are true or valid? What practical conclusions concerning personal behavior and social policy result from relating justified standards to relevant factual information? Once these distinctions among the perennial questions of classical moral philosophy are recognized, it becomes apparent that, whereas Durkheim attempted to enlighten all five of these traditional issues, his critics have chosen to focus their attack on his response to the fourth question, namely, his philosophical justification of ethical standards. With regard to Durkheim's explanatory theory of morality, his explanation of cross-cultural moral disagreements, his theory of moral education, and his practical conclusions, there seems to be considerable disagreement regarding the significance of Durkheim's contributions. Apparently, then, no accurate assessment of Durkheim's moral philosophy can be made in the absence of a careful and discriminating study of his moral thought as a complexly integrated whole.

Curiously, however, no major essay on Durkheim is devoted exclusively to these five interrelated aspects of his moral philosophy. As a consequence, none of the various elements of his moral philosophy, including his ethical theory, have received the careful attention and close scrutiny required to adequately assess his achievements in this field of scholarship. The present essay seeks to close this lacuna in Durkheimian scholarship by examining: his scientific theory of morality, his explanation of differing moral standards, his theory of moral education, his ethical theory, and his practical conclusions.

Chapter I lays the groundwork for this analysis by examining the methodological, philosophical, and sociological perspectives that domi-

5. See, for example, Georges Gurvitch, *Essais de sociologie* (Paris: Librairie du Recueil Sirey, 1938), p. 279.

nate Durkheim's work as a whole. His early dialectical resolution of the several basic philosophical issues examined in this chapter are essential for an adequate understanding of his moral and social thought.

The second and third chapters deal with the evolution of Durkheim's *science de la morale,* including his phenomenological description of moral experience and his explanation of it. Chapter II explores the young Durkheim's early assumptions regarding psychological motivation and socially induced moral obligation. Beginning with the moral theory in *Suicide,* Chapter III traces the gradual development of Durkheim's mature science of morality.

Durkheim's explanation of differing moral standards gets under way in Chapter IV. This explanation is related to his complex theory of social and moral evolution in various societies, including domestic groups, occupational associations, and political societies.

Chapter V explores Durkheim's response to the core question of moral education: how do we come to be moral both developmentally and pedagogically? Although Durkheim stressed pedagogical, as contrasted with developmental, factors in the emergence of moral man, both factors are involved, as they have been since the early days of Greek philosophy, in his treatment of this important issue.

Chapter VI analyzes Durkheim's treatment of specifically ethical issues as well as his utilization of justified norms to resolve several significant practical problems. Beginning with his brilliant critique of the dominant ethical theories of the nineteenth century, this chapter examines the development of Durkheim's own metaethical and normative theories. This development parallels that presented in earlier chapters of the present study.

Each of these major sections on salient aspects of Durkheim's moral philosophy concludes with a brief critical evaluation. The results of these several critical analyses are joined in the conclusion, which returns to the question posed at the outset of this introduction regarding the overall significance and value of Durkheim's moral philosophy.

I

Philosophical and Sociological Innovations

Methodological Characteristics

As a first step in untangling the complex threads in Durkheim's basic orientation toward the traditional issues of moral philosophy, several characteristics of his methodology must be noted. Although Durkheim saw himself as an empirical scientist and never failed to stress the importance of studying empirical facts, he was, like his great contemporaries Freud and Pareto, a philosophical system builder in the classical tradition of system builders. Accordingly, Durkheim not only tends to move back and forth, as most systematic scholars do, between philosophical assumptions, theoretical insights, and empirical observations, but he also follows other system builders in neither starting to solve, nor ultimately resolving, any major issue without implicitly committing himself to the solution of many others. It is an important characteristic of Durkheim's method to commit himself on ontological, epistemological, and ethical matters in the context of discussing strictly scientific issues.

A second characteristic of Durkheim's method is the dialectical manner with which he approaches virtually every major philosophical and theoretical issue. As Henri Peyre rightly observes, Durkheim was "a master of dialectics."[1] Despite his vigorous verbal opposition to the dialectical games popular among French philosophers in the late nineteenth century and despite his apparent use of the so-called *argumentum per eliminationem*,[2] Durkheim invariably sets forth antithetical views that are brilliantly criticized and seemingly discarded until they are joined, in modified form, in his own unique synthesis.[3]

1. Henri Peyre, "Durkheim: The Man, His Time and His Intellectual Background," in *Emile Durkheim*, ed. Wolff, p. 11.
2. For a discussion of Durkheim's apparent utilization of the *argumentum per eliminationem*, see Alpert, *Emile Durkheim*, pp. 87-89.
3. Durkheim's dialectical method is frequently mentioned in *mémoires* written by those who knew him best. Although Bouglé, Davy, Fauconnett, and Maublanc differ in their interpretations of Durkheim's thought, they all mention his ability to synthesize insights drawn from a wide range of sources. As Maublanc, who studied with Durkheim at the Sorbonne, recalls: "Il étudiait avec nous, en 1911, des questions variées du programme classique de philosophie: l'altruisme et l'égoisme, le concept, la croyance, les devoirs envers soi-même, l'utilitarisme, la

Durkheim's frequent use of the dialectical method has unfortunately passed unnoticed by most of his American interpreters. When his views are considered in relation to those contained in the works upon which he relied, however, there can be no doubt about either his tendency to glean insights from a broad range of philosophical and scientific sources or the perspicacious manner in which these views are joined in a unique synthesis. On the one hand, Durkheim was a true conservative (in the best sense of that misused term), desirous of preserving the insights of the past by seeking a delicate balance between opposing views. He did not hesitate, therefore, to go to Plato and Aristotle, Kant and Renouvier, Montesquieu and Rousseau for sustenance and support. They were concerned, as he was, with the great issues and, above all, with the moral quality of human existence. On the other hand, Durkheim was an intellectual radical who invariably rejected traditional formulas in favor of new, and often strkingly original, ideas. This makes his thought as a whole intense and vital, ambiguous and adventurous, characteristics that make his position on any issue difficult to grasp, much less to expound. Caution is necessary in attempting to understand Durkheim's views, although caution has not always been exercised.

The failure of most sociological interpretations of Durkheim to recognize the extent to which he was a dialectician apparently stems from two sources. The dialectical method he utilized to develop his most characteristic assumptions in early articles (those published between 1885 and 1893) has often been missed precisely because these articles, for some inscrutab‚é reason, have been widely ignored. Also, most interpreters have grossly overestimated the importance of *The Rules of the Sociological Method* for his work as a whole.[4] Preoccupied with emphasizing the scientific study of empirical facts, sociological students of Durkheim have generally approached him through several abstruse, positivist statements in *The Rules,* rather than through the dialectically constructed philosophical premises and theoretical assumptions elaborated during the decade of productive scholarship Durkheim devoted to

conscience morale, l'ascétisme, la famille, la patrie. En une heure, de quelques formules assénées sur l'auditoire, il renouvelait la question la plus rebattue, et, brassant tous les systèmes, faisait sortir de leur contradictions une synthèse neuve, la solution sociologique. Alors chacun des assistants, favorable ou hostile, aplati ou rebondissant, sentait obscurément qu'il avait devant lui un des grands héros de la pensée humaine, l'équivalent d'un Aristote, d'un Descartes, d'un Spinoza ou d'un Kant." (René Maublanc, "Durkheim Professeur de Philosophie," in a series of articles entitled "L'Oeuvre sociologique d'Emile Durkheim," by Célestin Bouglé *et al., Europe,* XXII [1930] , 297-298.)

4. For further discussion of this overestimation of the importance of *The Rules,* see Jack Douglas, *The Social Meanings of Suicide* (Princeton, N.J.: Princeton University Press, 1967), pp. 13-15, 22-25.

a careful critique of other social philosophers before publishing his first major book, *The Division of Labor,* in 1893 and *The Rules* in 1895. As a result, few scholars have recognized that Durkheim's avowed methodological ideal in *The Rules* only slightly resembles his actual method.

Whether Durkheim was aware of the crucial importance of his own dialectically formulated presuppositions has been questioned since, in concluding *The Rules,* he says that: "Because sociology was initially a product of great philosophical doctrines, it has retained the habit of depending on the philosophical systems with which it was formerly united. Thus, it has been successively positivist, evolutionary, and idealist, when it should have been content to be nothing but sociology . . . Sociology does not have to decide among the great hypotheses which divide metaphysicians. It does not have to embrace free will any more than determinism."[5]

It is not surprising that these lines, written at a time when Durkheim was anxious to establish the independence of sociology as an empirical science, should lead countless readers, and more than a few interpreters, to conclude that Durkheim felt that sociology could eschew all philosophical assumptions. Even the most sympathetic reader must admit that during the period between publication of *The Division of Labor* in 1893 and *Suicide* in 1897 the young Durkheim tended to slight the philosophical presuppositions underlying his actual approach to his subject matter. In fairness to Durkheim, however, it should be observed that the methodological views elaborated during this period presuppose the dialectically constructed premises presented in journal articles written by him between 1885 and 1893. The point of the passage cited above is not the complete independence of sociology from philosophy; it is, rather, that sociology has been vitiated by *excessive dependence* upon particular philosophical systems and by unwarranted metaphysical assumptions regarding determinism.

Durkheim makes it clear elsewhere in his early writings that, while an empirical science like sociology can eschew some philosophical issues, it ultimately rests upon several crucial assumptions. In addition to the major presuppositions that will be closely analyzed in subsequent sections of the present chapter, Durkheim explicitly includes among these assumptions the unity of nature,[6] the intelligible structure of the

---

5. Emile Durkheim, *Les Règles de la méthode sociologique* (Paris: Librairie Félix Alcan, 1895), pp. 172-173.
6. Emile Durkheim, "La Science positive de la morale en Allemagne," *RP,* XXIV (1887), 45. Cf. Durkheim, *Le Socialisme: sa définition, ses débuts, la doctrine Saint-Simonienne,* ed. Marcel Mauss (Paris: Félix Alcan, 1928), p. 138. *Le Socialisme* was written for a series of lectures delivered at the University of Bordeaux during the academic year 1895-96.

natural world,[7] the assumption that the human mind is capable of comprehending the logical articulation of natural phenomena,[8] the principle that a whole is greater than the sum of its parts,[9] and the principle of causality as expressed in the form "every scientific fact has a cause."[10]

Durkheim nowhere provides a systematic defense of any of these basic postulates. With Renouvier's dictum "il faut choisir" in mind, he simply confesses the necessity of selecting essential propositions at the outset of every inquiry.[11] The fact that Durkheim explicitly recognizes the inevitability of choosing presuppositions is, however, sufficient to demonstrate the error of assuming that, in attempting to establish the independence of sociology from metaphysics, Durkheim "begins by rejecting the assumption that sociology needs to rest on any philosophical presuppositions whatever."[12] Far from maintaining such a patently absurd position, Durkheim states that sociology, like every other discipline, rests upon philosophical postulates. What he denies is the assumption that the sociologist must begin his career by choosing among all "the great hypotheses which divide metaphysicians." This mediating position liberated Durkheim from the necessity of conforming to any single philosophical system, including French positivism. Thus freed, Durkheim could employ his considerable dialectical gifts criticizing other social philosophers and synthesizing ideas and insights gleaned from a wide range of philosophical and scientific sources.[13] This contention requires the supporting evidence provided by a careful analysis of the several major philosophical assumptions and theoretical insights contained within the articles published by Durkheim between 1885 and 1893.

7. Emile Durkheim, "Montesquieu's Contribution to the Rise of Social Science" (1892) in *Montesquieu and Rousseau: Forerunners of Sociology*, tr. Ralph Manheim (Ann Arbor: University of Michigan Press, 1960), pp. 10-13. This is a translation of Durkheim's Latin dissertation, *Quid Secundatus politicae scientiae instituendae contulerit*, which was printed originally at Bordeaux in 1892 by the Imprimerie Gounouilhou.
8. *Ibid.*
9. Durkheim, "Morale en Allemagne, p. 37; "Cours de science sociale: Leçon d'ouverture," *RIE*, XV (1888), 30.
10. *Ibid.*, pp. 26-28.
11. *Ibid.*, pp. 28, 46-47.
12. Emile Benoit-Smullyan, "The Sociologism of Emile Durkheim and His School," in *An Introduction to the History of Sociology*, ed. Harry Elmer Barnes (Chicago: University of Chicago Press, 1948), p. 501.
13. Realizing the importance of this approach in his own systematic work, Durkheim defended the dialectical method against narrow empiricism in his 1904-1905 lectures on "l'Histoire de l'enseignement en France." See Durkheim, *L'Evolution pédagogique en France* (Paris: Félix Alcan, 1938), I, 197.

Two interconnected philosophical perspectives lie at the heart of Durkheim's early writings. The first is his unique position concerning the issues at stake in the great nineteenth-century debate between idealists and naturalists regarding the place of values in the world of nature. For want of a better term, this aspect of Durkheim's basic perspective will be described as "neonaturalism." Closely related to this perspective is Durkheim's oft noted, but unique, conception of society as a reality *sui generis.* This second perspective will be referred to as "relational social realism," although it might also be described, from a historical point of view, as "neosocial realism." Taken together, these two basic perspectives, constitute the philosophical foundations upon which Durkheim's entire scholarship rests.

Neonaturalism

Durkheim's early position regarding the great debate in modern philosophy between naturalists and idealists is of particular interest, both for itself and for insight into Durkheim's thought. So significant is Durkheim's acceptance and critique of the major contentions of both idealists and naturalists that it is necessary to begin by placing his unique neonaturalist perspective within a broad historical context.[14]

While Durkheim's thought was maturing, philosophers and scientists were still meditating on several problems introduced by the rise of modern science, particularly the place of mental or spiritual phenomena in a world of brute facts. Scientists were preoccupied with the so-called external world of objective facts, while idealistically inclined philosophers treated the human mind or spirit in a metaempirical or nonscientific manner. Thus the world of objective facts was set against the realm of ideas and ideals, and matter was contrasted with spirit. These conflicts were, of course, essentially continuations of Cartesian dualism, which was itself a product of the new conception of nature introduced by Galileo and Newton. According to Galileo, nature was a purely mechanical system governed by the laws of dynamics. Nature, thus conceived, excluded everything qualitative, with the result that nature was set over against its knower, man. Man was regarded by Galileo as existing outside nature precisely because a natural world consisting of mere quantity obviously had to have its apparent qualitative aspects bestowed upon it from without, namely, by a human mind external to

14. For an excellent analysis of the various forms of naturalism discussed in this section, see Yervant H. Krikorian, ed., *Naturalism and the Human Spirit* (New York: Columbia University Press, 1944), esp. John Herman Randall, Jr. "Epilogue: The Nature of Naturalism," pp. 354-382.

it.[15] A fundamental dualism was thereby introduced between man's mind or spirit on the one hand and nature on the other. The rich varieties of human experience—artistic, moral, religious, even intellectual—became subjective, with the eventual result that "even the existence in man's experience of the science of mechanics itself became an enigma."[16]

Although a number of complex philosophical problems resulted from this subject-object split, it is sufficient to note one of several central issues: Can human ideas and ideals be equated with other natural phenomena? On this issue, materialists and evolutionary naturalists took the affirmative side against dualistic supernaturalists, monistic idealists, and nonrationalists. Unfortunately, the concept of nature shared by both protagonists and antagonists in this controversy permitted no adequate solution to the central problem at stake, namely, the status of human ideas and values in the world of nature.

According to early materialistic naturalists, all qualitative differences were reducible to quantitative differences, all mental phenomena to material entities, processes, and events. In other words, naturalism was identified with materialism and then employed in the systematic reduction of all distinctively human experiences, moral, aesthetic, logical, to blind mechanistic processes. In the late nineteenth century, other forms of naturalism, less metaphysically presumptuous than early scientific materialism, were developed. With regard to ultimate reality, these new forms of naturalism were frankly agnostic. Their advocates refused, for example, to assert that material atoms and their lawful dynamics constitute the whole of reality. Hence, the term "higher naturalism" was coined to designate these more modest claims.[17] In their interpretation of the world of the human spirit, however, these forms of naturalism (Darwin's biologism is an example) continued to perpetuate opposition to the spiritual or ideal that had characterized crude materialism. As a result, the spiritual factor in reality was still held to be dependent on nonspiritual causal factors. Thus, while these so-called higher forms of naturalism abandoned metaphysical materialism and tended to find more in nature than material particles, they persisted in explaining the higher by the lower, the distinctively human by the subhuman, the spiritual by the material or the biological.

15. See R. G. Collingwood, *The Idea of Nature* (Oxford, Eng.: Clarendon Press, 1945), pp. 102-103.
16. Randall, "Epilogue," p. 371.
17. I am indebted here to William Quillian's excellent discussion of "higher naturalism" in *The Moral Theory of Evolutionary Naturalism* (New Haven, Conn.: Yale University Press, 1945), ch. 1, pp. 1-12.

Against this reductionism, idealists and dualists of varying convictions maintained that thought or spirit composes, above the physical world, a moral, an intellectual, an aesthetic, a religious world, which is, nevertheless, real. Science deals only with facts; reason or spirit, with a realm that cannot be reduced to, or explained by, material elements or biological evolution. In this spirit, Émile Boutroux, Durkheim's esteemed teacher at the École Normale Supérieure,[18] directed a vigorous protest against "those overzealous 'fanatical' scientists who would reduce the universe to a mere mechanism governed by rigid physical necessity, who would place all things under the aegis of science, and who insisted that science is the only source of knowledge and that there can be no truth which cannot be expressed in mathematical terms."[19] Boutroux argued that another source of knowledge, more nearly infallible than science, is the human spirit or reason.

By the time Durkheim began studying philosophy and science in the 1870's and 1880's, several leading scholars on both sides of this controversy were beginning to formulate mediating perspectives which contained the seeds of the neonaturalist perspective some of their students would embrace.[20] Although numerous battles remained to be fought, some idealists like Boutroux were beginning to adopt a more favorable attitude toward the sciences. Boutroux, for instance, joined criticism of the metaphysical pretensions of materialism and biologism with celebration of strictly empirical studies. Far from discrediting science, Boutroux actually exalted "the mission of science by showing that its discoveries contributed to moral and intellectual advance, as well as to physical well-being."[21] In addition, Boutroux and other idealists began to search for a modus vivendi with the new scientific *Weltanschauung* by carefully analyzing the assumptions and methods of the several empirical sciences. In the process of adopting a less polemical attitude toward science, however, the philosophy of these idealists became increasingly scientific as they accepted some of the categories and methods of the sciences.

18. Durkheim expresses his high regard for Boutroux in the dedication of *De la division du travail social: étude sur l'organisation des sociétés supérieures* (Paris: Félix Alcan, 1893): "A mon cher maître M. Emile Boutroux: Hommage respectueux et reconnaissant." All references to *La Division du travail* are to the first edition unless otherwise indicated.

19. Lucy S. Crawford, *The Philosophy of Emile Boutroux* (New York: Longmans, Green and Company, 1924), p. 100.

20. John Herman Randall, Jr., provides an excellent historical analysis of the idealistic and scientific roots of this convergence toward a new form of naturalism in "Epilogue," pp. 372-374.

21. Crawford, *Emile Boutroux*, p. 100.

At the same time, scientists were showing an increased interest in avoiding metaphysics on the one hand and reductionism on the other in their explanations of psychological and cultural phenomena. This was especially true of social scientists in France, whose desire to contribute to national recovery after the humiliating defeat suffered during the Franco-Prussian War of 1870-1871 included a desire to avoid further internal dissension between idealists and scientists. The clarion call for a realistic sociological approach to the problems of France that was issued by Louis Liard after the war eschewed all hostility toward idealism.[22] In a genuine sense, leading scientists in France were arriving at the same qualified naturalism that science-minded idealists were reaching via another route.

Despite the idealist education he received at the École Normale Supérieure, Durkheim approached the time-honored conflict between idealists and naturalists from the naturalist or positivist side. With other naturalists, Durkheim began by assuming that everything that exists or occurs, however "spiritual" or "psychological," resides within one all-embracing system of nature. In other words, he agreed with other naturalists that all human phenomena occur within the natural world, against which such phenomena had so often been set. Durkheim was thus opposed to all dualism between nature and another realm of being, including the fundamental dualism between man and nature pervading modern thought. Opposition to dualistic divisions, however, is merely the negative side of Durkheim's naturalism. Positively, he advocates with other naturalists the extension of the scientific method into those regions from which it had hitherto been excluded. Despite the profound differences which separate Durkheim from earlier naturalists, then, he is united with them in his wholehearted acceptance of scientific method as the most reliable way of arriving at truths concerning the world of nature, society, and man.

22. For a brief discussion of this desire to avoid further internal dissension among scholars, see Célestin Bouglé, *The French Conception of "Culture Générale" and Its Influence upon Instruction* (New York: Bureau of Publications, Teachers College, Columbia University, 1938), p. 18. Bouglé notes that "Louis Liard, who was soon to group the Faculties into Universities, with the object of co-ordinating their efforts and spreading their influence, explained his action by saying that after 1871, France needed a bath in realism. What did he mean by that? Did he mean that the French should become utilitarian? Scarcely. That they should repudiate all idealism? He would not have gone so far, for he has demonstrated that positive science does not exclude, but on the contrary favors, metaphysics. But to begin with a better knowledge of social realities, in order to understand better the limits of the possible and the force of necessity—in other words, to remember that methodical and collective action implies before all else a knowledge of the groundwork—such was the program that he would have wished to give us."

However, Durkheim was sufficiently convinced by the major contentions of idealists to reject earlier forms of naturalism that either ignored higher forms of human thought and experience or simply explained them away. With the idealist critics of naturalism, he insisted that phenomenal data be accepted as given in experience. Consequently, Durkheim invariably accepted the phenomenological descriptions of moral and religious experience bequeathed to him by idealist philosophers. Yet he maintained, against idealists, that these higher forms of human experience are phenomena of nature.[23] Man himself, including his mind, is a part of the natural world. As a corollary, it follows that the subject matter of idealism, with all its sensitivity to the rich range of human experience, may be subjected to scientific analysis. To extend the scientific method into those sacred regions from which it was formerly excluded without, at the same time, ignoring or denying the distinctive characteristics of this immensely rich world of experience, was the goal of the young Durkheim. What is truly significant about Durkheim is not, then, his use of terms drawn from the worn baggage of naturalism and positivism, but his fundamental notion that "the faculty of ideation" is "a natural faculty for which conditions and causes can be found."[24]

Since Durkheim's chosen field of specialization was the study of morality, this neonaturalist perspective first appears in his early discussion of moral phenomena.[25] In the lengthy series of articles on "La Science positive de la morale en Allemagne," which established his reputation as a gifted scholar within French academic circles, Durkheim states that there are "only two kinds of moral theory in France: that of idealists and Kantians on the one side, that of utilitarians on the other."[26] The former have accurately described moral experience, although their transcendentalism precludes scientists from attempting to account for moral phenomena naturalistically. Thus, most German moralists "make psychic life something completely distinct from everything in the

23. "Or, pour la psychologie contemporaine, les faits psychologiques, moraux et sociaux, si élevés et si complexes qu'ils puissent être sont cependant des phénomènes naturels au même titre que les autres." (Durkheim, "Morale en Allemagne," p. 45.)

24. Emile Durkheim, "Value Judgments and Judgments of Reality" (1911), in *Sociology and Philosophy*, tr. D. F. Pocock (London: Cohen and West, Ltd., 1953), p. 96. Although this succinct statement is drawn from a relatively late work, similar observations can be found in Durkheim's early articles. See, for example, "Morale en Allemagne," pp. 33, 45, 278.

25. "Neonaturalism," in this context, refers to that form of naturalism that both accepts the rich complexity of phenomenal data as given in experience and avoids crude forms of reductionism.

26. "Morale en Allemagne," p. 33.

world. All of them more or less explicit admit that there is a complete break in continuity in the scale of beings; the word *Natur* indicates to them nature minus man."[27] Science-minded utilitarians, Durkheim continues, have correctly recognized the possibility of providing a naturalistic explanation of morality, but they have failed to accurately describe the phenomena in question. In short, "the Kantians make of morality a specific, but transcedent fact, which escapes science; the utilitarians [consider morality] a fact of experience, but one which is not specific."[28]

From the outset of his career, Durkheim's main problem was to explain scientifically the phenomena which he felt idealists had accurately described. In order to achieve this goal, the abandonment of dualism was necessary. Realizing this, Durkheim argued that as long as the spiritual aspect of reality was placed outside of nature, psychological and sociological analysis of morality and religion was impossible. The gulf separating man from nature had first to be overcome if psychologists and sociologists were to get on with their task.

People were for centuries so accustomed to thinking of such an abyss between the physical world and the so-called human world, they failed for a long time to accept the fact that the basic principles of the former are applicable to the latter. Whence the general tendency to put man and societies outside of nature, to make of the sciences of human life, whether individual or social, sciences set apart and without analogies even among the higher natural sciences . . . In order to surmount this obstacle, it was necessary to repudiate dualism; and the only way to accomplish this was to acquire and inculcate a lively sense of the unity of human knowledge.[29]

27. *Ibid.*, p. 48.
28. *Ibid.*, p. 278. Eleven years later Durkheim expressed essentially the same viewpoint in the course of discussing introspection and psychophysiology: "The old introspectionists were content to describe mental phenomena without trying to explain them; psycho-physiology explained them but dismissed their distinctive traits as negligible. A third school is being born which is trying to explain them without destroying their specificity. For the first mental life certainly had a nature of its own, but it was one that lifted the mental out of the world and above the ordinary methods of science. For the second school it was nothing in itself, and the role of the scientist was to pierce the superficial stratum in order to arrive at the underlying realities . . . It is [in the third school] . . . that this *spirituality* by which we characterize intellectual facts, and which seemed in the past to be either above or below the attentions of science, has become itself the object of a positive science, and that, between the ideology of the introspectionists and biological naturalism, a psychological naturalism has been founded, the legitimacy of which the present article will, perhaps, help to demonstrate." (Durkheim, "Individual and Collective Representations," [1898], in *Sociology and Philosophy*, pp. 32-33.)
29. Emile Durkheim, "La Sociologie en France au XIXe siècle," *RB*, XIII (1900), 610.

In brief, the sciences of man are founded on the assumption that "there are not two worlds in the world, one which is amenable to scientific observation, and the other which escapes it. The universe is one, and the same method must serve to explore it in all of its parts."[30]

To say that moral and religious phenomena occur within the world of nature and can be studied scientifically is one thing, but to assume that these phenomena can be completely reduced to, or explained by, material or biological factors is quite different. Durkheim explicitly rejected all traditional forms of reductionism. In the first edition of *The Division of Labor,* he states:

the major part of psychic phenomena does not derive from organic causes. This is what idealist philosophers have realized, and the great service that they have rendered science has been to combat all doctrines that reduce psychic life to a mere efflorescence of physical life. They have quite correctly perceived that the first, in its highest manifestations, is much too free and complex to be merely a prolongation of the second. Because it is partly independent of the organism, however, it does not follow that it depends upon no natural cause, and that it must be placed outside of nature.[31]

Similarly, Durkheim observes in the preface to *The Rules* that his position is closer to idealism than to materialism, for "Is not the essence of idealism in fact contained in the idea that psychological phenomena cannot be immediately derived from organic phenomena. Now our method is in part only an application of this principle."[32] Yet Durkheim refuses to describe himself as an idealist, stating in this context that "scientific rationalism" is the only designation he will accept. Durkheim's rationalism, however, is simply another form of his neonaturalism. Rationalism, he explained some years later, means that "there is nothing in reality that one is justified in considering as fundamentally beyond the scope of human reason."[33]

The first of the two basic philosophical perspectives that pervades Durkheim's work as a whole thus turns out, upon close analysis, to be the genuinely new, third, and mediating position between philosophical idealism and reductionistic naturalism which the term neonaturalism, as used in the present essay, is intended to express. With idealists, Durk-

30. Durkheim, *Socialisme,* pp. 138-139.
31. Durkheim, *Division du travail,* p. 389.
32. Durkheim, *Règles,* p. vii.
33. Emile Durkheim, *Moral Education,* tr. Everett K. Wilson and Herman Schnurer (New York: Free Press, 1961), p. 4. A translation of lectures delivered at the Sorbonne in 1902-1903 and posthumously entitled *L'Éducation morale* (Paris: Félix Alcan, 1925).

heim analyzes the distinctive qualities of moral and religious experience and rejects all traditional forms of reductionism. Yet he assumes, with naturalists, that the spiritual factor in reality occurs within the natural order. Years later, Durkheim himself succinctly summarized this point of departure:

Sociology moves from the beginning in the field of ideals—that is its starting-point and not the gradually attained end of its researches. The ideal is in fact its peculiar field of study. But . . . sociology cannot deal with the ideal except as a science. It does not set out to construct ideals, but on the contrary accepts them as given facts, as objects of study, and it tries to analyse and explain them. In the faculty of ideation (*faculté d'idéal*), sociology sees a natural faculty for which conditions and causes can be found . . . The aim is to bring the ideal, in its various forms, into the sphere of nature, with its distinctive attributes unimpaired.[34]

This starting point, as the last sentence indicates, was also the goal of Durkheim's work. It was his wish to be remembered for having achieved, in some limited sense, the aim of bringing moral and religious phenomena within the sphere of nature. An indication of fulfillment is the fact that his successors, despite significant differences, continue to invoke his name and his accomplishments in defense of similar ambitions. Thus, whatever the errors and lacunae in Durkheim's descriptive analysis and theoretical explanation of "ideation," he achieved his goal in one sense: he set social scientists in pursuit of the ideal.

Relational Social Realism

Durkheim not only discovered neonaturalism; he also discovered what had eluded earlier social scientists: a conception of society within which insights gleaned from several philosophical traditions could be fused and by which sociology could be launched upon new paths in the twentieth century. This is the cultural conception of society which Durkheim helped introduce into modern thought, a conception which is inseparable from the second basic philosophical perspective that dominates Durkheim's work as a whole, namely, "relational social realism."[35] Essentially, Durkheim's realistic conception of society rests

34. Durkheim, "Value Judgments and Judgments of Reality," p. 96.
35. For a careful analysis of Durkheim's relational social realism, see Alpert, *Emile Durkheim*, pp. 151-157. In summarizing his discussion, Alpert observes that relational or associational realism is "so termed because it claims that association is a real, generative process and that society as a system of relations is a reality" (p. 156).

upon the assumption that there exists, within the realm of nature, an entity designated by the term "society," defined as a system or network of relations, which is responsible for engendering collectively shared beliefs and norms. In other words, some (albeit not all) ideas and ideals not only occur within the realm of nature, but arise within, and function in relationship to, the relational system or whole denoted by the term "society." These social relations, as well as the phenomena engendered by them, are existent facts, that is, they have reality, though generally a spiritual or ideal rather than a physical or material reality.

This social entity, Durkheim further contends, is a reality *sui generis* which has a distinct existence and a nature peculiar to it.[36] As a corollary, argues Durkheim, it follows that collectively shared ideas or representations cannot be reduced to, or explained by, facts less complex than those governing social interaction. Just as the existence of physiological phenomena cannot be accounted for simply by the chemical properties of atoms, and just as the psychological phenomena of consciousness cannot be explained by the physiological properties of cerebral cells, similarly social phenomena cannot be explained by factors less complex than those governing social existence. The interaction of associated individuals gives rise to emergent phenomena, analogous to the way chemical elements combine in a genuinely new synthesis.[37]

In speaking of society as a reality *sui generis,* Durkheim voices a dominant note in the French sociological tradition stretching from Saint-Simon and Comte through Espinas.[38] Durkheim's realism is to be

36. Durkheim, "Morale en Allemagne," p. 37, "Cours de science sociale," p. 30, and *Socialisme,* p. 140.

37. Bouglé explains this aspect of Durkheim's thought in the following manner: "In Durkheim's eyes, true social reality depends on representations, but on collective representations, the particular characteristics of which must not be mistaken. They are due, not only to the contact of mind, but to a kind of chemical synthesis, which reveals more, when it has taken place, than is to be found in the constituent elements." (Bouglé, *"Culture Générale,"* p. 23.) For similar observations, see Tiryakian, *Sociologism and Existentialism,* pp. 14-15.

38. The following works contain admirable studies of the French social realist tradition: Durkheim, "Cours de science sociale," "Sociologie en France au XIXe siècle," and *Socialisme;* Raymond Aron, *Main Currents in Sociological Thought* (New York: Basic Books, 1965), I, chs, i, ii, iv, v; Emile Benoit-Smullyan, "The Development of French Sociologistic Theory and Its Critics in France," unpub. Ph.D. diss., Harvard University, 1937, I, chs. i, ii, pp. 1-130; Claude Lévi-Strauss, "French Sociology," in *Twentieth Century Sociology,* ed. Georges Gurvitch and Wilbert E. Moore (New York: Philosophical Library, 1945), ch. xvii; Lucien Lévy-Bruhl, *History of Modern Philosophy* (London: Kegan Paul, Trench, Trübner, and Company, 1899); Frank E. Manuel, *The Prophets of Paris* (Cambridge, Mass.: Harvard University Press, 1962); Robert A. Nisbet, *Emile Durkheim,* ch. i; Sheldon S. Wolin, *Politics and Vision* (Boston: Little, Brown and Company, 1960), ch. x.

distinguished from other representations of this tradition, however, insofar as he explicitly calls attention to the fact that his own version of sociological realism represents a third and mediating position between two extreme alternative conceptions of society. This time the two extremes are represented by sociological nominalism and "substantial social realism."[39] Despite Durkheim's vigorous rejection of the atomistic assumption that a society is simply an aggregate or sum of individuals, he does accept the nominalist contention that a human society cannot be separated from the individuals who compose it.[40] Accordingly, Durkheim rejects the substantialist interpretation of sociological realism according to which "society is an ontological reality, a substantial entity having corporate existence apart from, or, to use the traditional phrase, over and above, the individuals who comprise it."[41] Against this substantialist contention, Durkheim argues that a "society . . . has nothing metaphysical about it."[42] A social system "is not a more or less transcendental substance; it is a whole composed of parts . . . Since there are only individuals in society, they, and they alone, are the factors of social life."[43] In other words, Durkheim's position is one of "relational realism," where, by the latter term, is meant a conception of society which views a social system as a network of actual relations. These relations and the phenomena engendered by them are facts, albeit often nonmaterial facts, which genuinely exist. These facts exist neither apart from individuals nor in any single individual taken in isolation, for they only exist in and among associated individuals.

Durkheim views society in two different ways, which generally complement each other. On the one hand, he sees society as an interdepen-

39. "Sociological nominalism" may be defined as the philosophical doctrine that views society as merely a plurality or sum of independent individuals who, complete in their autonomy, derive nothing from their relatedness. For early statements by Durkheim regarding sociological nominalism, see "Morale en Allemagne," p. 37, and "Cours de science sociale," p. 30. In contradistinction to sociological nominalism, "substantial social realism" accords ontological reality to the social whole as against its parts. For a fuller definition of substantial social realism, see Alpert, *Emile Durkheim*, p. 151.

40. Durkheim, "Morale en Allemagne," p. 37, and "Cours de science sociale," p. 30. Alpert cites a number of later "occasions on which Durkheim insisted that 'individuals are the only active elements in society,' that 'it is an evident truth that there is nothing in social life which is not in individual consciousnesses,' that 'society is not possible without individuals,' that 'society can exist only in individual consciousnesses and through them,' that 'society exists and lives only in and by individuals . . . (and) has reality only to the extent that it has a place in human consciousnesses.' " (Alpert, *Emile Durkheim*, p. 152.)

41. *Ibid.*, p. 151.

42. Durkheim, "Gumplowicz, Ludwig, *Grundriss der Sociologie*," *RP*, XX (1885), 632.

43. *Ibid.*

dent set of beliefs and ideas. By uniting, acting and reacting upon one another, individuals give rise to linguistic symbols, religious beliefs, moral norms, and legal formulas shared by most, if not all, members of the society in question. Insofar as individuals think with and act on these intersubjectively shared ideas or representations, they think and act not as isolated self-contained individuals, but as participants within a larger cultural whole. On the other hand, Durkheim looks upon a society as a structural system composed of individuals or subgroups. Seen from this morphological angle, the structure or pattern of the group, the order or arrangement of its elements, gives to the group a characteristic physiognomy.

In noting both these aspects of a social system, Durkheim joins two very different traditions of nineteenth-century sociology. With the German school of *Völkerpsychologie,* Durkheim stresses the intellectual, emotional, and volitional unity of social groups. Yet, he also emphasizes the structural characteristics of social integration advanced by Spencer and other late nineteenth-century social organicists. Within the latter tradition, organic analogies were utilized in describing the unity of human societies. It was said that a society

is like an individual living body and unlike an inorganic system, in that it is a unity of differentiated and mutually dependent parts, each of which cooperates with the others for the benefit of the whole. The organization of a society involves both a differentiation individually, in classes, or in groups, of the human beings who compose it and a specialization of their activities. The total combination of these unlike and mutually dependent parts constitutes the structure of the society; their specialized and mutually dependent activities are functionally combined with reference to a common aim, which is the maintenance of the society as a unity in existence. There is a definite parallelism between social structures and functions and the structures and functions of individual organisms, in that both include sustaining, distributing, and regulating organs.[44]

From Durkheim's unique fusion of these two traditions emanates his characteristic claim that collective beliefs and norms "grow up around sustained patterns of social interaction," a contention which has been subsequently criticized for failing to distinguish between "patterns of social interaction, or social structures, and [cultural] patterns of moral beliefs or sentiments . . ."[45]

44. Florian Znaniecki, "Social Organization and Institutions," in *Twentieth Century Sociology,* ed. Gurvitch and Moore, p. 175.
45. Alvin W. Gouldner, "Introduction" to Emile Durkheim, *Socialism and Saint-Simon* (Yellow Springs, Ohio: Antioch Press, 1958), p. xxi.

If a social system may be described in terms of its ideational and structural characteristics, how does one define a social fact, and distinguish it from other phenomena? Unfortunately Durkheim does not explicitly discuss this question in his early writings. What he does say is sufficient to suggest, however, that "social facts" were initially defined by Durkheim as entities that satisfy certain requirements within the system of relations designated by the term "society." A social fact is anything produced by social interaction and serving social ends.[46] Durkheim, accordingly, distinguishes between the cause of a social phenomenon; the effects of the cause, that is, the phenomenon itself; and its social function.[47]

What, then, are the principal elements or "facts" within a social system? How are these various facts defined? How are they related to other phenomena? An admittedly tentative, but nevertheless extensive, response to these queries is provided by Durkheim in "La Science positive de la morale en Allemagne," "Les Études de science sociale," and "Cours de science sociale: Leçon d'ouverture."

For heuristic purposes, Durkheim classifies social phenomena under four broad categories: common ideas and sentiments, shared moral maxims and beliefs, juridical rules, and economic phenomena.[48] For each category Durkheim provides a brief definition as well as several "guiding" hypotheses regarding their genesis and functional consequences.[49] In view of Durkheim's later attempt, during the period between 1893 and 1897, to explain some changes in collectively shared representations in terms of substructural transformations, it is noteworthy that the young Durkheim calls explicit attention to the rich variety of causal factors and functional consequences that may be

46. See Durkheim, "Cours de science sociale," pp. 41-45. With respect to the collective function of a social fact, Durkheim states: "Pour qu'un fait soit sociologique, il faut qu'il intéresse non seulement tous les individus pris isolement, mais la société elle-même." ("Les Études de science sociale," *RP*, XXII (1886), 66.

47. For a careful analysis of these distinctions, see Albert Pierce, "Durkheim and Functionalism," in *Emile Durkheim*, ed. Wolff, pp. 154-169.

48. Durkheim, "Cours de science sociale," pp. 41-55. This fourfold classification of social phenomena represents a clarification of the following fivefold scheme presented several years earlier in "Études de science sociale," p. 78: economic phenomena, the state, law, morality, and religion.

49. That Durkheim was not unaware of the role of hypotheses in guiding the empirical scientist is indicated in the following passage: "si particuliers que soient les phénomènes qu'il étudie, il ne se contente pas de les décrire, il les enchaîne les uns aux autres, il en cherche les causes et les conditions. Pour cela, il fait des inductions et des hypothèses. Comment ne serait-il pas exposé à faire souvent fausse route, s'il procède empiriquement, s'il tâtonne au hasard, s'il n'est guidé par aucune notion sur la nature des sociétés, ... comment fera-t-il un choix? .... Si donc il les accueille tous indistinctement, il tombe dans la vaine érudition ... Or, pour opérer une sélection, il a besoin d'une idée directrice, d'un critérium ... " ("Cours de science sociale," pp. 46-47.)

studied in seeking to explain collective beliefs, norms, laws, and practices. In the first place, the fact that social phenomena are interdepen-
dent elements within a system makes it not only possible, but essential,
to study how shared religious beliefs, moral rules, legal codes, and so
forth "enter into relations," and "act upon one another."[50] This might
be done, for example, by studying the impact of religious beliefs and
moral rules on legal codes. Social phenomena may also be studied with
respect to the structural forms or the institutions responsible for engendering these phenomena, the aim of such a study being illumination of
the interrelationship existing between collective beliefs on the one hand
and social structures on the other.[51] Within this area of study, one
might investigate the interrelationship between ecclesiastical institutions and religious beliefs. Finally, the postulate that collective phenomena function not only in terms of one another but also in terms of
the whole society makes it desirable to study their broad functional
consequences. This area of study is described by Durkheim as "social
physiology," that is, the branch of sociology dealing with the broad
social functions of institutions and ideas.[52]

Taken together, these several causal and functional hypotheses concerning the interrelationship of beliefs, norms, laws, and economic
behavior express the basic postulates of contemporary structural functionalism. As Wilbert E. Moore has recently observed, structural functional analysis of societal systems rests upon the following propositions:

Human acts, groups, rules of conduct, and goals or values are interrelated, not isolated and autonomous variables. The interrelationships
constitute the major data for meaningful description or analysis of
social systems. They underlie so-called functional analysis, which asks
the systematic consequences of given patterns of action. By their predictability, their persistence, they constitute a major source of order, of
reliability in social affairs, that makes life tolerable if not wholly without risk and uncertainty. The establishment of the relationships among
social phenomena, the attempt to achieve precision in concepts for
elements and processes and to achieve precision in measuring the degree
of predictability from one set of variables to another . . . [are among]
the major concerns of contemporary sociology.[53]

50. Durkheim, "Morale en Allemagne," pp. 40-43, "Études de science sociale,"
pp. 79-80, and "Cours de science sociale," pp. 30-32, 33-35, 38-40.
51. Durkheim compares this type of structural study in sociology to morphology in biology in "Cours de science sociale," pp. 43-44.
52. *Ibid.*
53. Charles P. Loomis and Zona K. Loomis, *Modern Social Theories*, 2nd ed.,
with an editorial introduction by Wilbert E. Moore, Van Nostrand Series in Sociology (Princeton, N. J.: D. Van Nostrand Company, 1965), pp. xxii-xxiii.

Inasmuch as each of these propositions is contained in the writings of the young Durkheim, Radcliffe-Brown is clearly correct in according Durkheim the honor of founding structural functionalism.[54] Neither Radcliffe-Brown nor any other secondary writer has previously noted, however, that these theoretical views are clearly presented by Durkheim in works written long before those works usually cited in defense of according Durkheim credit for this theoretical insight: *The Division of Labor* and *The Rules.* As a result of this neglect of the structural functional hypotheses in Durkheim's early works, not only has the central importance of these hypotheses for Durkheim's thought as a whole frequently been missed,[55] but several of his more specific hypotheses regarding common ideas and sentiments, moral maxims, juridical rules, and economic phenomena have been neglected. It behooves us, therefore, to take a closer look at some of these more specific hypotheses with which Durkheim began and upon which he rested much of his subsequent research.

Common ideas and sentiments. According to Durkheim, these include "the popular legends, religious traditions, political beliefs, languages, etc." which are "transmitted from one generation to another."[56] In contrast with the collective psychological products of small, transient groups, these legends and traditions result from the association and interaction of a multitude of minds stretching across many generations. Normally, they are shared by all members of the collectivity and function to insure "the unity and continuity of collective life,"[57] although any single legend or tradition may, over time, lose its original unifying function. This is the case, for example, with many ancient religious beliefs.

Shared moral maxims and beliefs. In Durkheim's view, these are among the most important social phenomena since it is precisely through sharing and acting upon such maxims that individuals are most intimately related to others and a common life together becomes a reality.[58] Since Socrates, Durkheim observes, philosophers have more or less clearly

54. See A. R. Radcliffe-Brown, *Structure and Function in Primitive Society* (Glencoe, Ill.: Free Press, 1952), p. 178.

55. It is one thing to acknowledge that Durkheim first formulated principles subsequently accepted by structural functionalists; it is quite a different matter to recognize the central importance of these principles in his thought. A number of interpreters, including Talcott Parsons, have referred to Durkheim as a precursor of modern structural functionalism, although this is not a central theme in their presentation of Durkheim's thought. See, for example, Talcott Parsons, *Structure of Social Action*, pp. 301-450.

56. Durkheim, "Cours de science sociale," p. 42.

57. *Ibid.*; Durkheim, "Etudes de science sociale," p. 67.

58. Durkheim, "Morale en Allemagne," p. 38.

perceived the social necessity of shared moral concepts, but, in lieu of studying them scientifically, philosophers have tended to formulate subjectively conceived, abstract definitions. What interests us, says Durkheim, is not another abstract definition of the good, but the raison d'être of the major moral institutions of society.[59]

Like legends and traditions, moral norms or maxims are collectively engendered and commonly shared representations, although they differ from the former in several fundamental respects.[60] In the first place, moral rules are more exacting than customary beliefs. Maxims prescribe the things one ought to do, as against the things one is encouraged to believe. Secondly, moral maxims are protected against violation by sanctions of disapproval enforced by public opinion at large. Deviation results in penalties sanctioned by public opinion.

If public opinion is responsible for both the genesis and enforcement of moral maxims, what is the principal social function of these norms? With respect to this issue, the young Durkheim found himself in agreement with the German moralists, Wagner, Schmoller, and Ihering. Morality, he states, has the same function as other customary ways of behaving; its chief function is "enabling men to live together."[61] The principal "function of morality is to render society possible, to enable men to live together without too many bruises and conflicts, to safeguard in a word the great collective interests."[62] This is why sanctions are enforced on dissidents; sanctions are necessary to preserve those modes of behavior that are compatible with social consensus. The true function of morality, in short, is "to adapt individuals to one another and thus to assure the equilibrium and the survival of the group."[63]

Legal codes. If Durkheim found himself in close agreement with Wagner, Schmoller, and Ihering regarding the functional consequences of moral norms, he was equally impressed by the major contentions of the historical school of jurisprudence concerning the nature, genesis, and function of legal codes. Like Durkheim's own thought, the German historical school had evolved in opposition to the rationalist belief, held by many philosophical idealists, that philosophers could develop legal

---

59. Durkheim, "La Philosophie dans les universités allemandes," *RIE,* XIII (1887), pp. 334-335.
60. For a brief discussion of these distinguishing characteristics of morality, see Durkheim, "Etudes de science sociale," p. 68, and "Cours de science sociale," p. 42.
61. Durkheim, "Morale en Allemagne," p. 43.
62. *Ibid.,* p. 38.
63. *Ibid.,* p. 138.

codes applicable to all times and places by applying the moral principles
of pure reason to an ideal social being. Against this universalistic and
abstract approach to law, the principal representatives of the historical
school unequivocally affirmed an intimate connection between a
nation's positive law and its specific *Volksgeist*. Positive law, they
contended, could neither be understood nor effective apart from its
relation to the particular culture or society out of which law grows and
to which it is applied. When law is in conformity with the inner *geist* of
a culture, positive law is effective; when this is not the case, it tends to
be ineffective. The historical school's challenge to idealists was twofold.
They "opposed to armchair legislation the idea of continuity and
tradition, in interesting parallel to Burke's anti-revolutionary
deliverances"[64] and to the conservative school of French sociology
descending from de Maistre and de Bonald. And they "opposed to the
idea of a universal code the dependence of law upon the unique
characteristics and needs of each people."[65]

In stressing the deep origins of law in the stable beliefs and sentiments
of a particular people, Durkheim felt the historical school had both
correctly distinguished law from morality and rightly identified their
underlying relationship. In the first place, he believed the historical
school drew an essentially correct distinction between the codified laws
enforced by designated authorities and the living, moral maxims
governing group life. Durkheim thus follows several representatives of
the historical school in defining legal codes as sanctioned rules of
conduct enforced by "specially authorized representatives" of
society.[66] He also felt that the historical school correctly recognized
that law derives from, and is based upon, the inner moral convictions of
a culture. Although the *Volksgeist* doctrine seemed somewhat myste-
rious and unscientific to Durkheim, he did feel that it served an important purpose in highlighting the inverse functional relationship between
law and morals.

In Ihering's *Der Zweck im Recht,* the young Durkheim found several
specific suggestions concerning the social functions of legal codes that
were to assume great importance in his own thought. Ihering's most
important contribution to the sociology of law, in Durkheim's view,
was his functional interpretation of positive law. The most significant
function of law, Ihering maintained, is that of adapting the individual

---

64. Julius Stone, *The Province and Function of Law* (Cambridge, Mass.: Harvard University Press, 1950), p. 423.
65. *Ibid.*
66. Durkheim, "Cours de science sociale," p. 42.

or society to its millieu; by "millieu" Ihering meant not only the institutional, but also the cultural, environment from which positive laws grow and to which they are applied.[67]

Economics. Although this is repeatedly referred to by the young Durkheim as a major subdivision of the social sciences, his statements regarding economic phenomena are less sharply honed than those concerning popular legends, moral maxims, and legal codes. Basically, his contention is that the assumptions about the nature of economic motivation (rational self-interest, competition, and so forth) asserted by most nineteenth-century economists do not apply very well to the empirical world of economic activities.[68] These activities are seldom motivated, or determined, by purely economic motivations or exclusively rational considerations. Quite the contrary, economic activities are profoundly affected by the operation of noneconomic (moral, religious, and legal) factors that continually modify the operation of the economic system itself. As a corollary, it follows that economics must renounce its professed autonomy and become a social science. Once this occurs, Durkheim states, "the method and doctrine [of political economy] will change at once."[69]

Although the young Durkheim fails to specify precisely how economics will be transformed by recognition of the interaction of noneconomic and economic factors, he clearly indicates that economists should pay particular attention to the functional influences of economic phenomena on morality and vice versa. Schoenberg correctly recognizes, Durkheim notes in discussing the German economist's views, that financial security, wealth, and other economic factors have a profound influence on morality because they decisively affect the quality of family life, the character of child rearing practices, and the extent to which refined sentiments and manners are cultivated.[70] The young Durkheim is demonstrably less interested in the economic conditions influencing morality than in the moderating influence exerted by moral norms and legal codes on economic activities. He was especially intrigued, therefore, by Wagner and Schmoller who were also concerned with specifying how moral ideas and legal principles affect economic behavior. In this connection Durkheim cites Wagner's observation that moral norms respecting the dignity of the human person, by opposing "abusive and premature exploitation of children and women," have transformed eco-

67. See Durkheim, "Morale en Allemagne," pp. 49-58.
68. See Durkheim, "Cours de science sociale," pp. 28-29, and "Morale en Allemagne," pp. 35-46.
69. Durkheim, "Cours de science sociale," p. 43.
70. Durkhcim, "Morale en Allemagne," p. 35.

nomic practices by stimulating industrialists to replace men with ma-
chines.[71] Without understanding the profound effect of such moral
beliefs upon economic practices, Durkheim states, "one will form a
very false idea of economic development . . . For morality is not absorbed in political economy; all social functions, rather, contribute to
producing the form of morality to which economic phenomena have
had to submit while contributing to it."[72] Durkheim thus concludes his
explication of the economic theories of Wagner and Schmoller in opposition to laissez-faire and to Marx, by contending that moral norms are
more significant causal variables within economic systems than strictly
economic interests.

Three basic perspectives dominate Durkheim's entire work: his most
distinctive philosophical and theoretical presuppositions have been established by the dialectical method; his neonaturalistic approach to the
study of moral phenomena underlies the attempt to bring spiritual
phenomena, with their distinctive phenomenological attributes unimpaired, into the sphere of nature and scientific explanation; and, finally,
his relational social realism underlies the claim that society is a reality
sui generis. Among the phenomena generated by social existence are
common ideas and sentiments, moral maxims, legal codes, and economic practices. Each of these "social facts" has its own distinctive
nature, genesis, and function. The task of the social scientist, as Durkheim understood it, is to describe the essential characteristics of these
phenomena and to demonstrate how they come into being, enter into
relations, act upon one another, and compose coordinate social wholes.

71. *Ibid.,* p. 41.
72. *Ibid.*

II

Toward a Science of Morality, 1885-1893

Historically considered, the scientific theory of morality formulated by the young Durkheim between 1885 and 1893 represents an elaborate synthesis composed of insights and propositions gleaned from Comte's instinctual psychology, Kant's distinction between sensuous and noumenal aspects of the self, Renouvier's phenomenological science of morality, and Wundt's theory of collective representations.[1] As a scientific moralist, Durkheim thus stands among the great reconcilers in the recent history of scientific theories of morality. Like Kant, Renouvier, and Wundt, his principal aim is to provide a complete descriptive and explanatory account of "all those facts the moral nature of which is undisputed."[2] In pursuing this goal, which was never far from the center of his thought, Durkheim observes that "the facts of the moral life" include not only obligatory rules of conduct, but sentiments of sympathy and love, feelings of altruistic loyalty and disinterested devotion, emotional reactions of remorse and regret, and the conscious pursuit of order, harmony, solidarity, and well-being. In Durkheim's view, all these so-called "moral facts" must be accurately described and explained if the scientist, who specializes in this area, is to fulfill his task of explaining all the facts, the moral nature of which is undisputed.

Given this inclusive goal, it is scarcely surprising that the young Durkheim seldom criticizes other theorists for setting forth completely erroneous views. His critical point of departure is more often than not that the views perpetrated by his predecessors are inadequate because they ignore, or are incompatible with, other generally recognized moral phenomena. A few examples should be sufficient to demonstrate this point. Psychological hedonism is rejected by Durkheim not because it presents a completely false account of human motivation, but because it ignores "duties which involve a genuine disinterestedness, a more or less

1. Durkheim's systematic intentions are reflected in his praise of Wundt's attempt to reconcile diverse interpretations of morality. Wundt, Durkheim writes, "seeks to demonstrate the bonds that tie all these particular studies together," thereby restoring the unity that "this narrow specialization ignores and comprises." ("Morale en Allemagne," p. 114.)
2. Durkheim, *Division du travail*, p. 5.

complete forgetfulness of oneself."[3] Similarly, Wundt is praised for recognizing the importance of certain ends of conduct, but sharply rebuked for neglecting Kant's description of moral obligation.[4] For the scientist of moral phenomena to ignore such widely accepted phenomena as disinterestedness and obligation, says Durkheim, is to proceed like "a biologist who, instead of explaining biological phenomena, would contest their right to existence."[5] In other words, Durkheim's inclusive approach to the study of morality constitutes the fundamental criterion against which he evaluates other theorists and with which he supports his own contention that no philosopher or scientist has hitherto succeeded in accounting for all those facts, the moral nature of which is undisputed. Durkheim thus attempts to be as inclusive as possible in treating the two principal classifications of moral phenomena which he examines: psychological motivation and moral obligation.

Psychological Motivation

Durkheim's treatment of "motivation" is of considerable interest, both for its intrinsic merits as well as for the light it casts on the psychological foundations of social life. In the first place, certain basic inclinations or drives are instinctive in the sense that they are present from birth in every normal individual. In discussing these basic impulses, Durkheim avoids the tendency on the part of most nineteenth-century scientific moralists to reduce all innate inclinations to a single instinct such as self-preservation or organic equilibrium. There are, Durkheim states, several basic inclinations which have "their source in the very nature of man."[6] These include not only biological drives and egoistic instincts, but also social *penchants* which are expressed in the form of love, affection, sympathetic concern, and associated phenomena. Durkheim, therefore, rejects the Hobbesian claim that egoism is the basic human instinct, as well as the Darwinian and Spencerian assertion that social affection is a recent achievement of the human race.[7] In repudiating such claims, Durkheim notes that the egoistic hypothesis is incompatible with the social inclinations that are expressed wherever men associate together.[8] Taking his stand with Comte and several Ger-

3. *Ibid.,* p. 11.
4. Durkheim, "Morale en Allemagne," pp. 138-139.
5. Durkheim, *Division du travail,* p. 11.
6. Durkheim, "Morale en Allemagne," pp. 121, 56, 128, and "Études de science sociale," pp. 78-79.
7. Durkheim, *Division du travail,* pp. 11-14, 55-56, and "Morale en Allemagne," pp. 126-127.
8. "We have seen in effect that altruistic sentiments, whatever relationships they have with egoistic sentiments, do not derive from them. Each of them has its own source in the human heart from which each springs. Just as Rousseau's

man moralists, Durkheim approvingly cites Wundt to the effect that "there have been, since the beginning, social inclinations which have their source in the very nature of man. Every man has in effect a natural inclination for his fellows which is manifest as soon as most men wish to live together, that is, from the first days of humanity."[9] These inclinations cannot be reduced to egoism, for they are present from birth in every normal person.

In making a case for the existence of social as well as egoistic drives, Durkheim was scarcely an original theorist in the late nineteenth century. Comte and Wundt, to cite two of Durkheim's acknowledged precursors, had formulated similar views with respect to social propensities or instincts. Unlike these theorists, however, Durkheim refuses to elaborate a complex list of instinctual drives. The contrast between Durkheim and Comte on this score is especially illuminating. According to Comte, all men possess three purely egoistic instincts, four quasi-egoistical dispositions, and three nonegoistic tendencies.[10] For Durkheim, on the contrary, it is sufficient to recognize that there are non-egoistic, sympathetic inclinations in addition to biological instincts and egoistic drives. To be sure, Durkheim occasionally goes beyond this vague assertion and suggests, for purposes of clarification, that these nonegoistic propensities include such specific phenomena as sympathy, love, respect for others, and so forth. But Durkheim nowhere draws up anything resembling the various ad hoc lists of basic drives that were perpetrated throughout most of the nineteenth century, and well into the early decades of the twentieth century.

This admittedly modest claim that men are sympathetically inclined has considerable theoretical importance, however, for it is Durkheim's claim that enduring systems of human relations would be impossible unless men were somehow equipped with inclinations of a loving or, at least, of a friendly sort. "In fact, for men to acknowledge each other and to guarantee rights to one another, it is necessary, first of all, that they love each other, that for one reason or another they hold to each other and to the society in which they participate."[11] If men were not

---

solitary man has never existed, there has never been a human will in which egoism was the sole motive. The two inclinations are contemporaneous with one another and they are both contemporaneous with humanity." (Durkheim, "Morale en Allemagne," p. 128.)

9. *Ibid.*, p. 121.

10. Raymond Aron provides a convenient summary of Comte's instinctual theory in his *Main Currents,* I, 89. Comte's purely egoistic instincts include nutritive, sexual, and maternal dispositions. The four quasi-egoistical instincts are the disposition to overcome obstacles, the industrial or work instinct, the instinct to dominate, and the tendency to seek the approval of others. The three nonegoistical tendencies are friendship, veneration, and kindness.

11. Durkheim, *Division du travail,* p. 130.

naturally inclined toward their fellows, the whole fabric of society, its customs and institutions, would never arise, or, if by some alchemy society already existed, it would rapidly collapse. In the absence of social instincts, there would be no basis for association in the first place, no interaction capable of giving rise to shared rules of conduct, no notion of responsibility toward others. Moreover, it would be impossible, in the absence of such basic instincts, to socialize or moralize children.

It is of fundamental importance in interpreting Durkheim's motivational theory to recognize that while he appreciates the importance of basic instincts, he also observes that these drives are stimulated and profoundly modified by psychical representations. Men differ from animals, Durkheim contends, precisely because images and ideas intervene between innate inclinations and behavior. "Every motive is a sentiment," Durkheim states in this context, "but every sentiment is determined by a representation and varies with the kind of representation which determines it."[12] Apart from psychical representations, then, human motivation cannot be understood.

Without recognizing the theoretical significance of this stress upon psychical representations, it is difficult to appreciate the modernity of Durkheim's understanding of human motivation. What Durkheim is emphasizing in his doctrine of psychical representations is the fundamental principle of modern psychology that human behavior cannot be understood simply as an elaboration of biological instincts. We cannot even know our bodily urges, Durkheim suggests, unless they are "represented." In the absence of a perception or thought, an individual may "feel a vague and indefinable uneasiness, and sense the lack of something, but he does not know what."[13] These ideas or representations cannot be completely explained, Durkheim further contends, by biological phenomena precisely because psychological phenomena are realities *sui generis.* Durkheim's account of motivation thus stands in sharp contrast with the various theories advanced by biological psychologists in the last decades of the nineteenth century, wherein human motivation could be completely explained by visceral feelings, sexual instincts, hunger drives, and so forth. Against these views, Durkheim maintains that human behavior is elicited by psychical representations that mediate instinctual drives in various ways and canalize indiscriminate drives or inclinations in multifarious directions. Modification of motivational dispositions through learning thus acquired the importance in

12. Durkheim, "Morale en Allemagne," p. 132.
13. Durkheim, *Division du travail,* p. 303.

Durkheim's thought that it has subsequently acquired in social psychology.[14]

Durkheim distinguishes among three major types of purely psychological (noncollective) representations: ideas that represent the external world, ideas that represent states of the biological organism and the self, and ideas that represent others.[15] Inasmuch as "moral" sentiments ordinarily concern persons rather than things, it follows that ideas representing the self and those representing others are of primary concern to the scientific moralist.[16]

With respect to "representations that are purely personal," Durkheim observes that images of the self tend to excite self-regarding sentiments which are both agreeable and have the self as object. Because this "sphere of psychic life . . . varies from one man to another and remains peculiar to each," representations and sentiments of this sort constitute

14. For a comprehensive historical survey and contemporary analysis of socialization research and theory, see *Socialization and Society,* ed. John Clausen, (Boston: Little, Brown and Company, 1968).

15. This threefold distinction is implicitly assumed rather than explicitly formulated in Durkheim's early writings. See, for example, *Division du travail,* pp. 385-391 for the first and second, and pp. 55-56 for the third. Years later, Durkheim summarized his views regarding these three types of representations in the following manner: With regard to representations of the external world, the mature Durkheim states that "we cannot become attached to an external thing, whatever its nature, without representing it to ourselves, without having an idea of it, a sentiment about it, no matter how confused. By virtue of this fact alone—that we do represent an external object to ourselves—it becomes in certain respects internal. It exists in us in the form of the representation that expresses it, reflects it, is closely related to it. Thus . . . the object becomes an element of our consciousness." (*Moral Education,* p. 215.) Regarding representations of the self, Durkheim observes that "there are certain elements of ourselves that are . . . constitutive of our self, our strictly individual self; elements that bear . . . our imprint; that single us out as ourselves and not someone else—the form of our body, our social status, our character, etc." (*Ibid,.* p. 216.) As soon as a human being becomes conscious of these aspects of himself, Durkheim continues, "there is a subject who thinks of himself as distinct from everything that is not he—a subject who says 'I.'" (*Ibid.,* p. 217.) Finally, Durkheim argues that infants are naturally endowed with the ability not only to represent other human beings to themselves, but to emotionally identify and sympathize with them. "Indeed, this is how a bond of constant communication is established between the consciousness of the child and others' consciousness. What happens in the latter reverberates in the former. He lives their lives, enjoys their pleasures, suffers their sorrows. He is thus naturally induced to act so as to prevent or soften others' sorrows." (*Ibid.,* p. 220.)

16. This ready dismissal of the world of "things" from the realm of moral relations is revised in Durkheim's later writings. In *Moral Education,* for example, Durkheim argues that an infant's attachment to physical things, like toys, represents the first stage in the development of moral solidarity and disinterestedness. Between a child's sense of solidarity with, and loyalty to, his favorite toys, "and local patriotism, love of birthplace, of the paternal hearth—the moral and altruistic character of which nobody denies—there is only a difference of degree" (*Moral Education,* p. 218.)

the "foundation of all individuality."[17] As such, self-regarding sentiments have a place within the total economy of the moral life, though
they are clearly inferior, in Durkheim's view, to other-regarding or
altruistic sentiments.

In addition to purely personal images, images of other persons also
tend to generate, under appropriate conditions, favorable sentiments.
Not all images of others excite such favorable responses, but those that
do are the representations Durkheim considers worthy of special analysis. In this context Durkheim quotes Aristotle in support of his own
contention:

that we like those who resemble us, those who think and feel as we do.
But the contrary phenomenon is no less frequent. It very often happens
that we feel kindly toward people who do not resemble us, precisely
because of this lack of resemblance. These facts are so contradictory
that moralists have always vacillated concerning the true nature of
friendship, deriving it sometimes from the former, sometimes from the
latter. The ancient Greeks had already perceived this problem. "Friendship," says Aristotle, "causes much discussion. According to some, it
consists in a certain resemblance, and we like those who resemble us;
whence the proverbs 'birds of a feather flock together' and 'like seeks
like,' and other such phrases. According to others, on the contrary, all
those who are alike are opposed to one another . . . Heraclitus claims
that one can only unite those who are dissimilar, that the finest harmony is born of differences, and that everything comes into being
through variance."

These observations indicate, says Durkheim, that either resemblance or
difference may be a source of "natural friendship" or "moral solidarity." Not all differences among individuals, however, engender mutual
attraction and friendship. "Spendthrifts do not seek the company of
misers, nor just and honest people that of hypocrites and deceivers;
sweet and gentle spirits have no taste for sour and malevolent tempera-
ments." The only differences that foster mutuality and solidarity are
those which, instead of opposing and excluding, genuinely complement
each other.[18]

Both sentiments founded upon resemblance, as well as sentiments
based upon complementary heterogeneity, result from the fact that an
"image of another unites with ours," but the psychological processes
responsible for these two differing sentiments of interpersonal solidarity are somewhat different. With regard to sentiments resulting from

17. Durkheim, *Division du travail*, p. 216.
18. *Ibid.*, pp. 55-56.

likeness, "the union results from the resemblance of two images; it consists in an agglutination. The two representations unite because, being indistinct, totally or in part, they are confounded and become no more than one." In the case of sentiments of friendship and solidarity resulting from complementary differences, however,

the image of the one who completes us becomes inseparable from ours, not only because it is frequently associated with ours, but particularly because it is the natural complement of it. It thus becomes an integral and permanent part of our consciousness, to such an extent that we can no longer do without it and seek whatever is capable of increasing its strength. That is why we enjoy the society of the one the image represents, since the presence of the object that it expresses, by giving us an actual perception, enhances it.

Neither the sentiments nor the social relationships which derive from these two differing forms of psychological association are the same. Sentiments and relationships based upon resemblance result in a confusion between the self and the other, whereas sentiments and relationships based upon dissimilarity foster maintenance of self identity (might we say, in this case, "boundary-maintenance"?), while engendering a sense of mutual dependence. Both sentiments are equally "moral," however, since both elicit feelings of interpersonal solidarity and sympathetic concern.[19]

Moral Obligation

Thus far, Durkheim's account of morality has been based on natural human fellow feelings, extended by sympathetic sentiments elicited by images of other individuals. But Durkheim is not content to rest his analysis of morality with the insistence that men possess benevolent sentiments and motives. There remains the fact that men also possess a sense of moral obligation which, Durkheim recognizes, is quite different from other moral sentiments. This sense of moral duty Durkheim must still explain if his theory of morality is to contain a complete and adequate account of "the facts of the moral life."

Durkheim's descriptive account of moral obligation is based upon Kant's phenomenological description of moral duty. As Fauconnet observes, "Durkheim was personally, as Kant had been, above all a man of will and of discipline."[20] Accordingly, Durkheim maintains, with Kant,

19. *Ibid.*, pp. 63-64.
20. Paul Fauconnet, "Introduction to the Original Edition: Durkheim's Pedagogical Work," in Emile Durkheim, *Education and Sociology,* tr. Sherwood D. Fox (Glencoe, Ill.: Free Press, 1956), p. 43.

that men possess obligatory rules of conduct which exercise constraint on their wills quite different from the spontaneous sentiments studied by the Moral Sense School of psychology. With the German philosopher, Durkheim also maintains that these rules of conscience are irreducible to the instinctual life; they make their demands in their own right, independent of egoistic or other-regarding inclinations.[21] Duty, then, cannot be considered as dependent on natural inclinations, although Durkheim maintains, with Renouvier and against Kant, that obligatory rules generally fail to engender an appropriate behavioral response unless, by warming the heart, they set the will in motion.[22] Durkheim's problem is thus identical with Kant's: "how are we to explain the fact of moral obligation?"

Kant solved this problem by distinguishing between noumenal and empirical aspects of the self. As an empirical being, Kant maintained, man belongs to the realm of the sensuous, a realm in which he is subject to the play of impulse, habit, and desire. Insofar as man is a sensuous being, in Kant's view, he is subject to the laws of causality. But man is also—indeed, essentially—a rational being; that is to say, his nature is essentially noumenal or intelligible. As a rational being, man is capable of knowing and freely choosing an absolute and unconditional command or "categorical imperative." This rational moral law, says Kant, is subjectively experienced "like a voice from somewhere deeper, something behind our ordinary experience—a 'nonempirical experience.' "[23] In contrast with the bondage of the senuous self to the whims of desire and passion, the noumenal self is free insofar as its acts are based on a rational moral choice. Hence, Kant draws a sharp contrast between the sensous and the noumenal. "The essential thing in all determination of the will by the moral law is that the will as free should not only be determined without the cooperation of sensuous desires, but that it should even oppose such desires, and restrain all natural inclinations that might prevent the realization of law."[24] Moral duty is thus presented by Kant as harsh and uncompromising.

Although Durkheim was favorably impressed with, and deeply influenced by, Kant's distinction between noumenal and sensuous aspects of the self (Durkheim repeatedly criticizes other scientific moralists in his early publications for failing to account for this Kantian contrast),[25] he

21. Durkheim, "Morale en Allemagne," pp. 139, 278.

22. Durkheim, "Schaeffle, A., *Bau und Leben des Sozialem Körpers:* Erster Band," *RP*, XIX (1885), 100.

23. John Herman Randall, Jr., *The Career of Philosophy*, II (New York: Columbia University Press, 1965), p. 149.

24. *Ibid.*, p. 154.

25. See, for example, Durkheim, "Morale en Allemagne," pp. 138-139.

vigorously objects to the German philosopher's concept of the noumenal self. The principal theoretical reasons for this critique of Kant are
found in Durkheim's perspicacious treatment of the age-old problem of
the relationship between the individual and society.[26] Interpretations
of this relationship, Durkheim states on several occasions, have traditionally centered on one of two polar alternatives. One typical viewpoint conceives the self apart from community; the other understands
the self to be deeply conditioned by communal existence.[27] These two
alternatives have widespread consequences for the interpretation of
morality. The former, minimizing the interpenetration of selves that is
involved in community, tends to relate persons through innate moral
rules of conscience (natural law theorists), external institutional sanctions (Hobbes), or spontaneously engendered harmonious social relationships (the Manchester economists).[28] The latter concept of the relationship between the self and society is more organic in character, that
is to say, there is a real penetration of selves in one another.

Kant is described by Durkheim as being in agreement with Hobbes
and the Manchester economists insofar as he represents the former,
individualistic understanding of self and community, for the obvious
reason that Kant's conception of the self's relationship to society is,
like that of the economists, essentially unilateral.[29] The self, in its
freedom, affects what happens in society, but is not significantly
affected, in turn, by the sociocultural system in which it exists. Social
existence is not, then, a primary fact to be taken into consideration in
explaining either morality or other forms of human behavior.

26. Marcel Mauss informs us that Durkheim chose this problem of "the relationship between the individual and society" as his subject in 1883. (Marcel
Mauss, "Introduction" to Durkheim, *Socialisme*, p. *v.*)
27. Durkheim, "Morale en Allemagne," pp. 127-130.
28. See Durkheim, "Philosophie dans les universités allemandes," pp. 336-338,
and "Morale en Allemagne," pp. 33-48.
29. Durkheim, "Richard, G., *Essai sur l'origine de l'idée de droit*," *RP*, XXXV
(1893), 290. This identification of Kant with the economists does not mean that
Durkheim was insensitive to those aspects of Kant's theory of civil society that
differentiate his position from that of the laissez-faire theorists. Durkheim felt
that Kant was closer to the truth concerning the essential prerequisites of social
consensus than most other atomistic social theorists. In the first place, Kant
appreciated the fact that social order rests upon an intersubjectively shared morality. Kant, Durkheim states in this context, "éschappe en partie à l'individualisme
parce qu'il soumet l'individu à une loi que l'individu n'a pas faite, à une règle
objective, à une consigne impérative et impersonnelle." (*Ibid.*) Second, Kant realized, as laissez-faire theorists did not, that an external system of law is necessary
not only for social order, but for securing the freedom of individuals in society.
Appreciation of this Kantian insight leads Durkheim to argue in "Morale en Allemagne" and again in *Division du travail* that it is not freedom from law that
"grants to each individual a larger degree of personal liberty," but the existence of
appropriate laws, e.g., laws protecting individual rights. ("Morale en Allemagne,"
p. 42.)

This Kantian view, says Durkheim, is neither compatible with the real, concrete men we know nor with the cross-cultural diversity of moral rules:

Real and concrete men change with the physical and social milieu which envelops them, and naturally *la morale* changes with men. No doubt there are among *les morales* some common points, because there are similarities among the material and social conditions in which different societies have been and are currently situated. But each *morale*, nevertheless, bears the imprint of the particular milieu in which it originally appeared.

Kant's attempt to base the moral life on the requirements of reason alone thus fails, according to Durkheim, because the ideals of reason as well as the self of the actor both change with alterations in the social milieu. Moral reasoning is not, as Kant would have it, an entirely private affair of an isolated noumenal self existing in a realm of pure representations; it takes place, rather, in a community of shared moral rules. These communal moral concepts "efface at each moment the supposed line of demarcation which would separate our consciences. . . . The individual is an integral part of the society in which he is born; the latter penetrates him from all sides; to isolate and abstract oneself from society is to diminish the self."[30]

To contest Kant's concept of the noumenal self on these grounds, Durkheim notes, is not to contend that man is totally determined. Durkheim was quite willing to accept Kant's claim that the self is free, in some sense, to choose. To see man as a being-in-society, he states, "it is not necessary to believe that the human personality is totally absorbed in the bosom of the collective being." Why? What prevents the self from being totally determined by his social milieu? Durkheim's answer here is essentially Kantian, although it derives immediately from Wundt. "It is the will which prevents it [the self] from being thus absorbed into the milieu which surrounds it. Once the will emerges, it reacts in its turn on all those phenomena which come to it from outside and which are like the common inheritance of society; it makes them its own."[31]

What Durkheim objects to, then, is not Kant's doctrine of free will, but, rather, the German philosopher's assumption that man is by and large an abstract, isolated creature content in himself. Man, Durkheim

30. Durkheim, "Philosophie dans les universités allemandes," p. 337.
31. Durkheim, "Morale en Allemagne," p. 129.

contends, is a social being. This is the fundamental qualification of his existence and the delimitation of his being as a man. The human self is born into a community of selves which is partly characterized by shared conceptions of the good and the right. These shared meanings, and the sentiments engendered by them, penetrate the individual "from all sides."[32] The moral rules of conscience are held in "common with our fellows, and chiefly with those among them who are nearest to us, like our parents and our compatriots."[33] In brief, there is a real penetration of selves within communal relations such that it is impossible to separate the moral self, as Kant would have it, from other selves "by an abyss."

Durkheim uses the ambiguous term *la conscience collective* to denote shared moral rules and maxims. The collective conscience thus refers, in part, to shared moral rules widely held throughout a given society, that is, a large percentage of the people, not necessarily all, accept them and act according to them in ordering their social relations. Insofar as this is the referent of the collective conscience, Durkheim covers much the same ground with this term that cultural anthropologists like Malinowski, Kroeber, and Redfield cover with their various definitions of a cultural item.[34] Unlike these latter-day anthropologists, however, Durkheim associates epistemological and phenomenological connotations with the collective conscience, which enables him to employ this concept in explaining moral obligation.[35]

With respect to its epistemological meaning, Durkheim claims that the collective conscience refers not only to shared moral norms, but to the individual's "awareness of" cultural norms or the "re-presentation" in consciousness or conscience of shared moral meanings. Seen in this

32. Durkheim, "Philosophie dans les universités allemandes," p. 337.
33. Durkheim, "Morale en Allemagne," pp. 128-129.
34. This is the thesis of Paul Bohannan's essay, "Conscience Collective and Culture," in *Emile Durkheim*, ed. Wolff, pp. 77-96.
35. The pivotal position of *la conscience collective* in Durkheim's thought is largely due to the cultural, epistemological, and moral assumptions associated with the term. As Georges Gurvitch observes: "La théorie de la conscience collective est le fondement crucial de la sociologie de Durkheim, son point décisif, la racine de toute sa conception de la spécificité du social et de son irréductibilité à d'autres secteurs du réel. Elle est à la base de sa méthode sociologique, de son opposition de la solidarité mécanique et de la solidarité organique, de sa sociologie juridique et de sa sociologie religieuse, de sa théorie du suicide et de son interprétation du Totem et du Mana, enfin de sa science des faits moraux et de sa théorie des valeurs. Nulle conception de Durkheim ne fut aussi décisive pour l'orientation qu'il avait donnée à la sociologie, et pourtant nulle de ses thèses n'a rencontré une opposition aussi vive et aussi étendue que celle-là. Certains sociologues sont même allés jusqu'à accepter toutes les conclusions de la doctrine de Durkheim, sans accepter leur base indispensable—la théorie de la conscience collective." (Gurvitch, *Essais de sociologie*, p. 115.)

way, the ambiguous French term *conscience* is more or less equivalent to the English "consciousness,"[36] since the collective conscience, in this usage of the term, refers to the individual's perception of cultural norms. Durkheim thus draws a sharp analytical distinction between collective and individual aspects of consciousness, an interesting parallel to Kant's distinction between noumenal and empirical aspects of experience. "There are in each of our *consciences*," Durkheim states in *The Division of Labor*, "two *consciences:* one which is shared in common with our group in its entirety, which, consequently, is not ourself, but society living and acting within us; the other, on the contrary, represents only that in us which is personal and distinct to us, that which makes an individual of us."[37] The former is, as it were, a more or less accurate reflection of the shared rules of one's society.

Durkheim also associates various qualitatively distinct phenomenological experiences with this representation in consciousness or conscience of collective norms. Because collective rules enjoy the moral prestige individuals spontaneously associate with all collectively shared beliefs, and because these norms are invariably imposed upon the subject by public opinion, they engender sentiments that are qualitatively different from those evoked by individual representations. These are precisely the qualitative characteristics Kant associates with moral duty. A normal mind, Durkheim observes, cannot consider moral maxims without considering them as obligatory.[38] Moral rules have an "imperative character"; they "exercise a sort of ascendancy over the will which feels constrained to conform to them."[39] This constraint is not to be confused with physical force or compulsion; the will is not forced to conform to the norms it entertains even if these norms are enforced by public opinion. Moral "constraint does not consist in an exterior and mechanical pressure; it has a more intimate and psychological character."[40] But this intimate, psychological sense of obligation is, nevertheless, none other than the authority of public opinion which penetrates, like the air we breathe, into the deepest recesses of our being.

Because collective norms have an intensity and compelling force which far exceeds that of any privately formulated rule, Durkheim further contends, we naturally assume that they derive from, and are enforced by, some power, real or ideal, which is superior to us. This explains the transcendent aspect of moral experience.

36. Bohannan, "Conscience Collective and Culture," pp. 78-79.
37. Durkheim, *Division du travail*, pp. 138-139.
38. Durkheim, "Morale en Allemagne," p. 134.
39. Durkheim, "Cours de science sociale," p. 42.
40. Durkheim, "Morale en Allemagne," p. 56.

By virtue of their collective origin, their universality, their permanence in time, and their intrinsic intensity, these sentiments have exceptional power. They are thus radically separated from the rest of our *conscience,* which consists of much weaker mental states. They dominate us. They possess, as it were, something superhuman, and, at the same time, they bind us to objects that are outside our temporal life. They are experienced as an echo in ourselves of a force which is foreign to us, and which is superior to what we are. We are thus forced to project them outside ourselves, to attribute what concerns them to some external object.[41]

Projections of this sort, however, are nothing more than symbolic representations of the real moral forces which act upon individual members of society, namely, those exercised by public opinion.

The intensity with which obligatory states of consciousness are imposed by public opinion also explains the phenomenological experience of remorse, in contrast with regret. Remorse is a much more intense and painful experience than regret, because the collective representations responsible for it are stronger. Whereas regret is merely self-reproach inflicted for neglecting some desirable, self-imposed value, remorse is a severe moral condemnation for a serious infraction of an obligatory collective norm. Both sentiments are based upon punishment, "but the second is a violent pain due to the wound we have made with our own hands to the living parts of our moral conscience; the other is reduced to regret for having allowed a delightful joy to escape. One arises because an irretrievable loss has been suffered; the other because we have missed an opportunity to enrich ourselves."[42] These internal distinctions between remorse and regret stem from the greater intensity with which the obligatory norms responsible for engendering remorse are imposed by public opinion, in comparison with the moderate discomfort or regret an individual experiences when his behavior does not measure up to individually posited ideals.

In speaking in these various ways of the collective conscience, Durkheim often leaves the reader of his early writings with the impression that a society constitutes an external, moral environment within which individuals function. There is an important complement of Durkheim's theory of the collective conscience, however, which considerably modifies this thesis. When infants and adolescents first obey cultural norms, they are influenced by the external social milieu in which they live, but

41. Durkheim, *Division du travail,* pp. 107-108; cf. his *Moral Education,* pp. 89-91.
42. Durkheim, *Division du travail,* p. 29.

these rules may, through repeated observation, become internalized. When this happens, obligation is no longer due to the representation in consciousness of external norms or to the enforcement of these norms by society, for the norm, in this case, has become a "norm" of character, or the formula which expresses the way in which the individual spontaneously acts. Society does not need to constrain the individual to act once this occurs precisely because it has conquered his personality; obligation is internal, and the individual's own personality supplies the motivation to act in the socially approved manner. The mechanism responsible for this phenomena is habit: "When we have repeated a given action a certain number of times, it tends to be reproduced in the same manner. Gradually, by the effect of habit, a given form of behavior becomes an imperative with the force of a moral obligation. We feel ourselves obliged to always cast our action in this mold."[43] Talcott Parsons is quite correct, then, in suggesting "that Durkheim must be accorded, with Freud, the credit for what undoubtedly is one of the most fundamental of all *psychological* discoveries, namely, that of the fact of internalization of culture as part of the structure of the personality itself, not simply as providing an 'environment' within which the personality or the organism functions."[44]

Durkheim himself provides the most succinct summary of the foregoing aspects of his early theory of moral sentiments and obligation in his review (1887) of Guyau's *L'Irréligion de l'avenir: étude de sociologie*. In this brief but important article Durkheim distinguishes between two species of moral sentiments. "The first joins each individual to the personality of his fellow citizens; they are manifest in the interior of the community through the relations of daily life, such as senti-

43. Durkheim, "Morale en Allemagne," p. 40.
44. Talcott Parsons, in the "Foreword" to Durkheim, *Education and Sociology* (p. 9). George Simpson has recently criticized this comparison of Durkheim with Freud: "Talcott Parsons' statement, in his introductory remarks to the English translation of Durkheim's essay on education, that Durkheim must be credited with Freud for one of the most fundamental of all psychological discoveries—the internalization of culture in the structure of personality—is certainly stretching the point. Durkheim was unaware of the psychodynamics of the unconscious and of introjected imagery as systematically worked out by psychoanalysis, so that his conception of 'internalization of culture' cannot be put in the same class as Freud's." (Simpson, *Emile Durkheim* [New York: Thomas Y. Crowell Company, 1963], p. 3.) Although Simpson's point is essentially correct, it entails a misinterpretation of Parsons. The latter nowhere suggests that Durkheim's concept of internalization is as sophisticated as Freud's; his point is rather that Durkheim, in speaking of internalization, realized, as did Freud, that society is not simply an external environment. The real problem with Parsons' interpretation of Durkheim lies elsewhere, namely, with his assumption that the discovery of the fact of internalization occurred rather late in Durkheim's career. This assumption, which derives from Parsons' interpretation of *The Rules*, is refuted both by the above

ments of esteem, of respect, of affection . . . that we are able to experience for one another."[45] These sentiments of friendship or solidarity are referred to by Durkheim at this stage in the evolution of his moral theory as "interindividual" or "intrasocial" sentiments.

Those moral sentiments referred to in this early article as "intersocial," but elsewhere as "collective" and "social," are very different. They derive from representations engendered by a number of individuals acting and reacting upon one another over an extended period of time. These representations are collective in two senses: they are the emergent products of social life, and they are shared in common by participants in a collectivity. Normally, these collective representations are experienced as obligatory, although the moral "constraint" felt is only slight, if perceptible at all, when they are fully internalized.

These two diverse forms of morality affect individual members of society very differently: "The first leaves my autonomy and personality pretty nearly intact; it undoubtedly renders me *solidaire* with others, but without my losing much of my independence. On the contrary, when I act under the influence of the second, I am no more than a part of a whole, whose movements and influences I am obliged to follow."[46] This explains why only the latter can give rise to the idea of obligation.

Moral Relationships in Diverse Societies

When viewed in terms of the major elements in Durkheim's early theory of morality, *The Division of Labor,* which was one of two doctoral dissertations submitted by Durkheim at the Sorbonne in 1893, further clarifies several important themes in his early theory by demonstrating how societies differ with respect to the moral relationships

---

cited quotation from "La Morale en Allemagne" as well as by Durkheim's peculiar use of the term "external" in his early writings (including *The Rules*). When Durkheim maintains that social facts are "external," he does not mean that they are, at any given moment, "outside" the individual. For Durkheim, social phenomena are external in both of the following two respects, neither of which assume that they are now "outside" the consciousness of the individual. First, social facts are external in the sense of being *collectively engendered,* that is, "their source is not in the individual," but in society. (*Règles,* p. 8.) Secondly, social facts are external in that they "*come to us from without,*" i.e., they initially require representation within the individual's consciousness. (*Ibid.,* p. 9.) To be sure, social facts may be external in the sense of being *outside* the consciousness of any single individual if they are shared by others, but not by the person in question. This last sense of the term "external," however, is not the one stressed by Durkheim in discussing the externality of social facts. His main point is rather that internalized social phenomena are collectively engendered and introjected from without.

45. Durkheim, "Guyau, M., *L'Irréligion de l'avenir*," *RP,* XXIII (1887), 309.
46. *Ibid.*

existing among participating members. One major question before Durkheim in *The Division* may be formulated thus: How do different societies affect the moral sentiments, obligations, and loyalties of their members? As we shall see, Durkheim handles this issue by arguing that the various elements in his early theory of morality are combined in diverse ways in different societies.

Two very different societal types, primitive and advanced societies, are contrasted and compared in *The Division*. The former are said to be characterized by "mechanical solidarity"; the latter, by "organic solidarity." These two types are not, Nisbet and other interpreters to the contrary, mutually exclusive.[47] They are, rather, ideal types representing two extremities on the tree of societal evolution. Strictly speaking, there are no societies in which both types of integration are not present. Nevertheless, Durkheim claims that "we may legitimately refer to a given society as being integrated on the basis of the one or the other of these principles, if we are able to establish that that particular type of cohesion is the fundamentally significant one in the society under consideration," that is, "the one that operationally insures the cohesion of the group."[48]

In primitive societies, Durkheim argues, moral solidarity among participants is based upon similitude. In societies at this end of the historical continuum, individuals resemble each other partly by virtue of their common humanity, but primarily because they believe in the same values, feel the same collective sentiments, and perform similar functions. Similitude is maintained by the collective conscience, or the

47. Robert Nisbet's claim that Durkheim reverses the major thesis of *Division of Labor* in midstream is based upon the incorrect assumption that Durkheim initially interprets mechanical and organic forms of solidarity as mutually incompatible types. The following passage on page 277 of the English edition (a translation of the fifth French edition published in 1926) is thus interpreted by Nisbet as representing a reversal of the original argument of the book: "The division of labor can be produced only in the midst of pre-existing society. There is a social life outside the whole division of labor, but which the latter presupposes. That is, indeed, what we have directly established in showing that there are societies whose cohesion is essentially due to a community of belief and sentiments, and it is from these societies that those whose unity is assured by the division of labor have emerged." (Cited by Nisbet, *The Sociological Tradition* [New York: Basic Books, Inc., 1966], pp. 85-86.) Commenting upon this passage, Nisbet observes: "Although it is true that he [Durkheim] has been concerned with the type of cohesion he has labeled *mechanical*—analyzing its modes of law, custom, and belief—it is hardly true that he has been stressing the continuing necessity in modern organic society of sinews of stability that are mechanical in character." (*Ibid.*, p. 86.) Durkheim himself, however, clearly indicates at the outset of the first French edition of *Division du travail social* (p. 138) that "these two societies in other respects make up only one. They are two aspects of one and the same reality, but they must be distinguished nonetheless."

48. Alpert, *Emile Durkheim*, pp. 182-183.

beliefs and sentiments common to all members of the group. The pervasive influence of these traditional beliefs is such that individuals more or less blindly acquiesce to the dictates of public opinion. Individual differences scarcely exist since each member of society is dominated by the collective will. Where individual differences are expressed in the form of deviant behavior, repressive sanctions are brought to bear upon dissenters. Societies of this type are said to be characterized by "mechanical solidarity," not because unity is produced by mechanical or artificial means but because their coherence is analogous to the solidarity of like elements or similar molecules in physical bodies. In other words, the term "mechanical solidarity" calls attention to the fact that individuals resemble and hence like each other, resemblance being due, in this case, to the psychological similarity that results from sharing identical beliefs and norms.

Moral solidarity in primitive societies has a twofold source, natural sentiments of friendship engendered by resemblance and the collective conscience, which clearly derives from Durkheim's early theory of morality. However, the important hypothesis introduced for the first time here is that psychological resemblance is produced by shared beliefs and norms.[49] The second element in Durkheim's earlier theory, the collective conscience, is thus employed in *The Division* to explain interpersonal similarity. Durkheim continues to maintain, however, that other-regarding sentiments founded upon resemblance and rooted in the nature of man spontaneously emerge once similitude is engendered by the collective conscience.

Very different is that type of society (that is, modern) in which differentiation and organic solidarity prevail. Here, the social homogeneity reinforced by traditional mores is virtually nonexistent, and the repressive legal sanctions enforced by small communities constitute a less important source of unity. Freed from the primitive "yoke of tradition," diverse subgroups flourish and individual differences abound. Accordingly, institutional pluralism and individualism are the dominant features of a societal system of this sort. Within such a framework, "the cult of the individual" and moral rules associated with human rights are the primary examples of commonly shared religious and moral principles. Moral solidarity rests not on common beliefs and norms, but, rather, on the fact that individuals, be specializing, develop complementary differences which, in turn, evoke sentiments of solidarity founded upon heterogeneity.

49. Durkheim, *Division du travail*, pp. 138-140.

Moral solidarity in advanced societies, according to *The Division of Labor*, is a more complex affair than in primitive societies. The principal source of solidarity is based on natural sentiments engendered by complementary dissimilarity. This type of dissimilarity is now traced, however, to a social factor, namely, to the progressive development of the division of labor, a development primarily responsible for the evolution of differentiated personalities. In addition to this primary source of solidarity, however, there is a second, operationally less significant, basis of moral cohesion in advanced societies that is similar to the mechanical solidarity prevailing in primitive groups. Because the various subgroups that emerge in advanced societies tend to develop their own collective moralities, individuals within these groups resemble and like each other because they share common interests, beliefs, norms, and so forth. Accordingly, sentiments of friendship based on resemblance continue to exist in modern societies alongside sentiments founded upon dissimilarity.[50]

Insofar as these are the central themes of *The Division*, the work clearly rests upon Durkheim's early moral theory. The major difference is contained in the thesis that both similitude and complementary dissimilarity are engendered by social factors, that is, the collective conscience and the division of labor. There is another thread in Durkheim's somewhat tangled discussion of moral solidarity in *The Division*, a thread that becomes increasingly important as the argument of the book progresses. In addition to interpersonal friendship ties and normative rules of behavior, Durkheim introduces a third aspect of morality— loyalty to society as a collective entity.[51] "Not only do citizens love each other and seek out each other in preference to strangers," Durkheim asserts, "but they love their country."[52] This sense of devotion to society is variously referred to as "altruism," "social solidarity," and "moral solidarity," terms also used to describe interpersonal, other-regarding sentiments. By virtue of this linguistic ambiguity, Durkheim tends to shift back and forth between friendship ties among persons within group formations and loyalty to the group as a whole.[53] A case

50. *Ibid.*, pp. 84-85. Though the persistence of solidarity based on resemblance in the subgroups of modern societies is a minor theme in *Division of Labor*, it is, nonetheless, implied throughout Durkheim's treatment of similitude (Book One, chs. 1, 2) as well as throughout his discussion of the emergence of the division of labor (Book Two). Durkheim's first sophisticated treatment of secondary group solidarity is contained in *Suicide*.

51. This third aspect of morality is also suggested in several earlier publications by Durkheim. See "Philosophie dans les universités allemandes," pp. 436-437, and "Morale en Allemagne," p. 131.

52. Durkheim, *Division du travail*, p. 113.

53. This linguistic ambiguity may be intentional, for Durkheim seems to assume that loyalty to others naturally includes devotion to the group engendered by communication with them.

in point is his treatment of altruism in primitive societies. On the one hand, Durkheim refers to the following acts as examples of altruistic behavior: "the irresistible desire which compels the widow of India to follow her husband to the grave, the Gaul not to survive the chief of his clan, the old Celt to free his companions of a useless parasite by voluntary death."[54] Here the stress is clearly upon interpersonal ties. On the other hand, Durkheim argues that these examples indicate a strong sense of dependence upon, and devotion to, society as a whole. This second argument is best expressed in the following passage:

Because the individual is not sufficient unto himself, it is from society that he receives everything necessary to him, as it is for society that he works ... Thus a very strong sentiment of the state of dependence in which he finds himself is formed. He becomes accustomed to estimating himself at his true value, that is to say, he considers himself as only part of a whole, the organ of an organism. Such sentiments naturally inspire not only those ordinary sacrifices which assure the regular progress of daily social life, but even, on occasion, acts of complete self-renunciation and total self-denial.[55]

In other words, Durkheim's discussion of interpersonal relationships within social groups tends to fade, in *The Division of Labor,* into a discussion of sentiments of dependence upon, and loyalty to, the group as a reality *sui generis.*

Apparently, this shifting focus stems from Durkheim's acceptance at this point in his career of Comte's subtle, if somewhat ambiguous, distinction between sympathy and altruism. In Comte's work, sympathy refers to an innate sense of fellowship while altruism is a broader concept including "not only every sort of fellow feeling, but also active devotion to the service of others" and to one's group.[56] Altruism or "social benevolence," Comte further maintains, results from an intensification and transformation of the instinct of sympathy. This intensification occurs when the individual, transcending himself, feels and acts as a member of a group, or as a part of a social whole which is not simply an association but a union. Similarly, Durkheim generally, although not uniformly, refers to altruism as love of society as a whole in contrast with affection for individual members. The important point here, however, is that these two sorts of phenomena—love for others and loyalty to society—are simply not sharply distinguished in *The Division of Labor.*

54. Durkheim, *Division du travail,* p. 215.
55. *Ibid.,* p. 250.
56. Wilhelm Wundt, *Ethics* (London: Swan Sonnenschein and Company, 1906; New York: Macmillan Company, 1906), II, 149.

Interpersonal sympathy, moral obligation, and group loyalty are the three principal types of phenomena included within Durkheim's early theory of morality. The first results from spontaneous sentiments elicited by the image of another; the second, from the normative rules imposed by the collective conscience; the third, from sentiments of loyalty evoked by social groups or by representations produced by groups. All of these moral phenomena are significantly affected by the specific nature of the society in which they occur. These early views are refined and elaborated in Durkheim's mature writings.

III

Toward a Science of Morality, 1897-1917

Durkheim's second major empirical study, *Suicide,* inaugurated a new phase in the evolution of his scientific account of morality, a phase characterized by two developments in his thought: further clarification and refinement of his understanding of moral phenomena, and a more idealistic conception of society that eventually resulted in the formation of several new explanatory hypotheses. Lectures and articles written between the publication of *Suicide* in 1897 and Durkheim's untimely death in 1917 elaborate on these developments.

Moral Theory in Suicide

With respect to the first of these lines of thought, *Suicide* stands out among Durkheim's early works for its neglect of psychological sentiments of a sympathetic and friendly sort and its unequivocal stress upon the individual's attachment to social groups (in contrast with attachment to individuals within group formations). Where the young Durkheim frequently refers to natural sentiments spontaneously attaching "each individual to the personality of his fellow citizens,"[1] his stress in *Suicide,* and thereafter, is clearly upon sentiments evoked by the group as a whole. In place of interpersonal sentiments of sympathy and affection, Durkheim speaks almost exclusively in *Suicide* of the sentiments of attachment and adherence, loyalty and devotion, love and affection evoked by collectivities. Durkheim's most extreme statement in *Suicide* concerning group loyalty seemingly reverses his original position regarding the sympathetic ties upon which a common life together is founded. It is "the influence of society," he states at one point, which has "aroused in us sentiments of sympathy and solidarity drawing us toward others."[2] This statement is a rather typical example, however, of Durkheim's penchant for overdramatizing his position. He continues to presuppose the existence of natural sentiments of a

---

1. Durkheim, "Guyau, *L'Irréligion,*" p. 309.
2. Durkheim, *Suicide: A Study in Sociology,* tr. John A. Spaulding and George Simpson (Glencoe, Ill.: Free Press, 1951), pp. 211-212.

friendly sort and to assume that social life would never arise in their absence, but these sentiments are now relegated to psychology.[3] This latter field is said to be outside the immediate concern of the sociologist qua sociologist, although developments in psychology were never outside the ken of Durkheim's own inclusive perspective. Without abandoning his early motivational theory,[4] Durkheim begins in *Suicide*, and especially in *Moral Education*, to turn his attention to how innate sympathetic instincts are transformed by social existence.

In order to avoid misconstruing Durkheim's stress on the individual's attachment to those social groups of which he is a member in *Suicide*, it is necessary to keep in mind a second development in his theory of morality. In *Suicide* and subsequent works Durkheim places increasing emphasis upon the idealistic nature of group life.[5] To be sure, Durkheim continues to confuse participation in social structures with loyalty to collectively shared ideas, but he begins, with *Suicide*, to lay increasingly heavy emphasis upon collectively shared ends (in addition to shared norms) of moral action. Thus, Durkheim frequently speaks, in *Suicide*, of attachment to one's group in terms of devotion not to others or to the structural properties of the group, but to the moral concepts of the society in question. These concepts are interpreted as ideal ends of action.

These new aspects of Durkheim's moral theory are apparent in his treatment of egoistic and altruistic forms of suicide. Both suicidal types are defined in terms of *attachment* to collectively shared moral con-

3. Durkheim's first systematic attempt to distinguish between psychology and sociology by relegating general characteristics of human nature to the former discipline is contained in *The Rules of the Sociological Method*. "It is clear," he asserts, "that the general characteristics of human nature participate in the work of elaboration from which social life results. But they neither create it nor give it its special form; they only make it possible. Collective representations, emotions, and tendencies are caused not be certain states of the consciousnesses of individuals, but by the conditions in which the social group in its totality is placed. Undoubtedly, collective representations, emotions, and tendencies can only be realized if individual natures are not resistant to them; but these individual natures are merely the indeterminate material that the social factor molds and transforms. Their contribution consists exclusively in very general mental states, in vague and consequently plastic predispositions which, by themselves, if other agents did not intervene, could not take on the definite and complex forms which characterize social phenomena." (*Règles*, p. 130.) Durkheim further explicates his reasons for rejecting psychological explanations of social phenomena in "L'Origine du mariage dans l'espèce humaine, d'après Westermarck," *RP*, XL (1895), 606-623, and *Suicide*, Book One, chs. 1, 2, 4.

4. That Durkheim did not abandon his early motivational theory is indicated in his discussion of general characteristics of human nature in *Règles* (pp. 128-137) and his treatment of child psychology in *Moral Education* (pp. 216-222).

5. This interpretation of Durkheim's *Suicide* is persuasively developed by Jack Douglas in *Social Meanings of Suicide*, esp. pp. 33-73.

cepts, egoistic suicide being due to insufficient attachment to shared moral beliefs and altruistic suicide being the result of excessive solidarity with, and devotion to, group ends. These types are contrasted with anomic and fatalistic forms of suicide, which are defined in terms of *normative control*. Anomie or normlessness, as the term itself implies, is due to insufficient normative control whereas fatalistic suicide is the result of excessive group surveillance and lack of individuation. Inasmuch as Durkheim further clarifies and refines his moral theory in differentiating among these several types of suicide, a close analysis of the revised moral theory upon which this fourfold differentiation is based follows.

Egoistic suicide. This type is traced by Durkheim to the psychological disorientation resulting from the disintegration of the collective moral life of one's group. Once socialized man, by participating in the religious, political, and moral beliefs of a community, has become deeply attached to these higher forms of human activity, Durkheim maintains, he cannot be detached from society without experiencing a loss of direction, a sense of apathy, an absence of attachment to life itself.

Social man necessarily presupposes a society which he expresses and serves. If this dissolves, if we no longer feel it in existence and action about and above us, whatever is social in us is deprived of all objective foundation. All that remains is an artificial combination of illusory images, a phantasmagoria vanishing at the least reflection; that is, nothing which can be a goal for our action . . . Thus we are bereft of reasons for existence; for the only life to which we could cling no longer corresponds to anything actual; the only existence still based upon reality no longer meets our needs. Because we have been initiated into a higher existence, the one which satisfies an animal or a child can satisfy us no more and the other itself fades and leaves us helpless. So there is nothing more for our efforts to lay hold of, and we feel them lose themselves in emptiness.

In this situation, the individual, thrown in upon himself, is left with nothing but his own egocentric goals which become preponderant over those of the community; he recognizes no other rules of conduct than those based upon his private interests. "If we agree to call this state egoism, in which the individual ego asserts itself to excess in the face of the social ego and at its expense," Durkheim writes, "we may call egoistic the special type of suicide springing from excessive individualism."[6]

6. Durkheim, *Suicide*, pp. 213, 209.

Although virtually any group may have a prophylactic effect on suicide, Durkheim maintains that groups may be distinguished with respect to the relative degree to which they tie their members to collective ideas, ideals, and goals. Religious communions provide a case in point. Although Roman Catholic and Protestant churches equally condemn suicide, the former has a greater prophylactic effect on suicide, not because of its doctrinal proscription of the act, but because it sustains a more vital and extensive moral life. Catholicism protects its members against suicide because of the number and vitality of the beliefs and practices common to all the faithful. By way of contrast, Protestant churches, which are characterized by fewer beliefs and practices, attach the individual less firmly to group ideas. "The Protestant," Durkheim observes in this context, "is far more the author of his faith. The Bible is put in his hands and no interpretation is imposed upon him."[7] These internal differences are expressed in higher suicide rates for Protestants than for Catholics.

Altruistic suicide. If egoistic suicide results from insufficient moral integration, altruistic suicide results from excessive integration. In the former case there is too much individuation and reliance on self; in the second, there is too rudimentary individuation and an excessive devotion to societal ends. An example is provided by the excessive development of patriotic sentiments during wartime. Great social disturbances and great popular wars, Durkheim argues, "rouse collective sentiments, stimulate partisan spirit and patriotism, political and national faith, alike, and concentrating activity toward a single end, at least temporarily cause a stronger integration of society . . . As they force men to close ranks and confront the common danger, the individual thinks less of himself and more of the common cause." Impersonality is here carried to its highest pitch. The individual strips himself of his personal interests in order to be engulfed in something which he regards as more important than his personal existence. When such persons renounce life, "it is for something they love better than themselves."[8]

Anomic suicide. Durkheim's emphasis in *Suicide* upon attachment to group ideals, as well as his attempt in the work to reconcile this new position with his early, essentially normative, conception of the collective conscience, makes the statement introducing the chapter on anomic suicide particularly enlightening: "Society," Durkheim writes, "is not only something attracting the sentiments and activities of individ-

7. *Ibid.*, p. 158.
8. *Ibid.*, pp. 208, 228.

uals with unequal force. It is also a power controlling them."[9] This "power" is the authority with which moral rules are enforced by public opinion. Anomic or normless suicide is, quite simply, the result of insufficient moral regulation.

Although the examples of anomic suicide offered in *Suicide* are drawn primarily from the economic realm, it is clear that anomie, like other forms of suicide, may occur in any group. Normally, Durkheim contends, there is, at any given moment in history,

a dim perception, in the moral consciousness of societies, of the respective value of different social services, the relative reward due to each, and the consequent degree of comfort appropriate on the average to workers in each occupation. The different functions are graded in public opinion and a certain coefficient of well-being assigned to each, according to its place in the hierarchy. According to accepted ideas, for example, a certain way of living is considered the upper limit to which a workman may aspire in his efforts to improve his existence, and there is another limit below which he is not willingly permitted to fall unless he has seriously demeaned himself . . . A genuine regime exists, therefore, although not always legally formulated, which fixes with relative precision the maximum degree of ease of living to which each social class may legitimately aspire. However, there is nothing immutable about such a scale. It changes with the increase or decrease of collective revenues and the change occurring in the moral ideas of society.[10]

As long as societies succeed in fulfilling these ideal expectations, Durkheim maintains, there is a general feeling of calm, active happiness, pleasure in existing and living which characterize health for societies as well as for individuals.

But there are times in history when actual success either exceeds or falls below the limits set by public opinion to such an extent that individuals intuitively sense that things are not as they should be. An economic disaster is an obvious example. On the one hand, an economic disaster forces some previously successful individuals to suddenly reduce "their requirements, restrain their needs, learn greater self-control."[11] On the other hand, economic crises provide an opportunity for previously less successful individuals to suddenly increase their power and wealth. Either situation, Durkheim maintains, may be a source of sufficient unhappiness to result in suicide. For the disinherited, life becomes intolerable due to the sufferings resulting from their reduced

9. *Ibid.*, p. 241.
10. *Ibid.*, pp. 249-250.
11. *Ibid.*, p. 252.

form of existence. For the successful, unchecked aspirations, freed from the moderating influence of social regulations, quickly exceed reasonable expectations.

But then their very demands make fulfillment impossible. Overweening ambition always exceeds the results obtained, great as they may be, since there is no warning to pause here. Nothing gives satisfaction and all this agitation is uninterruptedly maintained without appeasement. Above all, since this race for an unattainable goal can give no other pleasure but that of the race itself, if it is one, once it is interrupted the participants are left empty-handed . . . How could the desire to live not be weakened under such conditions?[12]

Durkheim thus arrives at one of the basic insights of contemporary sociology, namely, that the gap between anticipated expectations and reality may be as great a source of pain and unhappiness as an unexpected tragedy.

Fatalistic suicide. Although Durkheim confines his analysis of fatalism to a footnote at the conclusion of his chapter on *anomie*, this form of suicide, by rounding out his typological scheme, further clarifies the moral theory upon which this scheme is based. This fourth type of suicide results from too much normative control, from a societal restraint that tends to be oppressive and, therefore, unbearable. "It is the suicide deriving from excessive regulation, that of persons with futures pitilessly blocked and passions violently choked by oppressive discipline." Although examples are hard to find in modern societies, Durkheim cites several historical examples: "Do not the suicides of slaves, said to be frequent under certain conditions . . . belong to this type, or all suicides attributable to excessive physical or moral despotism?" Fatalism is thus contrasted with anomie just as altruism is contrasted with egotism, that is, fatalism and altruism are due to the excessive influence of society, whereas anomie and egotism result from insufficient social regulation or devotion.[13]

Two general conclusions may be drawn from this analysis of the moral theory in *Suicide*. The first is Durkheim's insistence, in his description of altruism and egotism, that collectivities constitute ideal ends capable of attracting disinterested sentiments of devotion. Although this aspect of morality is not absent from *The Division of Labor*, it clearly recieves an emphasis in this work lacking in Durkheim's early writings. The second conclusion to be drawn from *Suicide*

12. *Ibid.*, p. 253.
13. *Ibid.*, p. 276, n25.

is that "collective representations" are here presented for the first time as ideal ends or values as well as obligatory norms. To be sure, Durkheim tends to shift back and forth in *Suicide* between society as a structurally desirable system and society as a cultural set of ideals, but it is, nevertheless, significant that Durkheim's early ambivalence concerning interpersonal sentiments and collectively engendered sentiments is here supplanted with an ambivalence vis-à-vis differing forms of collective existence (for example, societal structures and collectively shared ideals). If, indeed, the foregoing interpretation of the various forms of suicide is correct, the emphasis in this work ultimately falls upon socially engendered ideal ends of conduct rather than upon society as a structurally significant value. This notion of society as a foyer of ideals capable of eliciting moral devotion is increasingly stressed in Durkheim's later writings.

Final Refinements

The year 1898, during which Durkheim published his celebrated essay on "Individual and Collective Representations," is often interpreted as representing a fresh point of departure in the maturation of Durkheim's thought. Benoit-Smullyan succinctly summarizes this widespread interpretation of Durkheim's thought:

Around 1898, Durkheim entered on a new and distinct phase of his work. It is characterized, in the first place, by a more idealistic conception of the social group, with more emphasis on "collective representations" and less on the internal social milieu; and, in the second place, by adventurous speculation concerning the social origin of morals, values, religion, and knowledge. The social group is successively endowed by Durkheim with the characteristics of hyperspirituality, personality, creativity, and transcendence. The inception of this phase is marked by the publication of Durkheim's paper on individual and collective representations.[14]

Insofar as Benoit-Smullyan is concerned with Durkheim's increasingly idealistic interpretation of social groups and with the adventurous speculation contained in his mature works, he is undoubtedly correct. In view of the foregoing analysis of *Suicide,* however, Durkheim's subsequent works represent less of a turning point in his career than a clarification and refinement of ideas that were clearly present in his thought by 1897.

Durkheim's phenomenological description of moral experience is one

14. Emile Benoit-Smullyan, "The Sociologism of Emile Durkheim," p. 510.

issue that undergoes considerable clarification in his mature writings. In several articles and lectures, especially *L'education morale,* Durkheim further refines his earlier Kantian characterization of moral obligation as well as his treatment of altruism in *Suicide.* The result is an extremely sophisticated phenomenological description of both moral obligation and valuation.

The sense of ought. In his 1902-1903 lectures on moral education, Durkheim elaborates upon his early description of moral obligation by carefully distinguishing among four principal aspects of ought experience. In the first place, moral duties are said to be experienced as *"coercive prescriptions,* strict and harsh, the instructions one must obey [italics mine]."[15] This "must" of moral duty, however, is distinguished from physical pressure, as when a command is imposed by force, "for it is an altogether inner state, that is to say, an idea suggested." This idea is experienced like a command emanating from outside the self and directed to the self. It is like "a voice that speaks to us, saying: that is your duty." And, "because it speaks to us in an imperative tone we certainly feel that it must come from some being superior to us; but we cannot see clearly who or what it is."[16]

This command is experienced as *impersonal* in the sense of being independent of "personal predispositions." Moral duties are experienced as standards that ought to be obeyed independently of one's wishes, urges, and desires. When we feel such a claim, Durkheim contends, we do not consider it appropriate to count the personal cost of obedience. Indeed, to do so would be to question the legitimacy of the claim itself by considering one's egoistic interests and wishes above those of the command. It is in the nature of moral duties "that they are

15. Durkheim, *Moral Education,* p. 94. This reference to strict and harsh prescriptions is not meant to imply that moral obedience is unpleasant. Quite the contrary, Durkheim associates an element of eudaemonism with moral duty. "We find charm in the accomplishment of a moral act prescribed by a rule that has no other justification than that it is a rule. We feel a *sui generis* pleasure in performing our duty simply because it is our duty. The notion of good enters into those of duty and obligation just as they in turn enter into the notion of good." (Emile Durkheim, "The Determination of Moral Facts," in *Sociology and Philosophy,* p. 45.) But this pleasurable aspect of moral obedience is carefully distinguished from hedonistic pursuits: "This desirability peculiar to moral life participates of the preceding characteristic of obligation, and is not the same as the desirability of the objects that attract our ordinary desires. The nature of our desire for the commanded act is a special one. Our *élan* and aspiration are accompanied by discipline and effort. Even when we carry out a moral act with enthusiasm we feel that we dominate and transcend ourselves, and this cannot occur without a feeling of tension and self-restraint." (*Ibid.*)

16. Durkheim, *Moral Education,* pp. 142, 89.

to be obeyed, not because of the behavior they require or the probable consequences of such behavior, but simply because they command. Thus, it is only their authority that accounts for such efficacy as rules may have; consequently, any inability to feel and to recognize such authority wherever it exists . . . is precisely the negation of genuine morality."[17]

Moral duties, Durkheim further explains, have a *constant or invariant quality* in several different respects. In the first place, they are constant in the sense of being invariant over time in contrast with "momentary impulses" or dispositions of the moment. "Morality is basically a constant thing, and so long as we are not considering an excessively long time span, it remains ever the same. A moral act ought to be the same tomorrow as today, whatever the personal predispositions of the actor." Moral duties are also situationally constant insofar as the situations in question are not radically different. "Morality thus presupposes a certain capacity for behaving similarly under like circumstances, and consequently it implies a certain ability to develop habits, a certain need for regularity."[18]

Finally, Durkheim observes that moral obligation is usually experienced as *a direct and immediate claim* upon the self rather than as a rational conclusion deduced from some general ethical formula.[19] Durkheim, accordingly, criticizes rationalists for uncritically assuming that moral claims are a result of abstract deductions. Ordinarily, he maintains, moral acts are based upon particular rules that are imposed upon us in specific situations. In making most of our daily decisions, "we do not refer back to the so-called general principle of morality to discover how it applies in a particular case and thus learn what we should do. Instead there are clear-cut and specific ways of acting required of us." For example, we conform to the rule forbidding incest without deducing it from some fundamental axiom of morality. Similarly, we accept daily responsibilities for our children without deducing these responsibilities from an abstract notion of paternity or harking back to the ultimate foundation of morality. We do not have to logically justify specific rules because "they already exist, they are already made, they live and operate around us and impose themselves upon us." If this were not the case, Durkheim continues, we would be forced to

17. *Ibid.,* p. 34.
18. *Ibid.,* p. 27.
19. This aspect of moral experience was first recognized by Durkheim in 1893. See his *Division du travail,* p. 17.

construct new rules on an ad hoc basis whenever we were confronted with a new situation. Under these conditions, however, life would become unbearably complex.[20]

To say that specific rules of conduct are ordinarily imposed in this manner is not to deny the existence of genuine moral problems and uncertainties. Durkheim readily acknowledges that conscientious men are often perplexed and confused by alternatives. But he claims that these moments of perplexity seldom result from confusion regarding the validity of the rules that ought to be obeyed. More often than not, the problem is not whether a rule is valid, but, rather, "what is the particular rule that applies to the given situation, and how should it be applied?" In explaining why he interprets moral uncertainty in this manner, Durkheim states: "Since each rule is a general prescription, it cannot be applied exactly and mechanically in identical ways in each particular circumstance. It is up to the person to see how it applies in a given situation. There is always considerable, if limited, leeway left for his initiative." However, if no rule of conduct prescribes what ought to be done, moral obligation does not exist.[21]

In delineating these subtle phenomenological characteristics of moral experience, Durkheim reaches conclusions remarkably similar to those perpetrated by modern Gestalt psychologists. According to Fritz Heider (who summarizes the conclusions of this school of psychology), when a person has "the conviction that he ought to do *x* he recognizes a vector in the environment, a vector which is like a wish or a demand or a requirement on the part of some suprapersonal order and which has the validity of objective existence."[22] In specifying what he means by describing the experience of moral obligation as an experience of a demand on the part of a suprapersonal objective order, Heider points to the impersonal and invariant character of an ought experience. In Heider's view, oughts are impersonal, as they are for Durkheim, precisely because they "refer to standards of what ought to be done or experienced, standards independent of the individual's wishes."[23] But oughts are experienced not only as impersonal, but also as invariant, that is, "the same ought holds among a variety of situations as long as the variation is felt to be incidental, or extrinsic as far as the ought requirements are con-

20. Durkheim, *Moral Education*, p. 26. Talcott Parsons sees this thesis as an important building-block in Durkheim's case against the utilitarian theory of action in his *Structure of Social Action*, p. 313.

21. Durkheim, *Moral Education*, p. 23.

22. Fritz Heider, *The Psychology of Interpersonal Relations* (New York: John Wiley and Sons, 1958), p. 219.

23. *Ibid.*

cerned."[24] Durkheim, however, goes beyond Heider in stressing the experience of a direct and immediate claim upon the self as well as in grappling with the issue of moral uncertainty.

The sense of value. If Durkheim's phenomenological account of moral obligation in his mature writings elaborates upon his earlier account, his description of disinterested dispositions undergoes a dramatic transformation. In his earliest writings (1885-1893), it will be recalled, Durkheim speaks of disinterested sentiments of sympathy and group loyalty. In *Suicide,* the notion of altruistic attachment to collective ideals is introduced for the first time, although this thesis is not clearly differentiated from either sympathetic sentiments or sentiments of attachment to structural institutions. Although *Moral Education* preserves this tendency to fuse clearly distinct phenomena, Durkheim's treatment of valuation in "Value Judgments and Judgments of Reality" (1911) suggests a new point of departure, one which presumably would have been further clarified had Durkheim lived to complete *La Morale.*[25]

At the outset of this 1911 essay, Durkheim draws an important distinction between the objective, impersonal nature of a sense of value on the one hand, and subjective personal preferences and desires on the other:

When I say, "I like hunting," "I prefer beer to wine," "an active life to one of repose" etc., I express judgments which might appear to be based upon estimations but which are, in fact, simple judgments of reality. They merely report my relations with certain objects: that I like this or prefer that. These preferences are facts as much as the heaviness of bodies or the elasticity of gas. Such judgments do not attach value to objects but merely affirm the state of the subject. Also the predilections which are expressed are not communicable. Those who experience them can say that they experience them or, at least, that they think they do; but they cannot communicate their experience to others. It is part of their personality and cannot be divorced from it.

It is quite a different matter when I say: "This man *has* a high moral value, this picture *has* great aesthetic value, this jewel is *worth* so much." In all these instances I attribute to the people or things in question an objective character quite independent of my own individual feelings at the time of making the judgment.

24. *Ibid.,* pp. 220-221.
25. Durkheim's outline of *La Morale* indicates his intention to elaborate upon his earlier discussion of valuation. Several chapters were to be devoted to this issue. See Durkheim, "Introduction à la morale," *RP*, LXXXIX (1920), 80.

In an attempt to strengthen his description of a sense of value as objective and impersonal, Durkheim points to the distinction between liking something and valuing it. In instances of valuation, he states, one may not personally attach any value to the object,

but its value is not the less for that. I as an individual may not be highly moral in my behaviour, but that does not prevent me from recognizing moral value when I see it. By temperament I may not be very sensitive to art, but that is no reason why I should deny that there can be aesthetic value. All these values exist then, in a sense, outside me. Thus when we are in disagreement with others over judgments in such matters we try to communicate our convictions. We are not satisfied with merely affirming their existence; we try to demonstrate their validity by supporting them with impersonal arguments. Implicitly we recognize that these judgments correspond to some objective reality upon which agreement can and should be reached. These *sui generis* realities constitute values, and it is to these realities that value judgments refer.[26]

This clarification of the phenomenological sense of valuation leads Durkheim toward an implicit distinction between a sense of ought and a sense of value. Within the phenomological realm, an obligation is a claim upon the self calling for action, whereas a value is a property of an object (this man, picture, or jewel *has* value) that elicits a disinterested judgment on disposition. Heider suggests a similar distinction in the following passage:

In distinguishing value from ought, we can begin with the idea that value is linked with actions in a much less specific way than is ought. That is, "*p* values *x*" can give rise to many different actions, or to none at all, whereas "*p* ought to do *x*" means there is an actual objective force present. The relation between "*p* values *x*" and "*p* ought to do *x*" is analogous to the relation between "*p* likes *x*" and "*p* wants to do *x*."

In further explicating this distinction, Heider observes that

there is a difference between "I like *x*" and "I want *x*" . . . The same difference differentiates "I value *x*" from "I ought to do *x*." If we . . . [treat] the objective order like another person, then we can say that a value is that which the objective order likes, or which is of relevance to the impersonal reality, whereas an ought is that which the objective order wants.[27]

26. Durkheim, "Value Judgments and Judgments of Reality," pp. 80-81.
27. Heider, *Psychology of Interpersonal Relations*, pp. 224, 225.

With this explication of the sense of value, Durkheim's foregoing account of valuation clearly agrees.

Valuation and obligation, in Durkheim's view, are invariably combined in actual moral experience, but the resulting combinations vary with different circumstances, epochs, and individuals. There are moments of enthusiastic devotion when the element of goodness in valuation predominates to such a degree that the sense of obligation is at a minimum. There are other occasions when the idea of duty finds maximum support. "The relation between these two elements also varies with time; thus in antiquity it would appear that the notion of duty was on the wane; in the systems of morality, and perhaps in the everyday life of the people, the idea of the Sovereign Good predominated." In any given epoch, the relation of valuation and obligation may also vary widely in different individuals. For individuals have varying sensitivities to these two aspects of morality. Indeed, it is rare for one individual to be equally sensitive to both elements. "There are those for whom moral acts are above all good and desirable; there are those with a greater feeling for the rule itself who enjoy discipline, loathe anything indeterminate, and wish their lives to follow a rigid programme and their conduct to be constantly controlled by inflexible rules."[28]

This peculiar duality of moral value and obligation is also found in the religious realm: the sacred is experienced as both an object of high moral value and an object which inspires, if not fear, at least awe and respect. On the one hand, the sacred is a worthy object that attracts us. On the other hand, it inspires us with a religious respect that keeps us at some distance; any encroachment upon the legitimate sphere of the sacred is regarded as a sacrilege.

This comparison of the sacred with morality is not simply an interesting analogy. For morality, in Durkheim's view, cannot be understood unless it is related to religious experience.

For centuries morals and religion have been intimately linked and even completely fused. Even today one is bound to recognize this close association in the majority of minds. It is apparent that moral life has not been, and never will be, able to shed all the characteristics that it holds in common with religion. When two orders of facts have been so closely linked, when there has been between them so close a relationship for so long a time, it is impossible for them to be dissociated and become distinct. For this to happen they would have to undergo a

28. Durkheim, "Determination of Moral Facts," p. 46.

complete transformation and so change their nature. There must, then, be morality in religion and elements of the religious in morality.[29]

But the sacred and the moral are distinguished by the fact that the sacred in morality does not lift it above criticism, as it does religion. Morality is not simply an emotional reaction to sacred values and axioms; genuine morality requires rational deliberation. "Circumstances are never the same, and as a result the rules of morality require intelligence in their application."[30] Thus, the sacred element in morality does not involve blind or slavish submission.

Society as the Source of Morality

If a sense of obligation and a sense of value are the two principal aspects of moral experience, how are these phenomenological experiences to be explained? That Durkheim invokes the name of society in replying to this question scarcely comes as a surprise to anyone who has followed the logic of his thought into his mature works. What arguments, then, are adduced by Durkheim in support of this still current claim?

In addition to reiterating his earlier observations regarding the cross-cultural diversity of moral standards in support of his contentions vis-à-vis the social origins of morality, Durkheim introduces several additional arguments in his mature works that presuppose the doctrine of man set forth in "Individual and Collective Representations," "The Dualism of Human Nature," *Pragmatisme et sociologie*, and *The Elementary Forms of the Religious Life*. In these publications, the fundamental assumption is set forth that the human self or personality is composed of two very different poles.

In every age, Durkheim contends, man has been at least introspectively aware of the constitutional duality of his nature:

He has, in fact, everywhere conceived of himself as being formed of two radically heterogeneous beings: the body and the soul. Even when the soul is represented in a material form, its substance is not thought of as being of the same nature as the body. It is said that it is more ethereal, more subtle, more plastic, that it does not affect the senses as do the other objects to which they react, that it is not subject to the same laws as these objects, and so on. And not only are these two beings substantially different, they are in a large measure independent of each other, and are often even in conflict.[31]

29. *Ibid.*, p. 48.
30. Durkheim, *Moral Education*, p. 52.
31. Emile Durkheim, "The Dualism of Human Nature and Its Social Conditions," in *Emile Durkheim*, ed. Wolff, p. 326.

Durkheim contends that this phenomenological distinction between the body and the soul, widely recognized by Western philosophers and theologians, has yet to be adequately explained.

This duality can only be explained, Durkheim asserts, by sharply distinguishing between sensory appetites and reason, between a faculty for perceiving sensory demands (sensations, perceptions, images) and a faculty for thinking in universal and impersonal terms. There is in each individual both a bodily self, derived from sensory feelings, and a spiritual self, derived from representations that express something other than our bodily organisms.

These two aspects of our psychic life are, therefore, opposed to each other as are the personal and the impersonal. There is in us a being that represents everything in relation to itself and from its own point of view; in everything that it does, this being has no other object but itself. There is another being in us, however, which knows things *sub specie aeternitis,* as if it were participating in some thought other than its own, and which, in its acts, tends to accomplish ends that surpass its own. The old formula *homo duplex* is therefore verified by the facts. Far from being simple, our inner life has something that is like a double center of gravity. On the one hand is our individuality—and, more particularly, our body in which it is based; on the other is everything in us that expresses something other than ourselves.

Acts in conformity with the former pole are egoistic; they have the satisfaction of biological drives alone as their object. "When we satisfy our hunger, our thirst, and so on, without bringing any other tendency into play, it is ourselves, and ourselves alone, that we satisfy." Actions in accordance with impersonal representations of conceptual thought are disinterested inasmuch as they are neither motivated by biological drives nor do they involve attachment to sensations arising from our bodily selves.[32]

States of consciousness of the latter type, Durkheim asserts, must derive from society, inasmuch as a society is the only entity in nature that sufficiently surpasses the individual in terms of complexity and moral superiority to engender psychic phenomena of this sort. These collectively engendered states of consciousness are experienced as *objective* precisely because they do in fact come to the individual from without, that is, from the collective consciousness.[33] They are experienced as *impersonal* partly because they do not depend upon individual desires, but primarily because the symbolic elaborations of a collectiv-

32. *Ibid.,* pp. 327-328.
33. *Ibid.,* p. 337.

ity are, by definition, concepts or universals. "Concepts," Durkheim
states in this connection,

are always common to a plurality of men. They are constituted by
means of words, and neither the vocabulary nor the grammar of a
language is the work or product of one particular person. They are
rather the result of a collective elaboration, and they express the anony-
mous collectivity that employs them. The ideas of *man* and *animal* are
not personal and are not restricted to me; I share them, to a large
degree, with all the men who belong to the same social group that
I do. Because they are held in common, concepts are the supreme
instrument of all intellectual exchange. By means of them minds
communicate.[34]

These states of consciousness are also experienced as *invariant or constant* because they change slowly, being "the result of an immense
cooperation which stretches out not only into space but into time as
well; to make them a multitude of diverse minds has associated, united,
and combined their ideas and their sentiments; in them, long series of
generations have accumulated their experience and their knowledge."[35]
These ideals, whether they are experienced as obligatory duties or values, "are invested by reason of their origin with an ascendancy and an
authority that cause the particular individuals who think them and
believe in them to represent them in the form of moral forces that
dominate and sustain them ... Our feelings toward them are respect
and reverent fear, as well as gratitude for the comfort that we receive
from them; for they cannot communicate themselves to us without
increasing our vitality."[36] For all of these reasons, it is society that
moves the individual to transcend his bodily self and to participate in
the higher forms of moral life.

Arguments of this sort lie at the basis of the charge that Durkheim
concluded his career by conferring upon society a metaphysical, hyperspiritual status. Durkheim himself more or less admits as much in discussing the question: how do we know that the nonempirical, symbolic
system designated by the term "society" really exists? Basically, as
Durkheim himself was the first to observe, his answer represents a
revision of Kant's argument for the existence of God: if morality, or a
system of obligations and values, exists, a nonempirical entity qualitatively different from individuals must also exist. "Kant postulates God,

34. *Ibid.*, p. 327.
35. Emile Durkheim, *Les Formes élémentaires de la vie religieuse* (Paris: Félix
Alcan, 1912), pp. 22-23.
36. Durkheim, "Dualism of Human Nature," p. 335.

since without this hypothesis morality is unintelligible. We postualte society specifically distinct from individuals, since otherwise morality has no object and duty no roots."[37]

Does this mean that one must choose between God and society? In his early writings Durkheim carefully sidesteps this issue. In the first edition of *The Division of Labor,* for example, he declares: "It is possible that there is an eternal moral law, written in some transcendental mind . . . and that historical morality merely successively approximates the eternal law, but this is a metaphysical hypothesis that we do not have to discuss."[38] In *Suicide,* the traditional Roman Catholic distinction between first and secondary causes is invoked:

Just as the science of physics involves no discussion of the belief in God, the creator of the physical world, so the science of morals involves no concern with the doctrine which beholds the creator of morality in God. The question is not of our competence; we are not bound to espouse any solution. Secondary causes alone need occupy our attention.[39]

By 1906, however, the question of God or society is viewed as a fundamental issue calling for an existential decision: "Between God and society lies the choice. I shall not examine here the reasons that may be advanced in favour of either solution, both of which are coherent. I can only add that I myself am quite indifferent to this choice, since I see in the Divinity only society transfigured and symbolically expressed."[40] Henceforth, the spiritual transcendence and creativity traditionally ascribed to the Deity are increasingly attributed to society.

This gradual sanctification of society yields several additional claims that go beyond those associated with the social origins of moral objectivity, impersonality, and invariance. In *The Elementary Forms of the Religious Life,* Durkheim claims not only that socicty is the source of impersonal rules and values, but that it possesses all the spiritual characteristics necessary to arouse in an individual the sense of being in rela-

37. Durkheim, "Determination of Moral Facts," pp. 51-52.
38. Durkheim, *Division du travail,* p. 22.
39. Durkheim, *Suicide,* p. 318, n.14. A similar position is maintained by Durkheim in *Moral Education,* p. 61. "Unless the system of moral ideas is the product of a general hallucination, that being with which morality links our wills and which is the principal object of our behavior can only be a divine being or a social being. We set aside the first of these hypotheses as beyond the province of science. There remains the second, which, as we shall see, is adequate for our needs and aspirations and which, furthermore, embraces all the reality of the first, minus its symbolism."
40. Durkheim, "Determination of Moral Facts," p. 52.

tionship with a morally superior being. "Society has all that is necessary to arouse the sensation of the divine in minds, merely by the influence it exerts on them; for society is to its members what a God is to its worshippers." A religious person's sense of moral dependence on God thus results from his real, albeit unconscious, dependence on society.

Since it is by spiritual ways that social pressure is exercised, it could not fail to give man the idea that there exist outside of himself one or more moral and, at the same time, efficacious powers upon which he depends . . . Undoubtedly, if man could immediately see that these influences to which he submits emanate from society, then the mythological system of interpretation would never be born. But social action follows ways that are too circuitous and obscure, and employs psychical mechanisms that are too complex to allow the ordinary observer to perceive whence it comes. As long as scientific analysis does not come to teach it to him, man knows very well that he is acted upon, but he does not know by whom. So he must invent by himself the idea of these powers with which he feels himself in relation, and, from that, we are able to catch a glimpse of the way by which man was led to represent them under forms that are foreign to their nature and to transfigure them by thought.[41]

Society not only creates a sense of spiritual dependence, however, it also engenders the feeling of moral uplift and transcendence traditionally associated with religious worship. Just as "the man who has obeyed his god and who, for this reason, believes the god is with him, approaches the world with confidence and with the feeling of an increased energy," likewise, "social action is not limited to the sacrifices, privations, and efforts demanded of us. For the collective force is not entirely outside of us; but rather, since society can only exist in and through individual consciousnesses, this force must penetrate us and organize itself in us; it thus becomes an integral part of our being and in this way elevates and magnifies our existence."[42] As a corollary, it follows that the believer must be in error insofar as he understands "God" as being the source of these supernatural powers.

These chapters on Durkheim's moral theory constitute, primarily, a glimpse at his typical findings, an introduction to his phenomenological

41. Durkheim, *Formes élémentaires*, pp. 295, 298-299.
42. *Ibid.*, p. 299.

description of moral experience, and a sampling of the principal explanatory hypotheses that are the foundation of his theories and conclusions. The difficulties of such an effort are evident. Not only is much of the phenomenological data refined and revised in the course of Durkheim's intellectual maturation; not only are his explanatory hypotheses continually pushed beyond a fairly low level of abstraction into the realm of metaphysics; but coherent exposition has also required the "rethreading" of earlier insights that are introduced, in altered form, in Durkheim's mature writings.

What crucial issues and critical question emerge from this survey of Durkheim's attempt to delineate and explain the facts of the moral life? Although a complete survey of all the possible responses to this query is impossible in the present context, several central points deserve brief consideration. Durkheim is essentially correct in maintaining that a scientific study of morality must begin with a careful descriptive account of the phenomena to be explained, for any attempt to explain conscious mental processes must obviously be preceded by a careful description of the phenomena to be interpreted. Otherwise, the explanations are superfluous. Durkheim is further correct in his final description of the phenomenological nature of immediate moral obligation and valuation. Moral obligation does seem to involve an objective, impersonal, invariant demand for some sort of direct and appropriate response from the self. Values do appear, within the phenomenal world, as objective and impersonal properties of entities calling for a favorable judgment. The principal weakness of this descriptive work is Durkheim's failure to consider active moral judgment, that is, the rational justification of moral beliefs. By stressing immediate experience at the expense of active judgment, Durkheim fails to include rational moral decision making within his description of morality. Yet moral reasoning must be described and explained if an adequate science of morality is to be achieved. Despite this weakness, Durkheim's characterization of immediate moral experience is valid. The question remains whether his several arguments in favor of society as the sole source of moral beliefs and the experiences generated by them are tenable.

There are three principal objections regarding Durkheim's explanatory theory of morality. First, Durkheim's frequently repeated claim that moral standards vary cross-culturally is not a sufficient justification of the corollary that all moral standards are engendered by collectivities. That moral evaluations vary, no one will deny. But diverse evaluations are not necessarily evidence of a fundamental disagreement vis-à-vis the basic ethical principles of evaluation. It might well be the case that culturally diverse and seemingly opposed norms and values do not derive from any basic disagreement regarding fundamental ethical principles such as promise-keeping, truthfulness, beneficence, justice, and so forth. Cultural disagreements may rather result, as Duncker first observed in his now famous article of 1939 in *Mind,* from differences in the life situations of peoples or in the diverse meanings associated with identical contextual situations.[43] In other words, the diverse moral standards studied by sociologists and anthropologists may result from differing contextual interpretations cojoined with invariant moral standards rather than from fundamental ethical differences. For example, the fact that the Yahgan occasionally hasten the death of their relatives by strangulation does not necessarily demonstrate a fundamental ethical disagreement between the Yahgan and other peoples regarding the basic ethical duties of beneficence and not injuring others. Quite the contrary, strangulation is seen by the Yahgan as a kindly act in the best interests of their relatives as well as the long-term good of the tribe.[44] In this case, diverse cultural norms appear to derive not from fundamental ethical differences, but, rather, from diverse factual interpretations. If, however, it remains an open question whether or not cross-cultural moral disagreements are based upon fundamental ethical conflicts or differing contextual inter-pretations, it obviously cannot be assumed, in the absence of further theoretical and empirical arguments, that society is the sole source of moral principles. For the possibility remains that moral stan-dards are in fact cross-culturally invariant, socially diverse principles being the result of conflicting contextual interpretations rather than the prod-uct of fundamental disagreement about basic ethical norms and values.

Whether or not all moral disagreements are ultimately due to differing contextual interpretations, several recent studies suggest that there is far less cross-cultural moral variation than Durkheim supposed. Linton and Kluckhohn, for example, have both found several moral principles in all cultures.[45] Linton's list of universal principles includes norms re-specting reciprocity, fairness, parental responsibility, and filial obedi-

43. Karl Duncker, "Ethical Relativity," *Mind,* XLVIII (1939), 39-57.

44. Gerhard Lenski, *Power and Privilege* (New York: McGraw-Hill, 1966), p. 104.

45. See Ralph Linton, "The Problem of Universal Values," in *Method and Perspective in Anthropology: Papers in Honor of Wilson D. Wallis,* ed. Robert F. Spencer (Minneapolis, Minn.: University of Minnesota Press, 1954), pp. 145-168; Clyde Kluckhohn, "Ethical Relativity: Sic et Non," *Journal of Philosophy,* LII (1955), 663-677.

ence, as well as values regarding health, happiness, and knowledge. Kluckhohn adds several in-group prohibitions against killing, indiscriminate lying, and stealing. Kohlberg has recently argued, on the basis of several cross-cultural studies of moral discourse, that there are thirty basic moral categories, concepts, or principles in all cultures.[46] A minority of individuals in a given culture use all thirty categories, but some are used by everyone. Moral disagreements result either from employing different moral categories included within this limited range of thirty or from using these categories differently. These observations, incidentally, lead Kohlberg to reject Duncker's claim that all moral disagreements are due to diverse contextual interpretations, although he acknowledges that differing interpretations of this sort are responsible for some conflicting judgments. Moral disagreements are sometimes due to the use of differing moral principles. The thirty fundamental moral categories that people ordinarily use in moral discourse are found in all cultures, however.

Recent developments in psychology also render problematic the psychological assumptions underlying Durkheim's explanation of morality, especially those regarding the duality of human nature. Recent studies by Piaget and students following his approach, including Kohlberg, indicate that the phenomenological experience of objectivity, impersonality, constancy, and invariance associated with morality is not merely a product of collective concepts being impressed upon receptive organisms. In addition to cultural conditioning, the cognitive activity of the subject is necessary to constitute the experience. Piaget and Kohlberg conclude from their studies that the distinctive phenomenological character of moral experience is always as much a product of the cognitive construction of the subject as it is an accommodation to cultural conditioning by the subject.

In empirically verifying the validity of this basic insight, Piaget and Kohlberg have both demonstrated that the successive moralities of children are a product not only of social conditioning, but of the spontaneous restructuring of cognitive experience. Piaget, for instance, has convincingly shown that most children progress from heteronomous to autonomous forms of morality, a progression that parallels congitive development.[47]

46. Lawrence Kohlberg, "From Is to Ought: How to Commit the Naturalistic Fallacy and Get Away with it in the Study of Moral Development," in *Cognitive Development and Epistemology*, ed. T. Mischel (New York: Academic Press, 1971; in press.)

47. Jean Piaget, *The Moral Judgment of the Child*, tr. Marjorie Gabain (New York: Free Press, 1965).

According to Piaget, heteronomous morality is the morality of the young child between the ages of three and seven. At this stage, the child's limited cognitive development and respect for authority causes him to regard rules as sacred and unchangeable. Because rules are seen as unchangeable, all modifications, even if generally accepted, are resisted. Duty is understood as strict obedience to authority, with little regard to subjective intentionality or objective consideration of the consequences. Moral wrongness is interpreted in terms of sanctions; an act is bad because one is punished for it. Justice is served by expiatory punishment, that is, a punishment which is painful in proportion to the seriousness of the offense.

Heteronomous morality is eventually, at least in part, replaced by autonomous morality. With cognitive development and participation in peer group interactions, rules are no longer regarded as sacred, unchangeable laws; they are now seen as the outcome of free agreement and mutual consent. Rules become rational conventions that can be modified and adapted to serve orderly group action and cooperation. Moral behavior is now interpreted in terms of reciprocal rights and obligations, with intentions and consequences being viewed as important factors. Justice is now defined in terms of reciprocity; punishment takes the form of restoring the *status quo ante.*

Kohlberg, a student working within the Piaget tradition, has both refined the Swiss psychologist's stages and extended them into adolescence and adulthood.[48] Kohlberg's cross-cultural findings indicate that at least some adolescents and adults subordinate conventional social standards to internal moral principles formulated in comparative independence of the immediate social context. Adolescents and adults are capable of formulating abstract moral principles by which conventional moral standards may be judged. Particularly interesting in this connection is the last of Kohlberg's six developmental stages. The individual at this stage judges conduct in terms of ethical principles chosen for their logical comprehensiveness, universalizability, and consistency. If Kohlberg's analysis of morality is correct, Durkheim's assumption that all moral judgments simply reflect cultural standards cannot be accepted. Kohlberg's cross-cultural studies indicate that an individual at

48. Lawrence Kohlberg, "The Development of Children's Orientations Toward a Moral Order: I, Sequence in the Development of Moral Thought," *Vita Humana,* VI (1963), 11-33, "Moral Development and Identification," *Child Psychology,* 62nd Yearbook of the National Society for the Study of Education (Chicago: University of Chicago Press, 1963), "On Moral Education" (paper presented at the Conference on the Role of Religion in Public Education, Cambridge, Massachusetts, May 19 and 20, 1966), and "From Is to Ought."

this stage judges conventional morality in terms of abstract moral principles selected for their comprehensiveness, universalizability, and consistency in relative independence of the immediate social milieu.

Kohlberg's findings also indicate that all individuals, regardless of
culture, pass through the same order or sequence of moral development, with different principles and modes of reasoning being salient at
each stage. Individuals may become fixated at any stage, however, thus
failing to move on to the next. Most adults in the societies studied were
thus fixated at the conventional level described by Durkheim and by
Kohlberg in terms of obedience to shared rules that promote social
order.[49] Cross-cultural moral differences are attributed by Kohlberg to
the fact that societies provide diverse conditions for moral development; some retard, while others promote, development. Hence, the
stage attained by the majority in one culture may differ from the stage
attained by the majority in another. In other words, different societies
have seemingly diverse moral standards because their members are at
different stages of development. If Kohlberg is right, the major differentiating factor among cultures is not to be located in their diverse moral
achievements, but, rather, in the moral level of development achieved
by most individuals within the society. Instead of moral diversity being
due to the arbitrary creation of different collective moral standards, as
Durkheim supposed, Kohlberg proposes that the major source of moral
difference is developmental.

Inasmuch as this conclusion refutes Durkheim's thinking, it is important to observe that Kohlberg apparently underplays the role of society
just as Durkheim overplays it. While development may be the most
important source of moral diversity, cultural beliefs and practices
clearly guide development and nourish the formation of conscience.
Kohlberg acknowledges this important role of society, but his methodological procedures tend to preclude a careful sociological analysis of
the subtle ways in which cultural beliefs and practices both promote
development and affect individuals at the so-called "post conventional"
stages. Yet, whether or not an individual exercises his capacities for

49. Although Kohlberg relegates Durkheim's description of morality to the
fourth of his six stages, he praises Durkheim for providing a more accurate description of the social rule and authority perspective than Freud and Piaget. The
latter psychologists, Kohlberg contends, fail to distinguish between the primitive
"obedience to authority" perspective of the first stage and the more advanced
"rule and authority maintaining" perspective described by Durkheim. In this
more advanced stage, rules are obeyed not simply because they are commanded,
but because they are seen as necessary for social order. Durkheim is further
correct, Kohlberg suggests, in believing that the latter form of morality is the
"normal" adult morality in any society. (Kohlberg, "From Is to Ought.")

higher forms of moral reasoning depends in part upon the subtlety of his social milieu. Individuals at advanced stages are profoundly influenced by the quality of public debate regarding the justification of war, abortion, euthanasia, and so forth. In short, a fully adequate account of morality must further develop and extend Durkheim's seminal work by exploring the multifarious ways in which social conditions interact with psychological factors in the formation of morality.

What Piaget and Kohlberg have attempted to demonstrate is that cognitive development is as important, if not more important, in the formation of morality as social conditioning. Their conclusions are stated, in a somewhat different form, by Raymond Aron, who challenges Durkheim's assertion that man, without society, would be more or less indistinct from an animal. In this context, Aron rightly observes that while society is a necessary condition for the development of morality in the human species, this condition becomes sufficient only if man is endowed with capacities transcending those of other species. Moral comprehension and "communication obviously imply that there are several men, and in this sense a society exists, but the fact that there are several animals together is not enough to produce language, comprehension, and communication of the same type as in human society."[50] Animals live in groups, but this fact is not sufficient for the development of morality. Morality, therefore, depends in part upon the constitutive characteristics of human nature.

Finally, several critical questions must be raised regarding Durkheim's fundamental assumption that society is a relational entity, an objective and immanent reality *sui generis,* capable of imposing obligations upon, and creating values for, its individual constituents. Does a social reality of this sort actually exist? Today, social realists are widely accused of reifying or hypostatizing abstractions, of mistaking abstract concepts, like "society," for genuine realities. Durkheim is said to be guilty of this error insofar as he confuses "the social milieu for a *sui generis* reality, objectively and materially defined, when in fact it is merely an intellectual representation."[51] While it is true that Durkheim tends to regard analytical distinctions as embedded in reality when in fact the phenomena in question are often not existentially separable, this type of criticism begs the question whether social realism is an acceptable philosophical position. In lieu of simply condemning Durkheim for reifying analytical terms, it is necessary to critically examine social realism, which can only be done by distinguishing between legitimate and illegitimate forms of this doctrine.

50. Aron, *Main Currents in Sociological Thought,* II, 92.
51. *Ibid.,* pp. 88-89.

While it is enormously difficult to prove that anything genuinely exists, there is a sense in which "society" does appear to be more than an analytic fiction. There are, for example, patterned forms of social interaction and shared beliefs that apparently do really exist, although they would not exist if individuals did not think and act in specific ways. The purpose of sociological theory is not to create a heuristic fiction, but to grasp as accurately as possible existing social realities. No scientific theory provides a completely adequate representation of reality, but if a theory professes to be scientific, it must attempt to represent some aspect of reality. In reference to these issues, Parsons is undoubtedly correct in substituting "analytical realism" for "social realism," thereby calling attention to the fact that the general concepts of science are neither fictional nor exact copies of reality but, rather, attempts to "adequately 'grasp' aspects of the objective external world."[52]

Do sociological facts possess an ontological status irreducible to the thoughts and actions of specific individuals? Using the interaction of a depositor and a teller in a bank as an example, Maurice Mandelbaum has recently argued that the behavior of individuals in a typical social situation of this sort is unintelligible unless one assumes that there are genuine social facts involved which are not reducible to the facts of individual psychology.[53] When the depositor gives a withdrawal slip to the teller, both are behaving in terms of the teller's status and role, and these concepts of status and role are devoid of meaning unless they are interpreted in terms of the society in which they occur. Neither the behavior of the depositor nor that of the teller are reducible to how these individuals would ordinarily behave toward others or how others in turn would behave toward them. Whatever else the depositor may be thinking or doing when he presents his withdrawal slip, his behavior involves recognition of both the status of the man in the teller's cage and the role of a teller as an agent of the bank. To analyze or explain the depositor's behavior, one must have recourse to these societal concepts as well as to "bank," "legal tender," "contract," and others. The teller's behavior is similarly explicable only when these societal terms are employed. In exchanging money for the withdrawal slip, he is clearly not behaving as he ordinarily does with other persons since he obviously would not give money in return for such a slip presented to him at a cocktail party. Nor is the teller's behavior understandable solely in terms of the patterns of behavior that depositors exhibit in dealing with him, because then *their* behavior would have to be ex-

52. Parsons, *Structure of Social Action*, p. 730.
53. Maurice Mandelbaum, "Societal Facts," *British Journal of Sociology*, VI (1955), 305-317.

plained and an adequate explanation of their behavior would involve recognition or his status and role. If one wishes to explain this typical example of social behavior, one has to have recourse to social facts, in the form of societal concepts and patterned relationships, which are not reducible to how the individuals involved normally behave toward others or how others behave toward them. Thus, sociological concepts, like "status" and "role," are not merely heuristic devices, summarizing patterned behavior and nothing more; they refer to genuine and irreducible social facts of experience.

In further defending this moderate form of social realism, Mandelbaum employs Durkheim's argument that individuals are born into societies that have characteristics independent of them. These factual characteristics of society are not independent of other individuals, and it is only through the behavior of others that a specific individual learns accepted patterns of behavior. But the other individuals were also born into already existing organizations that were initially independent of them, and so it goes back to the beginning of time. Thus, socially oriented behavior is generally conditioned by an existing set of social facts.

In setting forth this moderate form of social realism, Mandelbaum defends himself against the usual objections to the ontological status of social facts. In the first place, this type of social realism does not assume that society is a whole greater than the sum of its parts, thus it is not subject to philosophical objections against the holistic doctrine. Second, the nonmaterial nature of these facts does not exclude them from the realm of existence unless one adopts an exceptionally narrow epistemological theory stating that only material objects are facts. A theory of knowledge of the latter sort, however, cannot account for our apprehending the nature of individual behavior and our gaining knowledge of human societies through observation of repeated patterns of individual activity. Finally, this moderate form of social realism does not deny individual initiative and other aspects of human behavior independent of social facts. Hence, it cannot be accused of seeing individuals merely as pawns of society.

Durkheim's brand of social realism is plausible insofar as it contains elements of this moderate form of relational social realism; it becomes untenable when pushed beyond these modest claims. Every society, he declares, is a reality *sui generis,* a creative synthesis superior in complexity to the individuals within it. This familiar holistic argument is nowhere supported by an adequate philosophical defense. Usually, it is supported, like most holistic sociological theories, not by logic, but by analogism, that is, by an escape into metaphorical language. Society is variously described as a conscience, a being, a superior life, even a deity in relation to its members, that is, as a superior being analogous to the human individual, and, more specifically, to "la conscience humaine." Society, however, nowhere exhibits the individual life-unity of the human mind or personality. The assertion that society is more complex than the subtle workings of an individual's mind and personality is scarcely a self-evident proposition; prima facie it appears to be wrong. In any case, one cannot existentially separate social phenomena, like culture, from the individual members of society and argue that one is more complex than the other.

In addition to arguing that every society is a reality *sui generis*, Durkheim insists that societies engender moral "forces." "A group is not only a moral authority which dominates the life of its members," he asserts, "it is also a source of life *sui generis*. A warmth emanates from it which animates or revives the hearts of its members, making them feel fellow sympathy and harmony, dissolving egoism."[54] It is one thing to say that society exists in the sense of patterned relationships and shared meanings, but it is quite another matter to assert that this reality is a source of moral forces that oblige and elevate amoral man. Durkheim's principal argument in favor of society as the source of all moral forces fallaciously extrapolates from the phenomenological facts. Because moral obligation and valuation exist, Durkheim argues, there must be a superior reality responsible for these phenomena. Neither the facts of phenomenological experience nor logical inference necessitate this conclusion. The phenomenological facts in question can plausibly be explained in terms of the constituted nature of the human psyche and its development in interaction with specific individuals from whom shared cultural meanings and patterns of behavior are acquired. An explanation of this sort does not need to have recourse to the notion that shared ideas somehow miraculously engender forces that dominate and elevate individuals. Nor does it require a leap of faith from the existence of x to the existence of y.

In the course of describing the moral forces of society, Durkheim depicts society as a morally superior reality:

A society is the most powerful compound of physical and moral forces to be seen in nature. Nowhere else do we find such a richness of diverse materials brought to such a degree of concentration. It is not surprising, then, that a more superior life emanates from it, which, reacting upon the elements [individuals] who produce it, elevates them to a superior form of existence and transforms them.[55]

54. Durkheim, *Division du travail*, 2nd ed., p. xxx.
55. Durkheim, *Formes élémentaires*, p. 637.

A few rhetorical questions should be sufficient to refute this assertion that every society is a morally superior entity. Are collective moral judgments usually considered ethically superior to individual moral judgments? An affirmative answer would appear to contradict our ordinary judgment of the parochial interests represented by labor unions, fraternities, political parties, national states, and so forth. Is the "religious" awe and respect men sometimes feel vis-à-vis societies really identical with genuine moral respect? The latter, genuine respect, appears to be distinguished from religious awe by the implicit assumption that the recommendations of wise or virtuous beings are generally right or good, that is, specific qualities are attributed to beings whom we deem worthy of genuine moral respect. Are these attibutes usually attributed to societies? If societies can engender evil rules and practices, how is it possible for the individual to distinguish between morally desirable and undesirable practices if their moral opinions are dependent exclusively on social conditioning? Common sense responses to these questions clearly indicate the error of assuming that societies are prima facie morally superior realities.

None of these objections to Durkheim's scientific theory of morality are intended to imply that social conditioning does not have a significant influence on moral experience and opinion. In this respect, Durkheim was right. But these objections do clearly indicate that neither cross-cultural moral diversity nor moral experience can be explained by an exclusively sociological perspective. While some aspects of Durkheim's social realism may be plausible, those used to explain moral experience are not. For these reasons, a psychosocial perspective is required to explain the phenomenological facts of moral life.

IV

Moral Societies

Durkheim's attempt to explain the psychological facts of the moral life and his conception of society as both the principal source of moral obligation and the prime object of loyalty convinced him that virtually every group is a moral community precisely because societies spontaneously engender moral rules and sentiments of devotion and attachment. Morality and social life are thus inextricably interwoven, and morality only begins with group life, or, to use Durkheim's formulation:

A system of morals is always the affair of a group and can operate only if this group protects them by its authority. It is made up of rules which govern individuals, which compel them to act in such and such a way, and which impose limits to their inclinations and forbid them to go beyond. Now there is only one moral power—moral, and hence common to all—which stands above the individual and which can legitimately make laws for him, and that is collective power.[1]

Reciprocally, moral rules, by providing shared concepts of the right and the good, render society possible by allowing individuals to live together without too many bruises and conflicts. In brief, neither morality nor society exists without the other, for morality only begins with social life and group life depends upon moral consensus.

Groups differ, however, with respect both to the content of their moral principles and the vitality of the ties by which they bind men together in social relationships. There is, accordingly, a second dimension to Durkheim's *science de la morale* that is interwoven with the abstract theoretical and philosophical analysis of the social determinants of morality presented in the two preceding chapters. This second dimension deals with the various social units or institutions that comprise moral communities in the sense that they engender rules as well as sentiments of moral attachment. In other words, this second dimension

1. Emile Durkheim, *Professional Ethics and Civic Morals*, tr. Cornelia Brookfield (London: Routledge and Kegan Paul, 1957), pp. 6-7.

examines specific moral communities rather than the moral influence that "Society" (*la Société*) exerts over its members. Insofar as differing moral principles are explained by Durkheim's work in this area, this second dimension of his sociology of morals answers another major question of classical moral philosophy: what factors account for the existence of conflicting ethical standards in different societies?

Two central questions lie at the heart of Durkheim's exhaustive research on moral institutions: What units of social organization constitute the most important moral communities? How do these social units differ cross-culturally, and within a given society at various stages in its evolution?

Moral Characteristics of Entire Societies

As a first step in answering these questions, Durkheim asks whether it is legitimate to consider entire societies as moral communities. With this specific issue as his starting point, Durkheim turns his attention to delineating the major characteristics of primitive and advanced societies. As previously indicated, the first of these two societal types is characterized by a strongly entrenched and repressive collective conscience that predominates in each member's mind over individual components of consciousness, negligible individuation, scant occupational differentiation, and mechanical solidarity founded upon resemblance. At the other end of the historical continuum are "higher" societies characterized by the dissipation of the communal conscience, the rise of individualism and egalitarianism, the emergence of occupational specialization, and the structural differentiation of the social system into a plurality of subgroups.

From this brief comparative analysis it is clear that primitive societies are moral communities in the Durkheimian sense since individuals are subordinated in such societies to collectively enforced rules of conduct and closely bound to their fellows by sentiments of attachment based upon resemblance. Whether modern societies also qualify as moral communities is still a question. It is this central problem that Durkheim's first major publication, *The Division of Labor: A Study of the Organization of Higher Societies,* was intended to resolve.

In attempting to bring to light what happens to the moral bases of advanced societies when individualism, occupational specialization, and social differentiation become progressively more important factors in social life, Durkheim was certainly not alone in the nineteenth century. Saint-Simon, Comte, Spencer, Wundt, and Tönnies had recognized the salient characteristics of modern societies cited by Durkheim, and each had wrestled, in his own distinctive way, with the moral implications of these factors for contemporary existence.

Herbert Spencer, for example, not only noted the rise of individualism and occupational specialization cited by Durkheim, he sought to relate his sociological analysis of advanced societies to his conception of contemporary morality. Starting from the assumption that social cohesion is based primarily upon the structural interdependence of individuals and groups, Spencer went on to suggest that modern, differentiated societies exhibit a closer unity than primitive societies primarily because modern societies are more complexly integrated. This thesis, which is based upon the English sociologist's famous evolutionary hypothesis that social aggregates move "from incoherent homogeneity to coherent heterogeneity," led Spencer to argue that advanced societies are becoming increasingly less dependent upon earlier forms of moral and legislative restraint. By virtue of the organic interdependence of individuals and groups in modern societies, Spencer contended, each individual unit contributes to the greatest good of the aggregate by pursuing his own rational self-interests. Hence, the moral bases of advanced societies are founded upon the miracle of ordering by which millions of self-interested producers and consumers spontaneously contribute to the social well-being of the greatest number.

Similarly preoccupied with the moral bases of individualistic societies, Ferdinand Tönnies attempted, with the publication of *Gemeinschaft und Gesellschaft* in 1887, to invert Spencer's theories. Starting from the crucial assumption that the relevant bases of solidarity in any society are not structural, but psychological, Tönnies argued that primitive societies exhibit a stronger form of coherence than modern societal systems. In the primitive *Gemeinschaft*, Tönnies observed, individuals are bound together by a community of ideas, volitions, and sentiments which make each of them think and act not as isolated, self-contained individuals, but as components of a larger whole. By way of contrast, isolated individuals in the modern *Gesellschaft* act not out of consensus and tradition, but in accordance with rational self-interest. History, Tönnies endeavors to demonstrate, appears to favor the extension of the *Gesellschaft* at the expense of the *Gemeinschaft*, but this evolutionary thesis is the reverse of Spencer's. For *Gemeinschaft* is understood by Tönnies as a living organism; *Gesellschaft*, as a mechanical aggregate or artifact.[2] Solidarity in the latter case is superficial and precarious because it is more or less limited to occasional "treaties and peace

2. Ferdinand Tönnies, *Community and Association,* tr. and supplemented by Charles P. Loomis (London: Routledge and Kegan Paul, 1955), p. 39.

pacts" enforced by the state.[3] Tönnies, whose world view was somewhat nostalgic, thus considers earlier forms of communal life morally
superior to those generally prevailing (outside small groups) in modern
societies.

Durkheim's analysis of the moral bases of advanced societies owes
something to both Spencer and Tönnies. The thesis of *The Division of
Labor* is, in fact, a synthesis of the views presented by these and other
scholars upon whom Durkheim relies for many of his early concepts
and theoretical propositions. With Tönnies, Durkheim argues that
common beliefs and values bind individuals less directly together in
modern, as contrasted with primitive, societies. Durkheim, accordingly,
rejects Spencer's evolutionary explanation of the emergence of
coherent heterogeneity from incoherent homogeneity. Spencer's
scheme is untenable, Durkheim argues, because the English scholar fails
to recognize that primitive societies "have a very strong collective life,
although *sui generis,* which manifests itself not in exchanges and contracts, but in a great abundance of common beliefs and practices."[4]
Despite this acceptance of Tönnies' thesis at Spencer's expense, Durkheim refuses to ascribe to Tönnies' views regarding the morally dispersive effects of individualism, specialization, and differentiation.

The rise of individualism does not necessarily lead to a breakdown or
weakening of the ties binding men together in modern societies
precisely because a new form of moral solidarity arises with the emergence of the division of labor. Tiryakian succinctly summarizes the
thesis of *The Division* on this point:

The transformation of the communal consciousness does not entail a
proportional weakening in social life, for societies may grow more conscious of their unity, which is the case in the rise of nationalism. As a
compensation for the relative decline of the importance of the collective consciousness in the face of increased individual differences, a new
social nexus emerges to bind the individual to society. This is the
division of labor, which provides the basis of a new type of society
based on what Durkheim terms "organic solidarity," a solidarity
founded upon individual differences rather than upon similarities
between social members. While societies increase in size and population
density, the constantly increasing division of labor (manifested in the
greater specialization of occupational tasks) maintains the cohesion of
society through a functional interdependence of its members.[5]

3. *Ibid.,* p. 88.
4. Durkheim, *Division du travail,* p. 195, n.2.
5. Tiryakian, *Sociologism and Existentialism,* p. 54.

This thesis, including the term "organic" solidarity, is strikingly similar to Spencer's analysis of advanced societies. It is noteworthy, however, that Durkheim complements Spencer's emphasis upon the structural nature of these ties by insisting that the organization of modern societies engenders sentiments of moral solidarity founded upon complementary differences and mutual dependence. This latter motif enables Durkheim, who is in this respect a true disciple of Comte, to part company with the basically egoistic picture of interpersonal ties in modern societies advanced by both Spencer and Tönnies.

Does this mean that the collective conscience withers away in advanced societies and with it the primacy of moral rules engendered by entire social systems? Although several interpreters of Durkheim have answered this question in the affirmative, there is little evidence to support their contention. It is, in fact, precisely the existence of collectively shared rules in modern societies that further distinguishes Durkheim's account from that perpetrated by Spencer.[6]

In the first place, Durkheim insists, with Tönnies, that advanced societies emerge from the chrysalis of earlier societies and that at least some traditional norms continue to remain in effect in modern societies. In other words, modern societies do not emerge within a moral vacuum, but within communities possessing norms which may modify or possibly even inhibit the emergence of individualism and specialization, a contention best expressed in the following passage:

The division of labor can be produced only in the midst of a preexisting society . . . There is then, a social life outside of the whole division of labor which the latter presupposes. This is, in effect, what we have directly established by demonstrating that there are societies in which cohesion is essentially due to the communion of beliefs and sentiments, and that it is from these societies that those in which unity is assured by the division of labor have emerged.[7]

Traditional norms and values, therefore, continue to persist and to modify changes within advanced societies.

That some collectively shared rules of conduct continue to be maintained in advanced societies is shown very clearly by Durkheim's discussion of changes in the nature of the communal conscience. In *The Division* (Part II, Chapter 5), Durkheim clearly states that his intention

6. For a careful analysis of Durkheim's criticism of Spencer for failing to recognize the importance of shared rules in advanced societies, see Talcott Parsons, *Structure of Social Action*, pp. 308-317.

7. Durkheim, *Division du travail*, pp. 306-307.

is not to demonstrate the disappearance of collective norms in modern societies, but, rather, to indicate changes in the nature of the collective conscience over time. Durkheim thus cautions against misunderstanding his thesis; it is not to imply that "the common conscience is in danger of totally disappearing."[8] His point is, rather, that collectively shared norms increasingly tend to consist of "very general and very indeterminate ways of thinking and feeling, which leave free room for a growing multitude of individual differences."[9] As societies increase in geographical size and in population density, collectively shared rules change from very specific, detailed regulations to relatively general, abstract principles. The chief reason for this transformation is that a large, relatively dispersed group of people "have fewer common denominators and share fewer common experiences and phenomena. Consequently, the more differences there are in the individual portraits which serve to fashion the composite portrait of society, the less precise or concrete will the latter be."[10] In the case of moral principles, for example, highly specific norms such as those regulating the coiffure of women and shaving give way to general rules respecting the rights of man, contractual obligations, property rights, and so forth. The latter principles, by virtue of being more universal, are more rational, and apparently less imperative, since abstract rules require the intervention of individual reflection "to apply them to particular cases."[11]

Further evidence that Durkheim does not envisage the withering away of the collective conscience in advanced societies is provided in his discussion of recent changes in the relative authority of public opinion. Superficial impressions to the contrary, Durkheim did not feel that collective authority is progressively being eliminated; instead, he suggests that the collective enforcement of rules of conduct in advanced societies is considerably weaker and less effective than in small, traditionalistic communities. The two principal factors that account for this dissipation of authority are increased mobility and urbanization. As exciting new opportunities in distant environments attract individuals from their places of birth, "a weakening of all traditions" generally follows, inasmuch as the defenders of tradition, older generations, are no longer in a position to transmit, inculcate, and enforce "ancestral customs." Urbanization further contributes to this general weakening of communal authority, since group surveillance of individual behavior is

8. *Ibid.*, p. 186.
9. *Ibid.*, pp. 186-187.
10. Tiryakian, *Sociologism and Existentialism*, p. 54.
11. Durkheim, *Division du travail, p. 164.*

considerably mitigated in large metropolitan areas. As the proverb, cited by Durkheim, puts it, "one is nowhere better hidden than in a crowd." These developments do not imply, however, the complete loss of collective authority. Strictly speaking, no societies lack rules of behavior enforced by public opinion; collective discipline is simply much weaker in modern societies than in traditionalistic communities.[12]

Changes in the relative generality of moral rules and in the authority of communal norms should not be taken to mean that all norms are similarly affected. One set of beliefs and norms has actually been progressively strengthened and clarified in the recent course of social evolution: collective representations respecting the dignity and worth of the human person. As other beliefs and rules progressively lose their former religiosity and as individualism gains strength in advanced societies, the individual progressively becomes "the object of a sort of religion" surrounded by protective rights. This is not to say that individual rights were not recognized until the modern period. If there is one rule common to all moral codes, Durkheim states, "it is certainly that which prohibits attacks against the person, for men who resemble each other cannot live together without each experiencing a sympathy for his fellows which opposes every act of a kind to make them suffer." It is to say, however, that at least in this one area the collective conscience has grown in strength and precision as it has increasingly stressed the rights and privileges of the individual.[13]

If Durkheim insisted, from the outset of his career, upon the central importance of the "cult of the individual" in modern societies, his theory concerning the causal conditions responsible for the emergence of this cult as well as its functional consequences underwent a significant evolution in the course of his intellectual development. According to the young Durkheim, the rise of the cult of the individual and the moral rights associated with it are ultimately due to quantitative changes in the size and density of modern societies. As societies grow larger in geographical size and as individual differences multiply with the progress of the division of labor, men discover that the only bond holding them together is their common humanity. But the resulting cult of the individual does not serve the same collective ends as the cult it replaces since it directs men to individual, rather than collective, goals.

It is thus, if one wishes, a common cult . . . in so far as it is shared by the community, but it is individual in its object. If it turns all wills

12. *Ibid.*, pp. 325-326, 330.
13. *Ibid.*, pp. 187, 180.

toward the same end, this end is not social. It therefore occupies a completely exceptional place in the collective conscience. It is clearly from society that it draws all its force, but it is not to society that it attaches us; it is to ourselves.[14]

In a word, the cult of the individual does not constitute a true social bond.

As a result of these early conclusions, Durkheim found himself attempting to defend paradoxical claims. In the first place, he faced the dilemma of maintaining that primitive religious and moral beliefs are realities *sui generis*, whereas the cult of the individual results from quantitative changes in the size and density of the population. He also was in the odd position of recognizing the primacy of the individual in contemporary morality, but denying any functional significance to this fundamental feature of modern societies. It was, perhaps, recognition of these difficulties that led Durkheim to considerably revise early hypotheses in his later writings.

This revision gradually unfolds in works written between 1897 and 1907 and introduces new hypotheses regarding both the causal conditions and functional consequences of the cult of man. Durkheim not only abandons his earlier attempt to explain this qualitative transformation of moral values in terms of quantitative changes, but he also frankly admits that Christianity was an independent causal factor in the emergence of the unique respect for the individual that dominates Western culture.[15] It was in Christian societies that the human personality first "acquired a kind of dignity which places him above himself as well as above society."[16] Durkheim now recognizes that this cult of man is not only a tie attaching us to ourselves, but an ideal which attaches us to society (now conceived as a foyer of ideals). "For man, as thus suggested to collective affection and respect, is not the sensual, experiential individual that each one of us represents, but man in general, ideal humanity as conceived by each people at each moment of its history."[17] Such an ideal Durkheim further contends, "draws him [the individual] beyond himself; impersonal and disinterested, it is above all

14. *Ibid.*, p. 187.
15. This is one of the principal theses of Durkheim's *Evolution pédagogique en France.*
16. Durkheim, *Suicide*, p. 333.
17. *Ibid.*, pp. 336-337. This statement is the earliest indication of Durkheim's mature conception of the collective conscience as a third term between the individual and society, a conception which is explicated and defended in *Pragmatisme et sociologie,* Cours inédit prononcé à la Sorbonne en 1913-14 et restitué d'après des notes d'étudiants par Armand Cuvillier (Paris: Librarie philosophique J. Vrin, 1955).

individual personalities; like every ideal, it can be conceived of only as superior to and dominating reality. This ideal even dominates societies, being the aim on which all social activity depends."[18] Henceforth, the values and rights associated with the individual constitute "the only system of beliefs which can assure the moral unity of the country."[19]

The young Durkheim's thesis regarding the moral bases of advanced societies can be briefly summarized from *The Division of Labor*. The most important moral ties binding diverse individuals together in modern societies are founded upon sentiments of solidarity engendered by complementary differences and mutual dependence. Although some traditional rules of behavior persist as modernization proceeds, these rules tend to become more abstract or rational and, therefore, less dogmatic and imperative. Counteracting this general tendency are those rules respecting the dignity and worth of the human person. These rules are gradually more carefully specified and more vigorously enforced than in earlier societies, although such rules are neither as numerous nor as all-pervasive as those that predominate in traditional societies.[20] In brief, modern societies continue to generate strong sentiments of solidarity (altruism), but they are comparatively deficient with regard to engendering and enforcing common rules of conduct (anomie).

In Durkheim's opinion, this diminution of collective authority is one source of the chronic social and moral disorder characteristic of modern industrial societies. Class conflicts and social unrest reflect in part the collapse of traditional sources of moral authority. More importantly, however, such phenomena reflect the failure of societies to establish new regulative, as opposed to authoritarian, controls in line with the relaxation of traditional authority engendered by societal differentiation.[21] Because societies have generally failed to establish new regulative agencies, the modern era is characterized by chronic moral and social disorder.

If modernization does not inevitably produce the unambiguous moral effects which the Manchester economists and Spencer associated with

18. Durkheim, *Suicide,* p. 337.
19. Durkheim, "Individualisme et les intellectuels," p. 10.
20. Durkheim, *Division du travail,* pp. 449-450. "As we advance along the evolutionary scale, the ties which bind the individual to his family, to his native soil, to ancient traditions, and to collective customs loosen ... To be sure, the whole of the common conscience does not, on this account, pass out of existence. There will always remain at least this cult of personality and individual dignity of which we have been speaking, and which, today, is the only rallying-point of so many people. But how little a thing it is, especially when one contemplates the ever increasing extent of social life, and, consequently, of individual consciences!"
21. *Ibid.,* Book Three, ch. 1.

"progress," the historical process by which societies are transformed, nevertheless, contains within itself a remedy for this breakdown of communal authority insofar as the process of structural differentiation spawns smaller communities within the larger social nexus. The spontaneous emergence of a common life together and of shared rules within smaller institutions in pluralistic societies is an exceedingly important subtheme running throughout Durkheim's early writings, the theme which leads him to draw a careful distinction between *la conscience collective ou commune* on the one hand and *la conscience sociale* on the other. The former refers to the system of ideas or norms held in common throughout an entire society while the latter and more inclusive term refers not only to beliefs and norms held in common, but also to institutionally engendered rules held by some but not all of the members of the larger collectivity. Durkheim formulates this contrast in *The Division:*

As the terms collective and social are frequently taken for one another, one is led to believe that the collective conscience is the whole social conscience, that is to say, that it extends as far as the psychic life of society, although, especially in advanced societies, it is only a very restricted part of the social conscience. Judicial, governmental, scientific, industrial, in short, all special functions are of a psychic nature, since they consist in systems of representations and actions. They are, however, clearly outside the common conscience.[22]

Each of these functionally specific groups has its own morality "so that morality is diversified with social conditions. There is one morality for each social stratum of the society."[23] Gurvitch is essentially correct, then, when he states: "whereas in mechanical solidarity, it is a matter of identical collective beliefs, in organic solidarity, it is a matter of collective beliefs differentiated in subgroups."[24]

From this analysis proceeds Durkheim's fundamental observation that subgroups constitute extraordinarily important moral communities in advanced societies. Such groups, by spontaneously generating shared norms and enforcing these obligations by their own authority, are, as it were, the moral equivalent in advanced societies of the collective or common conscience in primitive tribes since these groups are now primarily responsible for the specific duties that regulate most of our day-to-day activities in the family, the workshop, the university, and so

22. *Ibid.*, pp. 84-85.
23. Durkheim, "Morale en Allemagne," p. 123.
24. Gurvitch, *Essais de Sociologie*, p. 70.

forth. The rules of such secondary group formations are thus the natural complement of the highly general, abstract principles shared throughout modern societies and protected by public opinion at large. It is in this way that Durkheim succeeds in demonstrating that the rise of individualism, specialization, and differentiation does not necessarily lead to the morally dispersive consequences envisaged by Tönnies.

Secondary Group Morality

What was begun in *The Division of Labor* with respect to the secondary group bases of morality was further developed in *Suicide* and in lectures devoted to the family, occupational groups, the state, and educational institutions. In contrast with the limited attention accorded these groups in *The Division of Labor*, Durkheim's first, seminal treatment of them in *Suicide* stresses the importance of secondary groups in maintaining moral solidarity in advanced societies.[25]

In his lectures on the family, occupational groups, the state, and educational institutions, two basic themes predominate. First, moral rules and sentiments of solidarity are divided into several types, which are in turn related to the groups responsible for their emergence, development, and maintenance. Second, specific moral communities are studied historically in order to determine their current characteristics.

Central to Durkheim's discussion of morality in these lectures is his

25. In contending that *Suicide* further develops, but places greater emphasis upon, secondary groups than *Division of Labor*, I am explicitly disagreeing with those interpreters who maintain that *Suicide* represents a radical revision of Durkheim's earlier views regarding the secondary group bases of morality in advanced societies. According to this interpretation, *Suicide* associates characteristics assigned to the collective conscience of primitive societies in *Division of Labor* with secondary groups in modern societies. The principal problem with this interpretation is its failure to recognize the attention given in Durkheim's early writings, including the first edition of *Division of Labor*, to the persistence of the collective conscience in modern societies at the general societal level (individual rights and duties) and at the secondary group level (governmental, scientific, and industrial rules). What happens in *Suicide* and other later works is that a subordinate theme in *Division of Labor* becomes a major thesis. This is why Durkheim begins his famous "Preface to the Second Edition" of *Division of Labor* with this statement: " 'there is an idea, which remained in the penumbra in the first edition, and which it will be useful to bring to light, because it will clarify certain parts of the present work as well as those we have since published. It is the question of the role that occupational groups are destined to play in the social organization of contemporary peoples." In addition to Durkheim's own statement that *Division of Labor* recognizes the importance of secondary group morality but does not sufficiently develop this theme, the crucial significance of occupational group morality for modern social solidarity was clearly indicated by Durkheim a year before the completion of *Division of Labor* in 1893. See "La Famille conjugale: conclusion du cours sur la famille," *RP*, XCI (1921), 13-14. This was the last of seventeen lectures on the family that Durkheim gave at the University of Bordeaux in 1892.

distinction between universally applicable moral rules and particularistic moral codes.[26] The former apply to all men simply because men everywhere share the most universal traits of mankind. One subdivision of universally applicable rules pertains to the relation of the individual to himself, that is, those that make up the moral code called "individual." These include rules concerning responsibility, merit, suicide, and so forth. The other subdivision of universally applicable rules pertains to relations among individuals, such as rules prohibiting murder, protecting property rights, guaranteeing contractual agreements, and so forth. Durkheim contends that both types of universally applicable rules are engendered by entire societies and enforced by public opinion. They vary cross-culturally, although some, such as those prohibiting murder, are found in every society.

Particularistic moral codes only apply to those who belong to specific classes or secondary groups within society. In contrast with the universally applicable rules that apply to all men regardless of social role, particularistic codes delineate the responsibilities of professors, priests, soldiers, industrialists, scientists, and so forth. They tend to be more specific than universally applicable rules. Because functional responsibilities differ, the duties prescribed by particularistic codes vary considerably. For example, the scientist should develop a critical attitude independent of any authority other than reason; the priest or the soldier must demonstrate the opposite virtue of passive obedience within prescribed limits. The physician may be required to lie or not to tell the truth he knows, whereas other professionals have a contrary duty. Within every society, then, there are a plurality of specific moral codes that operate on parallel lines.

A distinguishing characteristic of particularistic rules is the general lack of concern with which the public consciousness regards them. Unlike the universally applicable rules engendered and enforced by public opinion at large, particularistic rules are always the affair of specific secondary groups and operate effectively only insofar as these groups protect them with their collective moral authority. They do not greatly concern the general public, partly because they are not common to everyone in society and partly because the general public does not possess the competence to ascertain appropriate responsibilities within specialized areas of competence. This explains why public opinion is seldom shocked by the violation of secondary group morality; most of

26. For Durkheim's discussion of this distinction between universally applicable moral rules and particularistic moral codes, see *Professional Ethics and Civic Morals*, pp. 3-6.

this behavior escapes the immediate knowledge and influence of public consciousness. Collective sentiments are only stirred "by transgressions so grave that they are likely to have wide general repercussions."[27]

Presupposed throughout Durkheim's discussion of particularistic rules is his basic assumption that moral norms are generated and sustained by stable patterns of interaction. This theoretical assumption also underlies Durkheim's further contention that the number and moral authority of these norms vary directly with the structural coherence of the group.

In general, all things being equal, the greater the strength of the group structure, the more numerous are the moral rules appropriate to it and the greater the authority they have over their members. For the more closely the group coheres, the closer and more frequent the contact of the individuals, and, the more frequent and intimate these contacts and the more exchange there is of ideas and sentiments, the more does a public opinion spread to cover a greater number of things. This is precisely because a greater number of things is placed at the disposal of all. Imagine, on the one hand, a population scattered over a vast area, without the different elements being able to communicate easily; each man would live for himself alone and public opinion would develop only in rare cases entailing a laborious calling together of these scattered sections. But when the group is strong, its authority communicates itself to the moral discipline it establishes and this, it follows, is respected to the same degree. On the other hand, a society lacking in stability, whose discipline it is easy to escape and whose existence is not always felt, can communicate only a very feeble influence to the precepts it lays down.[28]

Briefly, the greater the stability and the better the internal organization of the secondary groups in question, the stronger the particularistic rules.

To understand the secondary group bases of morality in advanced societies, a careful study of the historical development of these institutions is, according to Durkheim, absolutely indispensable. Durkheim was thus led by his interest in the social foundations of morality to engage in an exhaustive historical analysis of the secondary institutions which he considered to be the most important moral communities in Western civilization. The ultimate purpose of this vast research enterprise is perhaps best expressed in the following observation: "If we depart from the present, it is in order to return to it. If we flee the

27. *Ibid.*, p. 6.
28. *Ibid.*, pp. 7-8.

present, it is in order to see and to comprehand it better. In reality, we shall never lose this point of view. It is the goal toward which we shall constantly strive, and we shall see this goal being gradually realized as we advance."[29] If, then, one wishes to understand Durkheim's conclusions concerning the group bases of morality in modern societies, it is necessary to follow, with scrupulous care, his historical studies of the family, occupational groups, the state, and, also, of educational institutions.[30]

The Family

Durkheim's interest in the various institutional foundations of morality led him to devote considerable time and energy, during his early teaching career, to a thorough sociological analysis of family life. During the academic years 1888-1889 and 1891-1892 at the University of Bordeaux and again at the University of Paris in 1907-1908, Durkheim gave three different series of lectures entitled, respectively, "The Sociology of the Family," "The Family," and "The Evolution of Marriage." Unfortunately, Durkheim's original intention to publish a book based upon these lectures was never realized, and most of his lecture notes are no longer available. As a result, Durkheim's sociology of the family has been neglected by most American sociologists and anthropologists, despite the fact that it is possible to reconstruct his major theoretical hypotheses and empirical insights from various primary and secondary sources.[31]

29. Durkheim, *Evolution pédagogique en France*, I, 19. Durkheim did not believe contemporary social phenomena could be adequately understood in the absence of a sociological study of their genesis and historical development. In *Elementary Forms of the Religious Life*, he wrote: "we cannot arrive at an understanding of the most recent religions except by following the manner in which they have been progressively composed in history. In fact, historical analysis is the only means of explanation which it is possible to apply to them. It alone enables us to resolve an institution into its constituent elements, for it shows them to us as they are born in time, one after another . . . Every time that we undertake to explain something human, taken at a given moment of time—be it a religious belief, a moral rule, a legal precept, an aesthetic style or an economic system—it is necessary to commence by going back to its most primitive and simple form, to try to account for the characteristics by which it was marked at that period of its existence, and then to show how it gradually developed and became complicated, and how it became that which it is at the moment in question." (*Formes élémentaires*, pp. 4-5.)

30. Durkheim's historical analysis of domestic societies, occupational associations and political groups is presented in the present chapter. His research on the evolution of educational institutions is presented in Chapter V, Section 3.

31. The following are the principal primary sources on Durkheim's sociology of the family: "Introduction à la sociologie de la famille," *Annales de la Faculté des Lettres de Bordeaux*, X (1888), 257-281; "Famille conjugale," pp. 1-14; "Origine du mariage dans l'espèce humaine, d'après Westermarck," pp. 606-623; "La Prohi-

Durkheim's sociology of the family follows the broad comparative and evolutionary method represented by such men as Post, McLennan, Lubboch, and Morgan. Like these classical evolutionists, Durkheim posits several stages through which the family has evolved, although he explicitly rejects unilinear evolution. With Morgan, who was one of the first to recognize the significance of kinship relationships, Durkheim notes that an adequate typology of the family must be based upon an analysis of systems of kinship, primarily because kinship relationships define the various moral obligations of family members.[32] In other words, Durkheim appreciated the fact that "relationship terms" are among the basic social devices employed in the regulation of family life. By a "relationship term" is meant

the designation of an individual or a class of individuals that is socially significant. Every society of human beings is divided into social classes or groups, which, with reference to any individual in the society, are designated with kinship terms such as "uncle," "sister," "mother-in-law," etc. One's behavior toward one's fellows varies, depending upon the category of relationship in which the person stands. Since the categories are labeled with kinship terms, a close functional relationship obtains between kinship nomenclature and social organization and behavior.[33]

As these are among the basic postulates of most contemporary anthropologists, Durkheim's analysis of the family must be considered among the first truly modern studies in this field.

Despite his indebtedness to Morgan and others for several crucial methodological insights, Durkheim's own classification of kinship systems bears little resemblance to the prevailing evolutionary scheme per-

---

bition de l'inceste et ses origines," *AS*, I (1897), pp. 1-70; reviews on the family, marriage, sexual morality, and domestic organization in *AS* for 1897-1912: I, pp. 306-340, II, pp. 310-345, III, pp. 365-393, IV, pp. 340-365, V, 364-392, VI, pp. 342-369, VII, pp. 416-441, VIII, 408-432, IX, pp. 355-394, X pp. 320-440, XI, pp. 335-384, XII, pp. 410-441. The best secondary works are: Marcel Mauss, "In Memoriam: l'ouevre inédit de Durkheim et de ses collaborateurs," *AS*, New Series, I (1923), 7-29; Georges Davy, *Sociologues d'hier et d'aujourd'hui* (Paris: Félix Alcan, 1931), Part II, "Famille et la parenté d'après Durkheim," pp. 103-157.

32. "Voici en effet en quoi consiste un tel système de parenté. Il comporte l'usage de désigner d'un même nom, du nom de mère ou du nom de père par exemple, toute une classe de personnes (ma mère et ses soeurs, mon père et ses frères) vis-à-vis desquelles celui qui les désigne ainsi a des obligations définies, mais qui ne sont évidemment pas toutes avec lui dans le même rapport de consanguinité." (Davy, *Sociologues d'hier et d'aujourd'hui*, p. 125.

33. Leslie A. White, "Lewis Henry Morgan: Pioneer in the Theory of Social Evolution," in *Introduction to the History of Sociology*, ed. Barnes, p. 144.

petrated by Post, McLennan, Lubbock, and Morgan. According to these scholars, the primal human association was the promiscuous horde:

In the beginning was promiscuity. "Society" was without form; chaos prevailed and unregulated sex intercourse. Then groups of women, related or not, were looked upon as wives of groups of men, related or not. But the clans came forth; tribes were divided into these hereditary social units, and these were composed of blood relatives and also of some who were not so related. Thus social organization became more clearly formed. At first, and dominantly, this form was maternal in principle: the children belonged to the clan of their mothers. Later the gens developed: the children belonged to the gentes of their fathers. Finally, after all this had passed, the monogamous family (and the village) became the basic units of organization.[34]

When contrasted with this prevailing evolutionary scheme, the modernity of Durkheim's evolutionary theory is striking. He rejects the prevalent nineteenth-century hypothesis regarding a stage of primitive promiscuity. With modern anthropologists like Boas, Kroeber, and Lowie, Durkheim notes the absence of any evidence that this promiscuous state of affairs ever existed.[35] Even more important, he rejects the assumption, shared by most of his predecessors, that kinship is primarily and essentially a result of biological instincts. In this connection Durkheim persuasively argues that instincts are constant whereas kinship systems as well as the moral and juridical rules governing them vary cross-culturally.

Maternal love was the same among the Romans as among the Germans; and yet, in the Roman family, the mother was not legally related to her children. We have no reason to believe that paternal love was unknown among the Iroquois, and yet the father was legally a stranger to his own descendants.[36]

This variability can only be explained, Durkheim maintains, by considering the family, like any other social institution, as a social system with its own structure and morality. When the family is seen from this point of view, Durkheim states,

34. C. Wright Mills, "Edward Alexander Westermarck and the Application of Ethnographic Methods to Marriage and Morals," in *Introduction to the History of Sociology*, ed. Barnes, p. 656.
35. Durkheim, "Origine du mariage dans l'espèce humaine, d'après Westermarck," pp. 614-617.
36. *Ibid.*, pp. 609-610.

one does not consider the duration of sexual intercourse, but the regulation to which it is subjected; for it is in this that the great novelty which appears only with humanity consists. One does not ask why the sexes, in our species, cohabit for a fairly long period of time, but why, for the first time, their cohabitation, instead of being free, is subjected to imperative rules of conduct which are enforced by the ambiant clan, tribe, city, etc. . . . It is only in this sense that sexual relations interest the sociologist.[37]

Durkheim distinguishes six stages in the evolution of the family, each of which represents a further contraction in the extent of kinship relationships and in the number of moral duties associated with these ties: the diffuse clan, the differentiated family of maternal or paternal lineage, the joint family of agnates, the patriarchal family, the paternal-maternal family, and the modern conjugal-nuclear family.[38] In addition to representing a contraction in the extent of kinship ties, each of these stages also represents a contraction in the functional tasks performed by domestic societies. As the family becomes smaller, the diverse religious, political, economic, and moral functions originally performed by primitive kinship systems are lost to functionally specific groups such as the church, the state, occupational associations, and the like. This dual process of contraction in both kinship relationships and functional responsibilities is reflected in the basic symbols of identity or solidarity associated with these kinship types. As the family contracts in size and loses functions to other groups, the symbols of solidarity uniting family members become increasingly personalized.

The diffuse clan. Prominent in Durkheim's evolutionary theory of the family is his assumption that the diffuse clan was the original starting point of structural functional differentiation. Originally, the diffuse family clan was an autonomous, self-sufficient society. As such, it was

---

37. *Ibid.,* p. 614.

38. This six-stage scheme represents an attempt on the part of the present writer to synthesize slightly differing accounts of Durkheim's evolutionary theory of family types. According to Mauss, who bases his observations primarily upon the lectures given at Bordeaux on "The Sociology of the Family" in 1892, Durkheim advocated the following typology: the contraction of *"the amorphous exagamous clan,* a vast consanguineous group, to *the differentiated clan,* to families properly so-called, whether uterine or masculine; then to *the joint family of agnates;* to *the patriarchal family,* paternal and maternal; and to *the conjugal family"* (italics mine). Durkheim, "Famille conjugale," p. 6, n.2. Davy, who bases his presentation on later writings, formulates the following scheme: *the diffused clan;* the differentiated family of maternal and paternal descent; *the patriarchal family; the paternal-maternal family;* and *the modern conjugal family.* Davy treats *the joint family of agnates* as an intermediary stage between the second and the third stage.

responsible for the religious, political, moral, and economic functions normally found in any autonomous social system.[39] Within this group there is the "family" in our sense of the conjugal or nuclear, but Durkheim finds it weak in structural differentiation and lacking the cultural legitimation of the modern family.

Solidarity in the diffuse clan is based upon kinship, but kinship is an essentially religious or moral phenomenon.[40] The kinship system of the primitive clan is said to rest upon consanguinity, but consanguinity in this specific case is often purely fictional.[41] Consanguinity does not actually rest upon blood relatedness in primitive societies, but, rather, upon an imagined relationship based on shared religious beliefs concerning common origins and possession of the same name. The integrating religious symbol system of the diffuse clan is totemism.

The basis of the primitive family is totemism . . . In order to be a member of a family, it is necessary as well as sufficient to have something of the totemic being in oneself, that is, something of the divinized object which serves as the collective emblem of the group. While this participation can result from procreation, it can be obtained just as well by other ways: by tatooing, by all forms of alimentary communion, by blood communion, etc. These intitiation rituals are responsible for the extensive practice of adoption in primitive societies. Birth per se does not sufficiently integrate the child into the domestic society; it is necessary for religious ceremonies to be superimposed upon it.[42]

39. Durkheim's earliest reference to the manifold functions performed by the primitive family-clan is found in his first published article, a review of Schaeffle's *Bau und Leben* (pp. 88-89). In this review, Durkheim provides the following succinct summary of Schaeffle's views regarding the manifold functions performed by the primitive family: "As the family is the germ from which society is born, we should be able to find society there in an abridged form. And in fact, it has its tissues and organs. The family occupies a part of the soil which it appropriates to its needs. It has its protective and defensive institutions . . . It has an economic structure, an industry, and an intellectual life. The family is thus a sort of complete, social organism, which was once self-sufficient and the whole of society."

40. Against Frazer's hypothesis that marriage was the basis of kinship, Durkheim argues that "kinship and family are first based . . . on the mystic principle of totemic participation which constitutes the cohesion of the clan. It is . . . by the totemic clan, and not by marriage, that it is necessary to initially explain the family." (Davy, *Sociologues d'hier et d'aujourd'hui*, p. 125.) In *Elementary Forms of the Religious Life*, Durkheim further contends that "the primitive family organization cannot be understood before the primitive religious beliefs are known; for the latter serve as the basis of the former. This is why it is necessary to study totemism as a religion before studying the totemic clan as a family group." (*Formes élémentaires*, p. 148, n.2.)

41. Davy, *Sociologues d'hier et d'aujourd'hui*, p. 117.

42. Durkheim, "J. Kohler, *Zur Urgeschichte der Ehe: Totemismus, Gruppenehe, Mutterrecht*," AS, I, 317-318.

This is why cultic acts, rites, and other religious duties constitute the most important moral obligations in the diffuse family clan.

The differentiated family. This second stage in the evolution of the family gradually emerges out of the diffuse clan and can be of maternal or paternal descent. It generally occurs when nomadic hunting and fishing societies settle in a particular territory. As these territorially based societies increase in size, the clan tends to evolve "in a purely political direction, and the family in a purely domestic direction."[43] The resulting domestic societies are based upon actual consanguinity. In other words, solidarity in these differentiated families is based primarily upon actual blood relatedness. "This time," Durkheim states, "it is not only the name which is handed down to posterity . . . The entire organization of the family rests upon the principle of filiation.[44] This principal form of solidarity is backed up, however, by the survival of totemistic beliefs regarding lineal descent through either the maternal or paternal line.[45]

The joint family of agnates. This third, and further condensed, family type can be maternally or paternally descended. Kinship relationships and domestic obligations are less extensive in the joint family than in the differentiated clan, but members continue to be related to distant relatives inasmuch as joint families are composed of various subfamily groupings or collateral branches of the same lineage. Marriages among offspring fail to have a dispersive effect upon domestic societies of this sort because sons or daughters, upon forming their own families, "remain associated with the familial community of collaterals."[46]

---

43. Davy, *Sociologues d'hier et d'aujourd'hui*, p. 139.

44. Durkheim, "Grosse (Ernest), *Die Formen du Familie und die Formen der Wirthschaft,*" *AS,* I, 324.

45. This attempt to supplement solidarity based upon blood relationships with another source of family unity derives from Durkheim's opposition to sociological explanations based upon instinctual sentiments. In this context, the following passage is enlightening: "It is commonly believed that consanguinity is an exceptionally powerful cause of moral rapprochement. But we have frequently demonstrated that consanguinity does not have the extraordinary efficacy attributed to it. The proof is that in many societies non-blood relatives are found in numbers at the heart of the family . . . Inversely, it very often happens that very close blood relations are, morally and juridically, strangers to each other . . . The family does not owe its virtues then to the unity of descent; it is quite simply a group of individuals who happen to have been related to one another, in the midst of political society, by a particularly strong community of ideas, sentiments and interests. Consanguinity has been able to facilitate this concentration, for it has the natural effect of inclining consciences toward one another. But many other factors come into play." (Durkheim, *Division du travail,* 2nd ed. [Paris: Félix Alcan, 1902], p. xviii.)

46. Davy, *Sociologues d'hier et d'aujourd'hui*, p. 141.

Solidarity in the joint family stems neither from the totemic cult nor from consanguinity. It derives, rather, from common ownership of the domestic territory, home, or inheritance. "The community of inheritance, in this new and less extensive zone of kinship, plays the same role that the community of the totem played in the preceding community. This time it is a real tie that establishes the personal tie."[47] This "real" tie is, nevertheless, an ideal tie in the sense that it is the family field or ancestral home, together with all the memories and traditions associated with it, as "represented" to participating members that constitutes the principal basis of unity in the joint family. For this reason the fundamental obligation in the joint family is to protect and preserve the domestic patrimony.

The patriarchal family. The distinctive characteristic of this fourth and narrower type, as the term itself implies, is the presence of a single family head.[48] The best example is found in ancient Rome where the family was based solely upon agnatic descent and where matriarchal lineage was virtually unimportant. The patriarch's consort, in fact, was not really a member of her husband's family in this case. Inasmuch as the patriarchal family is restricted to the descendants of a living individual, kinship relationships and associated moral obligations are considerably more circumscribed than in the joint family of collateral families.

The major source of solidarity in the patriarchal family is "neither a mythic entity like the totem nor an objective element like inheritance, it is the authority of the father of the family." Even consanguinity itself is subject to parental control "since the father is free to accept or repudiate the child born to him" and "to bring into his family individuals who are not of his own blood." The real unity of the family is not based upon biological kinship, then, but, rather, upon a shared belief regarding the absolute monarchical authority of the patriarch; that is to say, solidarity is based upon an ideal concept, albeit one which relates family members to the personality of the father. The patriachal family thus represents an important stage in the gradual personalization of family ties, although these ties remain impersonal insofar as absolute obedience to the impersonal authority of the patriarch is the central moral obligation in such families.[49]

The paternal-maternal family. The fifth stage in the concentration of the family derives directly from the joint family of maternal descent in

47. *Ibid.,* p. 142.
48. For Durkheim's analysis of the patriarchal family, see *ibid.,* pp. 143-148, and "Famille conjugale," pp. 1-14, esp. the notes by Mauss.
49. Davy, *Sociologues d'hier et d'aujourd'hui,* p. 143.

societies that fail to develop in the direction of the patriarchal family. Durkheim refers to this domestic type as paternal-maternal.[50] The kinship system of the Germanic tribes represents the best example. Within the German tribes, says Durkheim, the nuclear family was the primary family unit. Unlike the Roman patriarchy, married sons and daughters formed independent and autonomous families of their own apart from those of their parents. Within these smaller family groups, kinship with the mother was as important as kinship with the father, that is, maternal kinship was placed on an equal plane with paternal kinship. This dual kinship system is traced by Durkheim to the fact that the Germanic family originated within, and retained traces of, the joint family of maternal descent, although it later developed in the direction of paternal kinship patterns. As a result, the mother was included, along with her husband and unmarried children, within the nuclear family. Solidarity in this case is even more intimate and personal than that found in patriarchal families. It is based upon symbolic legitimation of personal ties between both parents and their unmarried offspring.

The modern family. In Durkheim's view, this group represents the product of a long and complex process of concentration. Like other Western European institutions, the modern family represents a synthesis of Roman and Germanic social types; it combines Roman patriarchal features with German recognition of dual kinship. The modern family, however, is distinguished from earlier family groups by the intimate ties uniting husband and wife on the one hand, and parents with their children on the other. "Domestic solidarity becomes completely personal. We are attached to our family only because we are attached to the persons of our father, our mother, our wife, our children."[51]

Does this imply a strengthening or weakening of family solidarity? In his early lectures, Durkheim's initial response is rather ambiguous: "On the one hand, it is stronger, since kinship ties are now indissoluble. Yet, on the other hand, the obligations to which kinship gives rise are less numerous and important."[52] As early as 1892, however, Durkheim realized that it was impossible to deal with this question regarding the strength of familial solidarity without first distinguishing between two groups in the modern family and constrasting these groups with respect

50. For Durkheim's analysis of the paternal-maternal family, see *ibid.,* pp. 149-150, and "Famille conjugale," pp. 1-14, *passim.*
51. Durkheim, "Famille conjugale," p. 9.
52. *Ibid.,* pp. 8-9.

to both the nature and strength of moral solidarity. These two families within the modern family are the conjugal and the nuclear:

the family environment consists of different elements. For husband and wife alike the family includes: 1. the wife or husband; 2. the children ... In other words, the family consists of two different associations: the conjugal group and the family group proper. These two societies have not the same origin, nor the same nature, nor consequently, in all probability, the same effects. One springs from a contract and elective affinity, the other from a natural phenomenon, consanguinity; the former unites two members of the same generation, the latter unites one generation to the next; the latter is as old as humanity, the former was organized at a relatively late date.[53]

The strength of moral solidarity in these two cases is quite different.

It is Durkheim's contention that whereas the solidarity of the nuclear family continually "loses ground, marriage contrariwise becomes stronger."[54] With respect to conjugal solidarity, Durkheim maintains that "as we advance toward modern times, we see marriage developing. The circle of ties which it creates extends further and further; the obligations which it sanctions multiply ... The duty of fidelity is established ... Very complex rules fix the respective rights of each spouse."[55] Conjugal relationships become an increasingly important source of warm personal ties in modern societies, although these ties are not as strong as those that previously bound the individual to a large family group.

At the same time, however, the solidarity of the nuclear family has declined in importance as a vital source of interpersonal relatedness. In explaining this decline, Durkheim cites several causal factors, the first being that the sense of the unity of the family group has diminished. "Formerly, domestic society was not just a number of individuals united by bonds of mutual affection; but the group itself, in its abstract and impersonal unity. It was the hereditary name, together with all the memories it recalled, the family house, the ancestral field, the traditional situation and reputation, etc. All this is tending to disappear." This decline in the vitality of shared symbols and memories is not simply a result of the loss of earlier ties; it is also a result of the fact that shared meanings cannot be very intense in any extremely small social unit. The modern family cannot sustain a vital sense of solidarity

53. Durkheim, *Suicide*, p. 185.
54. Durkheim, "Famille conjugale," p. 14.
55. Durkheim, *Division du travail*, p. 61.

because there are simply not enough individuals within it to engender, maintain, and re-enforce similar ideas and sentiments. In other words, emotionally powerful symbols cannot be formed or maintained in a group like the modern family, which is not sufficiently large to permit "the active interchange of views and impressions" and "the circulation of these views and impressions from one person to another."[56]

This reduction in the size and moral solidarity of the family is explained in part by the mobility of modern youth. The home is often abandoned in modern societies by children from highly privileged backgrounds, who leave to commence or complete their education, and by children from impoverished areas, whose early departure is necessitated by economic hardship.[57] In addition to these early departures, young adults increasingly tend to establish their own homes and apartments away from their parents. The family thus tend to be reduced, in time, to the married couple alone. As a result, the nuclear family "plays a smaller role in life" and "no longer suffices as an object for life," not because "we care less for our children; but [because] they are entwined less closely and continuously with our existence."[58]

Despite these seemingly negative conclusions concerning the importance of the modern family as a source of moral solidarity, Durkheim, nevertheless, attributes several indispensable functions to modern domestic societies. The family remains an important source of moral obligations as well as a worthy object of altruistic devotion. By virtue of its status as a moral community, the family continues to provide emotional security for all family members. The importance of the family as a source of both morality and emotional security continues to show up in suicide statistics. Participation within a family circle, however small, has an important prophylactic effect on suicide. In addition, the family is a sort of elementary school for the moral training of children. Despite the loss of several significant functions in this area to educational institutions, the family, nevertheless, remains the primary school of moral education. And, the family protects the individual against unwarranted interference from other institutions, such as the state and economic groups. "Throughout all its [historical] transformations, the essential nature of the family always remains the same; it is an organization safeguarding certain individual interests, and, more generally, the natural place of shelter and support for the individual."[59]

56. Durkheim, *Suicide,* pp. 377, 202.
57. *Ibid.,* p. 199.
58. *Ibid.,* p. 377.
59. Davy, *Sociologues d'hier et d'aujourd'hui,* p. 153.

Durkheim recognizes that, while the family has gradually lost significant functions, it cannot simply be dismissed as a weaker version of its
former self. Although deprived of its former functional responsibilities
in the areas of religion, politics, and economics by the emergence of
functionally specific institutions in these fields, the family, nevertheless, remains a hothouse of moral and emotional relationships, a school
for the moral training of the young, and a fortress against the unwarranted interference of hostile forces bent upon the destruction of individual differences. Durkheim thus "adds an important principle to the
theory of structural differentiation—namely, that when in the course of
differentiation a unit appears to lose important functions, it is not
necessarily a weakened version of its former self; it may be a new, more
specialized unit, fulfilling important functions at a new level of complexity in the larger system."[60]

Occupational and Professional Groups

Durkheim's historical analysis of occupational groups is of considerable interest for several reasons. In the first place, Durkheim further
develops his study of the family in the course of tracing the emergence
of occupational groups to the gradual differentiation of the joint
family. In this context, he proceeds to explain why domestic societies
were more or less forced to yield their economic responsibilities to
functionally specific, economic associations. Durkheim then introduces
several suggestive hypotheses regarding the factors responsible for shap-
ing new moral communities. In doing so, he introduces the insightful
supposition that newly formed groups tend to be modeled after existing
societies. Finally, Durkheim introduces his reasons for believing that
occupational groups are uniquely qualified to fulfill indispensable moral
functions in modern societies. Taken together, these themes augment
the abstract, and, for that reason, the somewhat unsatisfactory treatment of social differentiation and economic group formation contained
in *The Division of Labor*.

The Roman guilds represent the first stage in Durkheim's evolutionary theory of occupational groups in the Occident. The causal conditions initially responsible for the emergence of these groups include the
formation of territorially based villages, the emergence of craft indus-
tries alongside agricultural activities, and the natural affinity of men for
each other.

60. Robert Bellah, "Durkheim and History," in Nisbet, *Emile Durkheim*, p.
163.

As long as industry was exclusively agricultural, it had its natural framework in the family and in the territorial group made up of contiguous families in the village. As a rule, as long as exchange or barter was little developed, the life of the husbandman did not draw him away from his home. He subsisted on what he produced. The family was at the same time a professional group.

With the appearance of specialized crafts, however, the craftsman found it impossible to confine his perspective and his activities solely to domestic relationships. Because customers were necessary in order to live by a craft, the craftsman had to take account of what craftsmen of the same trade were doing; he had to cooperate and compete with them. Thus a new form of social interaction was established outside the family, and we discover "a number of individuals who share the same ideas and interests, sentiments and occupations, in which the rest of the population have no part. When that occurs, it is inevitable that these individuals are carried along by the current of their similarities, as if under an impulsion; they feel a mutual attraction, they seek out one another; they enter into relations with one another and form compacts and so, by degrees, become a limited group with recognizable features, within the general society." For these reasons, a new group was formed in the heart of the Roman Empire.[61]

Initially, these emerging guilds, like other newly constituted groups, took as their model an existing social institution. As the family was the principal social institution of the day, the family rather naturally became the pattern on which the new groups were modeled. The first *collegia,* as the Roman guilds were called, thus resembled great families with their own banquets, festivals, worship, burial, and so forth. From the outset, however, these groups also possessed their own peculiar characteristics. Being primarily concerned with occupational or professional matters, they could only imitate the essential features of domestic societies. They could neither reproduce them exactly nor succeed, like the primitive family, in embracing all social functions. The distinctive characteristics of these specialized economic groups is not to be found in their domestic features, then, but, rather, in the moral sentiments inspired by these groups and in the moral rules by which they attempted, from the outset, to regulate economic behavior.

Initially, the *collegia* were extralegal societies. They were neither recognized by Roman law nor granted a significant function in the

61. Durkheim, *Professional Ethics and Civic Morals,* pp. 26, 23.

political structure of the Roman city. This is explained, Durkheim claims, by the agricultural and military nature of Roman society.

Over a long period the crafts were no more than a minor and subsidiary feature of collective activity in the Roman world. Rome was essentially an agricultural and military society. As an agricultural society it was divided into *gentes, curiae* and tribes. Assembly by centuries [meaning voting units in the assembly] reflects rather the military side. But it was quite natural that the industrial functions, at first unknown, then only rudimentary, should not affect the political structure of the City in any way. They were *cadres* set up late in the day alongside normal official *cadres:* the product of a kind of outgrowth from the very early social structure of Rome. Moreover, until a very late date in Roman history, the craft carried the mark of a moral obloquy; that fact puts out of court any idea that it ever held an official place in the State. Things did no doubt change with time, but the very way in which they changed clearly demonstrates what they were like at the outset. The craftsmen had to have recourse to irregular means to see that their interests were respected and to secure a status in keeping with their growing importance.[62]

Gradually, the growing strength of the guilds more or less forced the Roman state to recognize their existence and their achieved status within the rest of the social order, but the hierarchical and bureaucratic character of Roman society led to their being absorbed as cogs in the administrative machine. With this absorption, however, the character of these groups was changed, for "this dependence upon the State was not long in degenerating into an intolerable servitude that emperors could maintain only by force."[63] As a result, the Roman *collegia* did not survive the dissolution of the Empire upon whose political power and force they had become dependent.

An important revival of the guild system in Western civilization occurred in the eleventh and twelfth centuries. From their inception, the social milieu in which these new occupational groups were established was quite different from the Roman city-state. Instead of arising as subsidiary institutions within an essentially agrarian and military society, the medieval guilds emerged in towns which were specifically established by feudal lords as centers of manufacturing and trade. As a result, the medieval guilds were closely bound to the basically commercial character of urban centers in the Christian West.

62. *Ibid.,* pp. 32-33.
63. Durkheim, *Division du travail,* 2nd ed., p. x.

These nascent medieval guilds were not modeled, as in Rome, upon domestic societies, but, rather, upon the prototype provided by the church. One might describe them as *ecclesiolae in ecclesia.* "Rather often," Durkheim quotes from Levasseur's *Les classes ouviéres en France jusqu'à la Révolution,*

> the medieval corporations were established in the parish church or in a particular chapel and placed under the invocation of a saint who became the patron saint of the whole community . . . It was there that they gathered and witnessed with great ceremony the solemn masses, after which the members of the brotherhood went, all together, to end their day with a joyous feast.[64]

These religious features did not prevent the medieval guilds from developing more explicit occupational rules than those formulated in the Roman *collegia.* Quite the contrary, the religious legitimation of the corporation considerably aided them in realizing this specifically moral task. By virtue of the more favorable commercial and religious milieu in which they found themselves, the medieval guilds succeeded in formulating a fairly complex set of rules covering such things as the respective rights and duties of employers and employees, the rights and privileges of workers, and occupational honesty in consumer relations.

During the period stretching from the dawn of the High Middle Ages to the eve of the French Revolution, the guild system continued to grow in importance and dignity. For this remarkable flourishing of medieval economic corporations, several noneconomic causal factors are cited by Durkheim.[65] The guilds successfully met a perennial social need or function insofar as they succeeded in regulating commerce and industry, thus preventing the painful consequences of unregulated economic competition. They also filled an important lacuna in the moral life of the individual as the family gradually became, during this same period, a progressively less important source of moral authority. As family duties became increasingly restricted to interpersonal domestic relationships, the guilds provided their members with a fresh set of "occupational ethics" backed by collective authority. The corporation thus became, in a sense, the heir of the family, albeit an heir governing a less extensive field of behavior than that regulated by earlier domestic societies. Finally, the guild system grew in importance and dignity

---

64. *Ibid.,* p. xiv.
65. For Durkheim's analysis of the causal factors responsible for the emergence of guilds in the Middle Ages, see *ibid.,* xi-xx.

because it provided a milieu in which its members could enjoy the fruits of a common life and the pure joys of communing or associating together.

What accounts, then, for the collapse of the guild system at the outset of the industrial revolution? Durkheim finds his answer in the response of the guilds to the new economic ball game created by the emergence of large-scale manufacturing. With the discovery of new factory methods in the seventeenth and eighteenth centuries, it became not only possible, but desirable, to set up manufacturing facilities outside the framework of the medieval commune and to produce commodities for national consumption. As a result, industry gradually evolved to a point where it could no longer be regulated by the old municipally based guilds. If the guilds had become national organizations paralleling large-scale industry, they would presumably have survived. But this is precisely what they failed to do. Instead of reorganizing themselves on a national basis, the guilds chose instead to remain bounded by the walls of the city and hedged about, like prisoners, by archaic traditions. They thus became "a kind of dead substance or foreign body which only persisted in our social organism by the force of intertia" until they were abolished by the French Revolution.[66]

Two momentous consequences have resulted from this abolition of the guilds. The release of economic activity from secondary group regulation has given rise to recurrent industrial conflicts, ruthless competition, and other unfortunate economic practices. To be sure, industry has not been completely removed from all moral influences. There are general rules "about the fidelity and devotion workers of all sorts owe to those who employ them, about the moderation with which employers ought to use their economic superiority, a certain reprobation of all competition too openly dishonest, for all flagrant exploitation of the consumer," but these publicly supported rules have scarcely succeeded in regulating the war of all against all in the economic sector. "The most blameworthy acts are so frequently absolved by success that the boundary between what is permitted and what is prohibited, what is just and what is unjust, is no longer fixed, but, rather, subject to almost arbitrary dislocation by individuals."[67]

And, the numerous individuals, who spend the greater part of their lives in the industrial and commercial sphere, "have only a faint impress of morality, [since] the greater part of their existence is passed

---

66. Durkheim, *Professional Ethics and Civic Morals,* pp. 35-37.
67. Durkheim, *Division du travail,* 2nd ed., p. ii.

divorced from any moral influence."[68] Such a state of affairs cannot fail to be a source of severe demoralization or anomie if one assumes, as Durkheim does, that "human passions stop only before a moral power they respect" and that "only a constituted society enjoys the moral and material supremacy indispensable in making rules for individuals."[69] Given this assessment, it is scarcely surprising that Durkheim concludes his discussion of occupational ethics with a clarion call for a national *syndicat* charged with the moral responsibilities previously allotted to the medieval guilds.

Durkheim found that occupational groups, unlike the family, increasingly extended their moral and economic responsibilities during their evolution from illicit *collegia* to medieval guilds. The collapse of these associations has resulted in the loss of their three basic social functions: the regulation of industry, the establishment of occupational ethics backed by collective authority, and the formation of an enjoyable, collective milieu worthy of moral loyalty. Not only did this analysis add an important chapter to the sociological study of histor-ically significant economic institutions, it also added another hypothesis to Durkheim's theory of structural differentiation: when a unit that has performed essential functions is abolished, these functions may not be immediately assumed by another institution. Thus, the collapse of occupational associations has left a serious lacuna in the moral fabric of modern societies. As a result, industrial societies have gone through a lengthy period of unregulated economic activity, immoral economic behavior, and widespread anomie.

The State and Civic Morality

Durkheim's study of the state and civic morality presupposes the general theoretical background provided in his lectures on the family and occupational morality. Not only is Durkheim's definition of the state formulated in close relationship with his theory of structural func-tional evolution, but the state is said to qualify as a moral community, like the family and occupational groups, primarily because it engenders rules and inspires sentiments of attachment or loyalty. Yet, several theoretical refinements introduced by Durkheim in discussing the state and civic morality are sufficiently significant to deserve mention at the outset. First, he considerably alters his earlier treatment, in *The Division of Labor*, of the relationship between legislative statutes and

68. Durkheim, *Professional Ethics and Civic Morals*, p. 12.
69. Durkheim, *Division du travail*, 2nd ed., pp. iii, v.

public opinion. This alteration yields a more sophisticated theory of the complex nature of this relationship than that presented in his earlier writings. Secondly, he modifies his earlier thesis regarding the causal conditions responsible for the rise of individualism and the emergence of natural rights. Whereas *The Division* traces the rise of individualism primarily to morphological factors, Durkheim now claims that a state devoted to the protection of the individual from group tyranny is an essential prerequisite for the emancipation of the individual from the undifferentiated social mass. In this connection, Durkheim introduces the persuasive hypothesis that individualism requires a pluralistic society in which the existence of differentiated institutions precludes any single social unit from tyrannizing individual members. This new position enables Durkheim to develop a theory of civic morality that mediates between Spencer's atomistic individualism and Hegel's state absolutism. Finally, Durkheim introduces, in the context of discussing civic morality, the fundamental theoretical principle that groups posit ideals as well as rules. In moving from Durkheim's discussion of occupational ethics (where the stress is upon obligatory rules and sentiments of attachment inspired by the group as a whole) to his treatment of civic morality, we thus encounter the theoretical shift to the fundamental notion, examined earlier, that "attachment" is to be understood in terms of loyalty or devotion to shared "ideals." Civic morality thus represents an important step in the evolution of Durkheim's moral theory as a whole.

Inasmuch as the relevant social unit in the field of *la morale civique* is the state, Durkheim begins his discussion of this subdivision of morality with a careful definition of this political institution. The state is a specific, relatively autonomous, political institution, existing for the special purpose of maintaining a scheme of legal order and acting through laws enforced by prescribed and definite sanctions.[70] As a duly

70. Durkheim, *Professional Ethics and Civic Morals,* ch. 4. This characterization of the state as a distinct structural unit with political functions represents an attempt on Durkheim's part to distinguish the state from both domestic and occupational groups. Dissatisfied with previous definitions of the state in terms of territorial unity and the numerical size of the population, Durkheim observes that neither characterization provides a clear distinction between political institutions and others. With regard to Bluntschli's territorial definition of the state, Durkheim notes that this approach denies "any political character to the great nomad societies whose structure was sometimes very elaborate." (*Ibid.,* p. 43.) Moreover, a territorial definition fails to provide a clear distinction between political societies and domestic societies, since the latter are, in many countries, no less bound to the soil. Equally unsatisfactory is Rousseau's attempt to define a political society in terms of the numerical size of the population. In addition to the obvious fact that definitions of this sort are notoriously arbitrary and varying, Durkheim observes that they fail to draw any recognizable distinction between numerically large families and statistically small, but differentiated, societies.

constituted institution of this sort, the state does not, by definition, exist in the diffuse clan. True, political functions are performed in primitive societies, as in every society, but a specific institution responsible for the exercise of political functions is nonexistent at the earliest, undifferentiated stage of social evolution. Durkheim, therefore, criticizes Sumner Maine and Fustel de Coulanges for assuming that the state, in the modern and "proper sense of the term," exists in primitive kinship societies. A differentiated institution, like the state, can only exist, Durkheim maintains, in those societies formed by the coming together of a rather large number of secondary groups which are not themselves subject to any duly constituted authority.[71] In brief, a state only exists in a structurally differentiated society.

The distinguishing characteristic of the state is its right to represent the "supreme authority" which resides in the body politic as a whole. The state is not itself the "sovereign authority," but, rather, "the highest organ" within, or sovereign agent of, this authority. The state's principal function is to "think" and "act" for the rest of the society. In performing this principal function, states or, rather, agents of the state, deliberate in a rational and self-conscious manner upon the central beliefs and norms of the society they represent, as well as the collective issues facing the society as a whole. Having reached policy decisions, the parliamentary or the executive branch sets forth general principles or laws generally intended to advance the common good.

Does this mean that the state is merely passive in reflecting public opinion? As Durkheim altered his position on this issue, two different answers are contained in his writings. In his early articles and in *The Division,* Durkheim vigorously contends that the state normally just reflects public opinion. He thus unwittingly ascribes to the so-called "fallacy of legislative impotence," which Julius Stone aptly describes as the fallacy of overexaggerating "the role in legal development of popular consciousness as distinct from the consciousness of small groups whether of specialists or of a dominant class."[72] In his later writings, however, Durkheim alters his initial hypothesis regarding the inverse relationship between statutes and public opinion. While continuing to stress the obvious impact of public opinion upon governmental decisions, Durkheim notes, in *Leçon de sociologie,* that the state makes its own distinct contribution to the formation of laws and policies. The following passage best summarizes this mature position regarding the interrelationship between public opinion and the government:

71. *Ibid.,* p. 45.
72. Stone, *Province and Function of Law,* p. 442.

When a bill is carried in Parliament, when the government takes a decision within the limits of its competence, both actions, it is true, depend on the general state of social opinion, and on the society. Parliament and the government are in touch with the masses of the nation and the various impressions released by this contact have their effect in deciding them to take this course rather than that. But even if there be this *one factor* [italics mine] in their decision lying outside themselves, it is none the less true that it is they (Parliament and government) who make this decision and above all it expresses the particular *milieu* where it has its origin. It often happens, too, that there may even be discord between this *milieu* and the nation as a whole, and that decisions taken by the government or parliamentary vote may be valid for the whole community and yet do not square with the state of social opinion.[73]

Durkheim thus arrives at the important theoretical insight that while governmental decisions arise from, and sometimes reflect, public opinion, these decisions are made by partly autonomous institutions which independently influence social change. The state becomes, in Durkheim's mature writings, a partially independent causal variable with its own distinctive impact upon the nature of society and the character of social change.

At the outset of its historical evolution, the state was inextricably bound to religious beliefs. Civic morality was inseparable from religious morality. The aims of the state were seen as essentially religious, while religious beliefs deeply influenced politics:

The destiny of the State was closely bound up with the fate of the gods worshipped at its altars. If a State suffered reverses, then the prestige of its gods declined in the same measure—and vice versa. Public religion and civic morals were fused: they were but different aspects of the same reality. To bring glory to the City was the same as enhancing the glory of the gods of the City: it worked both ways.

As a result of this almost total devotion to nonempirical, sacred goals, the state, at this stage in history, was often indifferent to the needs and interests of individuals. The individual was viewed as part of the profane world in marked contrast with the sacred sphere of the gods. "What was prized by all, were the beliefs held in common, the collective aspirations, the popular traditions and the symbols that were an expression of them." Likewise, the individual, being absorbed as he was in the mass of society and counting his own private interests as rela-

---

73. Durkheim, *Professional Ethics and Civic Morals,* p. 49.

tively insignificant in comparison with the religious aims of the state, gladly and without demur subordinated "his own lot to the destinies of collective existence without any sense of sacrifice."[74]

The further one advances in the study of history, Durkheim maintains, the more one becomes aware of two processes. The individual, by gradually breaking away from "the depths of the social mass," expands the scope of his personal sphere of existence and acquires ever-wider control over his own behavior. The individual personality gradually emerges as "an autonomous centre of activity, an impressive system of personal forces whose energy can no more be destroyed than that of the cosmic forces." Paralleling these developments are certain major alterations in the moral values of society. From being ignored, the individual gradually becomes an exalted object of moral respect, acquiring ever-wider rights over his own person and over the possessions to which he is now given title. In brief, the cult of the individual replaces the cult of the gods of the city "as the pole-star for public as well as private conduct."[75]

In addition, the state continues to grow in size and importance. "As we read on in history," Durkheim states in this connection,

> we see the functions of the State multiplying as they increase in importance. This development of the functions is made materially perceptible by the parallel development of the organ itself. What a far cry from the instrument of government in a society such as our own to what it was in Rome or in a Red Indian tribe. In the one, a score of ministries with all their interlocking, side by side with huge assemblies whose very structure is infinitely complex, and over all, the head of State with his own particular administrative departments. In the other, a prince or a few magistrates, some counsellors aided by secretaries.[76]

The state, like the individual personality, has thus progressively become an autonomous center of activity with an immense influence upon the rest of society.

Recognition of the interrelationship between these two developments is essential, Durkheim contends, in order to accurately interpret the gradual emergence, in the modern era, of new moral ties uniting the state and its citizens. Unfortunately, neither the evolutionary theory of civic morality perpetrated by Spencer, nor that advanced by Hegel, recognizes this interrelationship. Spencer erroneously concluded from

74. *Ibid.*, pp. 55, 56.
75. *Ibid.*, pp. 57, 56.
76. *Ibid.*, p. 53.

his one-sided analysis of the rise of individualism that the duties of the state were becoming progressively limited to a wholly negative justice, whereas, in fact, the functions of the state are multiplying in number and importance. Equally unsatisfactory is Hegel's antithetical doctrine concerning the evolution of the all-powerful state. By neglecting the emergence of individualism, Hegel's conception of civic morality was distorted in the opposite direction:

it is argued that every society has an aim superior to individual aims and unrelated to them. It is held that . . . the State is to pursue the carrying out of this truly social aim, whilst the individual should be an instrument for putting into effect the plans he has not made and that do not concern him. It is to the glory of the society, for its greatness and for its riches he has to labour: he has to find recompense for his pains in the sole fact that as a member of the society he has some sort of share in the benefits he has helped win.

This Hegelian social ethic, which superficially seems identical with Durkheim's own, represents, according to Durkheim, an anachronistic effort to replace individualism with "the cult of the City State in a new guise."[77]

The truth concerning the evolution of civic morality, argues Durkheim, lies in a third position situated between the negative, individualistic doctrine perpetrated by Spencer and the absolutist conclusions advanced by Hegel. Far from having been progressively restricted to negative functions, Durkheim maintains against Spencer, the state has increasingly interfered in a positive manner to protect individuals against secondary group exploitation and despotism. "It is the State that has rescued the child from patriarchal domination and from family tyranny; it is the State that has freed the citizen from feudal groups and later from communal groups; it is the State that has liberated the craftsman and his master from guild tyranny."[78]

This is not to deny historical examples of state tyranny, or the possibility of state despotism developing again in the future, but it is to claim that, normally, where secondary groups exist and where these groups actively counteract this tendency toward state supremacy, the state has been responsible for the gradual emancipation of the individual. Durkheim thus sees "a dynamic balance between the state and secondary groups as maximizing individuality,"[79] although it is also

77. *Ibid.*, p. 54.
78. *Ibid.*, p. 64.
79. Bellah, "Durkheim and History," p. 165.

his claim that this dynamic balance is ineffective unless the state, in lieu of restricting itself to enforcing a purely negative justice, actively permeates "all those secondary groups of family, trade and professional association, Church, regional areas and so on ... which tend ... to absorb the personality of their members."[80] This nontyrannical intervention on behalf of individuals cannot be realized unless the state continues to expand its functional responsibilities.

The fundamental moral duty of the modern state has become the positive promotion, protection, and defense of the rights and privileges associated with individualism. This responsibility, as Hegel would say, is a collective aim superior to the individual qua individual, for "it is not this or that individual the State seeks to develop, it is the individual *in genere*, who is not to be confused with any single one of us." But it is not the state that is here the object of moral concern; it is, rather, a collectively shared ideal. Moreover, it is an ideal close to its devotees. This ideal is, as it were, a cult which

has all that is required to take the place of the religious cults of former times. It serves quite as well as they to bring about that communion of minds and wills which is a first condition of any social life. It is just as simple for men to draw together to work for the greatness of man as it is to work to the glory of Zeus or Jehovah or Athena. The whole difference of this religion, as it affects the individual, is that the god of its devotion is closer to his worshippers. But although not far removed, he does nevertheless still transcend them, and the rôle of the State in this respect is what it was formerly. It rests with it, shall we say, to organize the cult, to be the head of it and to ensure its regular working and development.

The cult of the human person, with all that such a cult implies with respect to the protection of individual rights and the promotion of his moral and physical well-being, is thus the fundamental ethical duty of the state, the polestar for moral guidance.[81]

If promotion and protection of the idealistic cult associated with individualism is the fundamental moral duty of modern states, what are the principal duties governing the citizen's relationship to the state? Obviously "patriotism" is one possible answer, but patriotism alters in the course of history. What form of patriotism increasingly characterizes the civic morality of contemporary societies? At the outset of his treatment of this question of modern patriotism, Durkheim notes the

80. Durkheim, *Professional Ethics and Civic Morals*, p. 65.
81. *Ibid.*, pp. 69-70.

recent emergence of a conflict between loyalty to the national state on the one hand and devotion to the human ideal and to mankind in general on the other—in a word, between patriotism and world patriotism. This modern conflict in loyalties was unknown to the ancient world with its cult of the state and the gods of the state:

For the [ancient] worshippers there was therefore nothing to allow of choice or hesitation. They could conceive of nothing above the State, above its fame and greatness. But since then, things have changed. No matter how devoted men may be to their native land, they all today are aware that beyond the forces of national life there are others, in a higher region and not so transitory, for they are unrelated to conditions peculiar to any given political group and are not bound up with its fortunes. There is something more universal and more enduring. It is true to say that those aims that are the most general and the most unchanging are also the most sublime. As we advance in evolution, we see the ideals men pursue breaking free of the local or ethnic conditions obtaining in a certain region of the world or a certain human group, and rising above all that is particular and so approaching the universal. We might say that the moral forces come to have a hierarchic order according to their degree of generality or diffusion.[82]

These observations are sufficient, Durkheim asserts, to justify the conclusion that national patriotism is gradually being superseded, in moral worth, by world patriotism, although there is no reason to believe that, as long as there are states, national patriotism will not continue to be a powerful moral sentiment.

Granted these observations, and the ever-present possibility of aberrational developments, Durkheim suggests that the only course for societies and for individuals in the immediate future lies in reconciliation of these two forms of patriotism. The national ideal must be merged with the human ideal, individual states must become the agencies by which the human ideal is carried into effect.[83] Then, and only then, will the conflicting loyalties implicit within our current civic morality be resolved, and the conflicts faced by citizens be overcome.

82. *Ibid.*, pp. 72-73. In *Formes élémentaires* (p. 609), Durkheim finds a nascent sense of international patriotism in primitive societies.
83. Durkheim, *Professional Ethics and Civic Morals*, p. 74. This belief in the necessity of fusing patriotism with humanism underlies Durkheim's opposition to narrow forms of nationalism. Although he viewed patriotism as a virtue, he explicitly rejected nationalist arguments based upon the alleged superiority of a given nation, including France. See his comments in "Pacifisme et patriotisme," Séance du 30 décembre 1907, *Bulletin de la société française de philosophie*, VIII (1908), 66-67.

These dichotomous loyalties would be reconciled, Durkheim suggests, if each "State had no other purpose than making men of its citizens, in the widest sense of the term." In a political milieu devoted to this exclusively domestic end, "civic duties would be only a particular form of the general obligations of humanity. It is this course that evolution takes . . . The more societies concentrate their energies inward, on the interior life, the more they will be diverted from the disputes that bring a clash between cosmopolitism—or world patriotism, and patriotism." As long as there are states, national pride will continue to exist, but societies can find their honor, "not in being the greatest or the wealthiest, but in being the most just, the best organized and in possessing the best moral constitution." In pursuing this humanistic goal, Durkheim contends, there is surely enough work to keep every society, and every publicly interested citizen, fully occupied:

The planning of the social *milieu* so that the individual may realise himself more fully, and the management of the collective apparatus in a way that will bear less hard on the individual; an assured and amicable exchange of goods and services and the co-operation of all men of good will towards an ideal they share without any conflict: in these, surely, we have enough to keep public activity fully employed.

In short, the moral duties of the state to the individual and those of the individual to the state should both merge in the human ideal. The only problem is that they have failed to do so![84]

In his lectures on the state and civic morality Durkheim contends that the history of the state is the history of the emergence of the individual from the social mass, the appearance of the cult of man, and the rise of world patriotism. Structurally, the state has tended to establish a dynamic balance among secondary groups that has greatly aided the development of individualism by preventing any single group from tyrannizing its members. Ideologically, the state has actively promoted and protected the natural rights and privileges associated with the cult of the human person. With the rise of world patriotism, the task of the modern state is to reconcile national patriotism with universal humanitarianism by devoting itself to internal justice, peace, and solidarity.

In evaluating Durkheim's evolutionary analysis of moral societies, critics have largely confined themselves to *The Division of Labor*. Sub-

84. Durkheim, *Professional Ethics and Civic Morals*, pp. 74-75.

sequent work on the history of the family, occupational groups, and the state has received scant attention from social scientists working in these fields. Consequently, Durkheim has been frequently criticized for themes that were later refined or repudiated. In fairness to Durkheim, these later revisions will be mentioned in evaluating his first major book. For expository purposes, however, *The Division of Labor* will be evaluated before proceeding to a critique of his research on specific institutions.

Three major objections can be raised in criticism of the evolutionary thesis of *The Division of Labor,* none of which refute its central claim that Western societies have evolved in the direction of greater structural differentiation, individuation, occupational specialization, and respect for individual rights. First, few of Durkheim's assumptions about primitive societies can be accepted in precisely the form in which they were stated almost eighty years ago. As Durkheim himself observes in *The Elementary Forms,* there is greater structural differentiation and individuation in these societies than his original characterization of mechanical solidarity suggests.[85] Subsequent research has also shown that the severe constraint and repression associated with the primitive collective conscience does not accurately portray the nature of social constraint in early societies. There is considerable evidence, in fact, that social constraint tends to increase as societies move beyond the primitive case, as the mature Durkheim more or less admits in describing constraint in Australian tribes. Cruel and painful punishments, he observes, are rare, partly because the revengeful deities that appear in later stages of religious evolution are absent but largely because these early societies are not "huge Leviathans which overwhelm a man by the enormity of their power and place him under a severe discipline."[86] Similarly, the repressive laws attributed to primitive societies in *The Division of Labor* are not particularly characteristic of these societies. In this context, Barnes has recently noted:

Durkheim took his evidence on legal codes from classical antiquity and early Europe, and some historical progression of the kind he had in mind may have taken place there, though even in this area Merton holds

85. In *Elementary Forms,* Durkheim acknowledges the presence of structural differentiation in the sections dealing with the various secondary groups in Australian tribes. See, for example, his *Formes élémentaires,* pp. 142-158, 215-216. Individuation is recognized in passages dealing with the individual totem and the way in which individuals develop their own distinctive ideas vis-à-vis collective beliefs. (*Ibid.,* pp. 606-607.) Individuation is said to be less developed in primitive societies than in advanced societies, but it is not absent. (*Ibid.,* p. 7.)
    86. *Ibid.,* p. 321.

he was mistaken. But this progression cannot be extended to the primitive world, where legal codes do not exist in writing, if at all. In stateless societies almost all jural rules are, in these terms, restitutive rather than repressive. Indeed, it is interesting that in an inquiry based on evidence from forty-eight societies, and aimed to test whether or not Toennies, Durkheim, Park, Small, Maine, Redfield and Riesman are all talking in different terms about the same dimension of societal complexity, the authors . . . examine eight variables in terms of greater or less societal complexity, as suggested by these theorists, and equate punishment by government action with greater complexity, and punishment by the person wronged with less complexity.[87]

Recognition of the error of attributing repressive laws to primitive societies may explain why Durkheim abandoned this theme after *1893*.

Another set of objections applies to the general theory of social change advocated in *The Division of Labor*. Despite the value of several specific hypotheses about urbanization and mobility, Durkheim commits a fundamental methodological error in presuming to establish causal links between the primitive and the modern case without considering intervening societies. He fallaciously assumes, moreover, that the complex factors involved in the evolution of entire societies can be reduced to a few simple causal factors. In addition, Durkheim clearly overestimates the role of morphological factors in social change, thereby underestimating the role played by ideational and moral factors. Fortunately, Durkheim's later research on intervening societies, as well as his mature multicausal theory with its clear recognition of religious and axiomatic causal variables, indicates that the mature Durkheim realized these weaknesses in his first, amateurish treatment of social change.

And, developments in Durkheim's own day, as in our own, render untenable his central claim that the division of labor engenders moral solidarity in advanced societies. As Georges Friedmann notes in this connection, a superficial examination of the way the division of labor is practiced in contemporary factories, mines, and offices clearly demonstrates that it is far from engendering the various virtues Durkheim attributed to it.[88] Not only does the division of labor often fail to

87. J. A. Barnes, "Durkheim's *Division of Labour in Society*," *Man* (Journal of the Royal Anthropological Institute), I (1966), 168-169. The reference to Merton is to Robert K. Merton, "Durkheim's *Division of Labor in Society*," *American Journal of Sociology*, XL (1934), 326. The second reference is to Linton C. Freeman and Robert F. Winch, "Social Complexity: An Empirical Test of a Typology of Societies," *American Journal of Sociology*, LXII (1957), 461-466.
88. Georges Friedmann, "La Thèse de Durkheim et les formes contemporaines de la division du travail," *Cahiers internationaux de sociologie*, XIX (1955), 52.

engender solidarity; the unequal rewards associated with it frequently engender feelings of exploitation rather than mutuality. In fact, during the eight decades following "the publication of this report, the forms taken by specialization in technical societies have only enlarged the gulf between the ideal consequences of the division of labor, as Durkheim explicated them, and the real effects that we observe in our societies."[89]

The last of these three major criticisms is the most damaging with respect to the validity of Durkheim's analysis of the moral bases of advanced societies inasmuch as it clearly indicates that he was wrong in assuming that the division of labor was responsible for the emergence of new forms of solidarity based upon complementary differences and mutual dependence. At the same time it must be acknowledged that Durkheim was quite correct in stressing the importance of shared norms in modern societies. For the most part, these norms are relatively general, abstract principles. Moreover, collectively engendered rules respecting the dignity and worth of the human person are central to contemporary morality in most Western societies. The young Durkheim may have been wrong in contending that this so-called cult of the individual is not a genuine social link, but realization of this error eventually led him to view this cult as the principal source of moral solidarity in contemporary societies.

Durkheim's historical analysis of specific moral institutions is some-what more difficult to evaluate than *The Division of Labor*. Several years ago it would have been fashionable to criticize him for even attempting, in these studies, to elaborate an evolutionary typology, but the recent revival of evolutionary theories in the social sciences mutes this criticism. Today, Durkheim's basic principles of analysis—structural differentiation, functional specialization, symbolic integration, norma-tive control—are generally accepted as necessary conceptual tools for the sort of evolutionary study that he undertook.[90] But these tools have yet to be applied in such a way as to extract an evolutionary scheme from the highly specialized studies on these groups published since Durkheim's death. Such a study would unquestionably yield a

89. *Ibid.*, p. 58. For reasons related to Durkheim's failure to sufficiently emphasize collective beliefs, Merton agrees with Friedmann's conclusion that he overestimates the role of the division of labor as the principal source of modern solidarity. (Merton, "Durkheim's *Division of Labor*," p. 324.)

90. Talcott Parsons defends the use of these and other Durkheimian concepts in his recent book, *Societies: Evolutionary and Comparative Perspectives,* Foundations of Modern Sociology Series, ed. Alex Inkeles (Englewood Cliffs, N.J.: Prentice-Hall, 1966).

much more complicated evolutionary theory than Durkheim was able to construct from the materials available to him, but there is considerable evidence that it would also confirm some of his principal theoretical and empirical insights.

Durkheim's treatment of the family is clearly incomplete, as he acknowledged by not publishing his lectures in this area.[91] But his major thesis regarding the gradual contraction in size and functional significance of this social unit would appear to be essentially correct. The recent work of Parsons and Bales on the nature and function of the family tend to confirm Durkheim's leading ideas.[92] In viewing "the modern type of family as a result of a process of specialization and its main functions as those of 'pattern maintenance' and 'tension management,'" these sociologists come close to Durkheim's basic position.[93] A number of other studies have confirmed the validity of Durkheim's thesis that increased social mobility, urbanization, and secondary group formation have considerably diminished the moral role of the family. Few contemporary students of the family, however, agree with Durkheim's psychologically naïve contention that a small social unit, like the modern family, cannot be an emotionally powerful source of moral authority and solidarity.

Durkheim's historical account of occupational groups is also essentially correct.[94] The Roman *collegia* began as illicit associations that underwent a modest evolution before disappearing with the

91. According to Marcel Mauss, Durkheim was urged to publish his lectures on the family shortly before World War I. He decided not to do so because too much research would be required to bring his work up to date. (Durkheim, "Famille conjugale," p. 1.)

92. See Talcott Parsons and Robert Bales, *Family Socialization and Interaction Process* (New York: Free Press, 1955), ch. 1; Parsons, *Essays in Sociological Theory*, revised ed. (New York: Free Press, 1964), pp. 421-422.

93. Bellah, "Durkheim and History," p. 163.

94. For the history and political theory of *collegia* and guilds, see: "Clubs, Greek," "Clubs, Roman," *The Oxford Classical Dictionary* (Oxford, Eng.: The Clarendon Press, 1949), pp. 204-205; John Figgis, *Churches in the Modern State* (London: Longman's, Green and Co., 1914), ch. 2; Otto von Gierke, "The Idea of Corporation," tr. Ferdinand Kolegar, in *Theories of Society*, ed. Parsons, Shils, Naegele, and Pitts (New York: Free Press, 1961), I, 611-626; Otto von Gierke, *Natural Law and the Theory of Society*, tr. with an introduction by Ernest Barker (Cambridge, Eng.: Cambridge University Press, 1934), I and II; Otto von Gierke *Political Theories of the Middle Ages*, tr. with an introduction by F. W. Maitland (Cambridge, Eng.: Cambridge University Press, 1900); H. J. Laski "The Early History of the Corporation in England," *Harvard Law Review*, XXX (1917), 575; E. G. Hardy, *Studies in Roman History* (London: Swan Sonnenschein and Company, 1906), ch. 9, pp. 129-150; Jean Pierre Waltzing, *Etude historique sur les corporations professionnelles chez les Romains depuis les origines jusqu'à la chute de l'empire d'Occident* (Louvain: Charles Peeters, 1895-1900), I-IV, and *Les Corporations Romaines et la charité* (Louvain: Charles Peeters, 1895).

collapse of the Roman Empire. Occupational associations were revived as guilds in the Middle Ages, when they succeeded in regulating moral relationships in the economic realm and in eliciting group loyalty. The main weakness of this analysis is not to be located in this historical account, but in Durkheim's conclusion that a restoration of analogous groups composed of employees and employers is essential in order to reinstitute these several moral functions in our time. Among the many difficulties posed by this conclusion, several strictly empirical observations are sufficiently important to bear brief mention here. Durkheim fails to envision the possibility that governmental agencies might perform the regulatory functions formerly assigned to the guilds. He also fails to entertain the possibility that trade unions might engender rules and sentiments of profound importance vis-à-vis the moral ordering of economic behavior. Syndicates composed of employers and employees do not appear to be the best means of regulating economic behavior if the term "moral" includes, as Durkheim contended, the concept of distributive justice. Historically, militant unions have been more successful in achieving this goal than any combination of interest groups. Nor is it true that men are destined to live in a state of moral anomie until the type of syndicate envisioned by Durkheim is established. Numerous economic as well as noneconomic voluntary organizations are clearly capable of providing individuals with rules as well as a sense of solidarity.

Durkheim's analysis of the state and civic morality contains a series of illuminating hypotheses and important empirical insights. His definition of the state as a specific, relatively autonomous, political institution existing for the special purpose of maintaining a scheme of legal order through laws enforced by definite sanctions is essentially correct. His carefully drawn distinction between the supreme authority of the body politic and the state as an agent of this authority fits into the mainstream of liberal political theory. The thesis that the state and secondary groups maximize individual liberty by counterbalancing one another must surely be classified as an important sociological insight. Certainly Durkheim was also right in maintaining, against Spencer, that the modern state has gradually extended its social responsibilities, especially in the area of civil rights. Few rational men of goodwill would contest Durkheim's hope that national loyalty might be fused with world patriotism, however unlikely his lofty thought that national states might find their honor in realizing humanistic ideals in their own domestic gardens.

There are, however, several problems with Durkheim's analysis of the state. He tends to vacillate between factual analysis and normative political theory. As a result, it is extremely difficult to decide upon the appropriate criteria to be employed in evaluating his work. Durkheim's definition of the state, for example, is a factually correct description, but it is not an adequate normative theory because it leaves out essential ethical elements, like the constitutional foundation of the state and the idea of justice upon which it is based. The contention that states normally emancipate and protect individuals from secondary group tyranny is a patently incorrect historical description of the role of the state in ancient Mesopotamia, Egypt, and Rome, not to mention more recent examples of tyrannical political establishments. A much better case for this historic role could be made for voluntary societies and revolutionary groups who, by challenging the monolithic power of the state, have freed individuals from the ever-present danger of state tyranny. As a normative element within a democratic political theory, however, the idea that states should prevent secondary group tryanny is a perfectly acceptable, ethically defensible assertion.

Nor did Durkheim paint a very precise picture of the relationship between society and the state, the state and secondary groups, and the state and its citizens. He was wise, therefore, not to have published the lectures that were posthumously edited, for they tend to raise more questions than they answer. What precisely is the relationship between the state and society, including cultural standards? How are cultural ideas actually employed in political discussions? How are moral ideals misused by political representatives to rationalize exploitation, partisan politics, and unjust foreign policies. How do various secondary groups (ranging from self-interest groups to voluntary associations devoted to the public good) influence and counterbalance the state? How do the various freedoms of speech, press, assembly, and religion actually operate in modern democratic societies? How do citizens make their opinions known to the state? These and a multitude of other exceedingly important questions are either left unanswered or inadequately sketched in Durkheim's brief analysis.[95]

95. For a sharp critique of Durkheim's brief treatment of these issues, see Raymond Aron, *Main Currents*, II, 70-97. Aron notes, but fails to sufficiently stress, the role of the cult of the individual in Durkheim's thought. As a result, his critique overemphasizes the collective side of Durkheim's political theory. Nevertheless, he raises several important criticisms. In objecting to Durkheim's tendency to translate difficult social and political issues into problems of organization and moralization, Aron correctly notes Durkheim's failure to appreciate

A somewhat different problem is Durkheim's typical nineteenth-century liberal confidence in "history as the immanent unfolding of institutions which enshrined all the values he held dear."[96] Seeing the desirable functions performed by the modern state and secondary groups, Durkheim ignored and, hence, underestimated the demonic aspect of political life. Believing in the progressive realization of liberal goals, he failed to perceive that struggle and even violence are often essential weapons in the good fight against entrenched proponents of systematic oppression and injustice.

Turning from specifics to the general purpose of this historical treatment of various moral societies, it is apparent that Durkheim's entire analysis is governed to a large extent by his desire to join the two very different sociopolitical traditions in which he stood. On the one hand, he was convinced by, and gave articulate expression to, many of the conservative sociological views elaborated in France and Germany in opposition to the excesses of the French Revolution, including the primacy of society, the organic nature of society, the dependence of morality and law on the mores of a specific people, the necessity for authority in state and society, and man's psychological and moral indebtedness to society for his ideas, language, morality, and religion.[97] On the other hand, Durkheim also sought to give expression to the central tenets of the great natural rights tradition against which these conservative theories were initially perpetrated, that is, to individual rights, personal liberty, universal brotherhood, and worldwide community.[98] Unable to accept classical arguments in support of these ideals, he sought to root them in a metaphysics of history. By demon-

---

the role of conflict in social life. Aron's interpretation of Durkheim's treatment of democracy leaves out the latter's discussion of sovereignty, but succeeds in pointing to important weaknesses in Durkheim's brief treatment of the relationship between society and the state. Durkheim's discussion of democracy as involving close communication between the mass of individuals and the state, Aron contends, tends "to devaluate properly political institutions, to regard the principle of legitmacy as secondary, to be indifferent whether the head of state is or is not called king, or whether he is appointed by birth or by election" (p. 84). Durkheim's proposal that direct universal suffrage might be replaced by indirect suffrage through newly established intermediary corporations is justly criticized for failing to forsee that such an arrangment might lead to the collapse of representative forms of power.

96. Richter, "Durkheim's Politics and Political Theory," p. 204.

97. For a discussion of the conservative views of the French sociological tradition, see Nisbet, *Emile Durkheim*, pp. 23-28; Benoit-Smullyan, "Development of French Socialistic Theory and Its Critics in France," pp. 1-130.

98. For a comparison of the European tradition of Natural Law and Right with the conservative sociological counterrevolution in Germany, see Ernst Troeltsch, "The Ideas of Natural Law and Humanity in World Politics," in Gierke, *Natural Law and the Theory of Society*.

strating that society had given birth to the rights of man and that social authority, while still necessary, was now subject to these ideals, Durkheim sought a means of doing justice, within a sociological context, to the values enshrined in the French constitution. At the same time, he also found a means of correcting the serious lacuna in the social theory of the natural rights tradition that his great contemporary, Otto von Gierke, had detected. Having read von Gierke's monumental *Das deutsche Genossenschaftsrecht*, Durkheim was aware of the German scholar's persuasive argument that the natural rights tradition had failed to formulate a natural right of association and, hence, an adequate political justification for the existence of those secondary groups that stand between the state and the isolated individual. By seeing these groups as the natural outcome of societal differentiation, Durkheim presumably felt that he had found a way of justifying the existence of such groups without falling into the state absolutism to which von Gierke ultimately succumbed.

The paradoxical quality of Durkheim's social and political thought derives from these and other dialectical resolutions. Man is of infinite worth, yet this value is not inherent within him; it is but a supreme fiction created by society. Man is totally dependent upon society for the qualities that make him human, yet society has increasingly freed him from group tyranny. Man has become "an autonomous center of activity," yet secondary group restrictions, by preventing anomie, actually increase his liberty. Patriotism is a fundamental duty, yet patriotism must be counterbalanced by humanistic ends. For the ambiguities, lacunae, and errors in some of these paradoxical formulations, Durkheim has been justly criticized, but it is no longer justifiable to attribute to him conservative doctrines unqualified by the liberal, and occasionally radical, elements in his thought.

V

Moral Education

From an early date, Durkheim defined philosophy as well as sociology broadly enough to include moral education. As early as 1887, in fact, he urged philosophers to introduce their students to the facts of morality, especially sympathy, sociability, and group morality.[1] At the same time he argued that the application of the scientific method to moral development would furnish new information for moral instruction. Later, after his appointment in 1902 to the Sorbonne as a deputy for Ferdinand Buisson, whom he succeeded in the chair of the *Science de l'Education,* Durkheim developed his own theory of moral education in several lecture series.[2] These lectures from the latter part of his career explore still another major question of classical philosophy: how do we come to be moral both developmentally and pedagogically? By specifying the various psychological and sociological processes involved in childhood moralization and by indicating the social factors responsible for the historical variation of educational ideas and institutions, these lectures add another dimension to Durkheim's moral philosophy

1. Durkheim, "Philosophie dans les universités allemandes," pp. 439-440. Durkheim consistently maintained that moral instruction in the universities and the lycées should be the responsibility of philosophers trained in science. See, for example, his "L'Enseignement philosophique et l'agrégation de philosophie," *RP,* XXXIX (1895), 138-141.

2. Durkheim taught educational theory and practice as well as sociology throughout his entire teaching career. In 1887 a special position was created for him in the *Faculté des Lettres* at Bordeaux, where he taught sociology and pedagogy until 1902. During this period he gave a weekly one-hour lecture on pedagogy. In 1902 he was appointed to the Sorbonne as a deputy for Buisson, whom he succeeded in 1906, in the chair of the Science of Education. In recognition of the new field of sociology, the title of this chair was changed in 1913 to the Science of Education and Sociology. During Durkheim's fifteen years at the Sorbonne, Fauconnet estimates that he devoted at least a third, often two-thirds, of his teaching time to pedagogy. As one of the most distinguished professors of of education in the Third Republic, his educational theories were utilized in both secondary and normal schools. His secular theory of moral education, in fact, became an integral part of the required normal school curriculum, leading one critic to remark: "The requirement that M. Durkheim's sociology be taught in the two hundred normal schools of France is the most serious national peril which our country has known for a long time." (Jean Izoulet, as cited by Célestin Bouglé, *Bilan de la sociologie francaise contemporaine* (Paris: Félix Alcan, 1935), p. 168, n.

and extend his evolutionary perspective to another major social group, namely, educational institutions.

In tackling the problem of moral education, Durkheim wrestles with issues hotly debated since the early days of Greek philosophy. What is the general nature and role of education, and what is moral education in particular? Is education primarily a process of socialization or spontaneous development? Is moral education learning obedience to authoritative standards or character training? How do, and how should, educational institutions function? Should the school encourage conformity or freedom and autonomy? These central questions obviously call for fundamental decisions concerning the nature of man and his development in relationship to both the physical and the social environment.

The Nature and Role of Education

Education, in Durkheim's view, is the lifelong process by which the individual learns to cope with his physical environment and, more importantly, with his sociocultural milieu. In every society, the education of children is of the first importance, essential both for the good of society and for the well-being of the individual. Since every society depends upon a measure of consensus among its members, the importance of inducing members of society to do willingly what they must do if the society is to function properly is obvious. But it is no less true that socialization benefits the individual by providing him with the accumulated wisdom of past generations, by teaching him to control his biological instincts, and by instructing him concerning the means of attaining desirable goals.[3]

Education, in brief, is virtually synonymous with "socialization," meaning the process by which the individual learns the ways of a given society or social group. More specifically,

education is the influence exercised by adult generations on those that are not yet ready for social life. Its objective is to arouse and to develop

3. To see education from this Durkheimian perspective "as a process of growth and development—taking place as a result of the interaction of an individual with his environment, both physical and social, beginning at birth and lasting as long as life itself—a process in which the social heritage as a part of the social environment becomes a tool to be used toward the development of the best and most intelligent persons possible, men and women who will promote human welfare, that is to see the educative process as philosophers and educational reformers conceived it. It is certainly the way that Kant, Pestalozzi, Froebel, Herbart, Herbert Spencer, G. Stanley Hall, and William James understood it." (Stella Van Petten Henderson, *Introduction to Philosophy of Education* [Chicago: University of Chicago Press, 1947] p. 44.)

*in the child a certain number of physical, intellectual and moral states
which are demanded of him by both the political society as a whole and
the special milieu for which he is specifically destined.*[4]

By definition, education involves learning, but learning is a process
which differs cross-culturally, and in any given society, at various points
in its evolution. Durkheim, accordingly, felt called upon to draw a
broad, but extremely important, distinction between two very different
types of learning.

Throughout the greater part of human history, one important form of
education has been more or less spontaneous.[5] Adults have educated
their children while pursuing their own tasks. Children have not been
directly taught. This spontaneous process suited the nature of learning
in primitive societies quite well and continues to suit the type of learning that takes place in the modern home. As long as social realities are
not excessively complex, the young can embrace facts and their relationships in their own way, at their own time, and according to their
own interests and initiative. This form of learning is continuous, since

there is no period in social life . . . when the younger generations are
not in contact with their elders and when, therefore, they are not
receiving from them some educational influence. For this influence
does not make itself felt only in the very brief moments when parents
or teachers are consciously, and by explicit teaching, communicating
the results of their experience to those who come after them. There is
an unconscious education that never ceases. By our example, by the
words that we utter, by the actions that we perform, we constantly
mold our children.[6]

By identifying, imitating, approving, and cooperating with adults, the
child readily learns what he needs to know without formal socialization.

Direct pedagogy, whether perpetrated by priests or scholars, is contrasted with spontaneous learning. The aim of direct pedagogy is to
teach what is more complex, abstract, and intangible. Puberty rites,
catechistic instruction, and formal lectures are examples of this type of
education.[7] The peculiar aspect of this form of instruction is that the

4. Durkheim, *Education and Sociology*, p. 71.
5. Although Durkheim uses the term "unconscious" rather than "spontaneous"
to describe this form of learning, the latter term accurately describes the processes
involved. See Durkheim, *Education and Sociology*, pp. 91-98, and *Moral
Education*, pp. 17-18., 129-148, 177.
6. Durkheim, *Education and Sociology*, p. 91.
7. How these examples of direct pedagogy evolved from spontaneous instruction in primitive societies is indicated by Durkheim in the following passage:

learner is under the pressure of the social milieu of a specific institution, as well as the pressure of the teacher, who, in this case, is the
agent of society. All social activities socialize participants, but direct
pedagogy specializes deliberately in instilling the intellectual concepts
and moral ideas which constitute the most important social bonds. For
these reasons, direct or formal pedagogy was the mode of instruction
that especially attracted Durkheim's own scholarly attention.

Character Formation

Although Durkheim's definition of education includes physical
education, cultural instruction, and moral training, the latter is the
principal focus of most of his lectures. Moral education, as understood
by Durkheim as well as by his philosophical precursors, is primarily
concerned with character formation in the ethical, as contrasted with
the psychological, sense. "In the psychological sense one's character is
his distinctive nature, that which makes him himself rather than
another. In this sense everyone has character. In the ethical sense the
term means that quality of human nature which makes for dependability. Character in this sense means an inner consistency or unity of
personality. It means constancy, steadfastness, dependability. It implies
stability."[8] The aim of moral education, according to Durkheim, is thus
to develop the "fundamental dispositions . . . at the root of the moral
life."[9]

Durkheim's richest and most sophisticated analysis of the various
ways in which the moral character of the child is formed under the
pressure of the social milieu of the classroom is contained in the
remarkable series of lectures on moral education that Durkheim offered

"under tribal conditions the essential characteristic of education is that it is
diffuse; it is given to all the members of the clan indiscriminately. There are no
specialized teachers, no special overseers entrusted with the training of the youth;
it is all the elders, the totality of the ascending generations that play this role. At
most it happens that, for certain particularly fundamental forms of instruction,
certain elders are more specifically appointed. In other societies, more advanced,
this diffuseness comes to an end or at least weakens. Education is concentrated in
the hands of special functionaries. In India, in Egypt, it is the priests who are
charged with this function. Education is an attribute of the priestly power. Now,
this first differential characteristic leads to others. When the religious life, instead
of itself remaining completely diffuse as it is originally, creates for itself a special
organ charged with directing it and with administering it, that is to say, when it
takes the form of a priestly class or caste, what is properly speculative and
intellectual in religion takes a development unknown until then. It is in these
priestly milieux that appeared the first precursors, the first and rudimentary
forms of science: astronomy, mathematics, cosmology . . . There is from then on
material for a specific instruction. The priest teaches the elements of those
sciences which are in process of being formed." (Durkheim, *Education and
Sociology*, pp. 96-97.)

8. Henderson, *Introduction to Philosophy of Education*, p. 325.
9. Durkheim, *Moral Education*, p. 21.

at the Sorbonne in 1902-1903. Fully half of this posthumously published work is devoted to describing and explaining the formation of three basic elements of moral character: discipline, autonomy, and attachment.

Discipline. In Durkheim's view, one important aspect of moral development involves formation of the two character traits associated with the term "discipline." By insisting on regular class attendance, homework, and similar measures, the school develops "a certain disposition in the individual for a regular existence—a preference for regularity."[10] In doing so, the educational system does not simply discipline a tabula rasa; rather, it builds upon one of the child's innate predispositions, namely, his enjoyment of habitual conduct.[11] By acting upon the child's character as a creature of habit, teachers assist in developing in the child a capacity for behaving uniformly under like circumstances, which helps him when he moves into other groups where a similar ability to develop habits is indispensable.[12]

This taste for regularity, however, is not the whole of the spirit of discipline. There is also the preference for moderation which derives from "the feeling that beyond him there are moral forces that set bounds for him, forces that he must take into account and to which he must yield." Development of this propensity is made possible by the child's innate openness to imperative suggestions from authority figures. "When the child has come to understand more clearly his moral

10. *Ibid.,* pp. 34, 148.

11. *Ibid.,* pp. 129-134. In defending this claim that the child is not a tabula rasa, Durkheim states: "if nature does not predispose the child in appropriate ways—in such a way that we have only to superintend and direct his natural development—if it leaves almost everything for us to do, we could not . . . succeed in our labors if the child's nature were opposed to us, if it were completely refractory to the orientation that must be developed in him. The child's nature is not so malleable that one can make it take on forms for which it is in no way fitted. So there must be in the child, if not precisely those conditions we must develop, at least certain general predispositions that help us in achieving the goal and that act as levers through which educational influence is transmitted to the roots of the child's consciousness. Were this not so, it would be closed to us. Through physical coercion, we can require the child to perform in certain ways; but the wellsprings of his inner life escape us." (*Ibid.,* p. 134.)

12. *Ibid.* In discussing the child's enjoyment of habitual ways of doing things, Durkheim introduces the following examples: "Once he [the child] has developed certain habits, they dominate his behavior to a far greater extent than with adults. Once he has repeated a given act several times he shows a need to reproduce it in the same way. He abhors the slightest variation. We know, for example, how the order of his meal, once established, becomes sacred and inviolable for him. He even pushes this adherence to habit to the point of the most compulsive detail. He wants his cup, his napkin in the same place. He wants to be served by the same person. The slightest deviation distresses him . . . He will reread the same book to the point of satiety. He will dwell on the same pictures without becoming bored. How many times have we told our children the same old stories." (*Ibid.,* p. 135.)

dependency vis-à-vis his parents and his teachers, his need for them, their intellectual superiority over him, and the worth of that superiority, then the ascendancy with which they are henceforth continually invested communicates itself to their prescriptions and re-enforces them." Development of this propensity is fostered when the teacher conveys his or her own respect for the impersonal rightness of moral rules, thus conveying to the child an appreciation of the fact that rules transcend personal dispositions.

The teacher must therefore be committed to presenting it [the rule], not as his own personal doing, but as a moral power superior to him, and of which he is the instrument not the author. He must make the students understand that it imposes itself on him as it does on them; that he cannot remove or modify it; that he is constrained to apply it; and that it dominates him and obliges him as it obliges them. On this condition alone will he be able to evoke a sentiment that . . . is or ought to be at the very foundation of the public conscience: this is the respect for legality, the respect for impersonal law deriving its ascendancy from impersonality itself.

By thus learning to respect moral rules in school, the child learns to respect rules in other social situations.[13]

This characteristic Durkheimian emphasis upon discipline sounds unduly restrictive, as Everett Wilson puts it, to "a generation suffering post-Victorian recoil and invoking the wrath of Viennese gods upon the superego."[14] It is important to note, therefore, that Durkheim denies the widespread assumption in his era, as well as in ours, that discipline is incompatible with self-realization, freedom, and happiness. Discipline, by restraining limitless ambitions and by canalizing limited reserves of psychic energy in pursuit of determinate goals, is the indispensable means without which regular realization of human potentialities would be impossible. And, genuine psychological freedom, in Durkheim's view, is only possible through self-mastery of the unlimited power of unrestrained appetites. Let us imagine, he writes,

a being liberated from all external restraint, a despot still more absolute than those of which history tells us . . . By definition, the desires of such a being are irresistible. Shall we say, then, that he is all-powerful? Certainly not, since he himself cannot resist his desires. They are masters of him, as of everything else. He submits to them; he does not dominate them. In a word, when the inclinations are totally liberated,

13. *Ibid.*, pp. 139, 140, 156.
14. Editor's introduction, *ibid.*, p. ix.

when nothing sets bounds to them, they themselves become tyrannical, and their first slave is precisely the person who experiences them. What a sad picture this presents. Following one upon the other, the most contradictory inclinations, the most antithetical whims, involve the so-called absolute sovereign in the most incompatible feelings, until finally this apparent omnipotence dissolves into genuine impotence . . . Self-mastery is the first condition of all true power, of all liberty worthy of the name.[15]

Finally, Durkheim argues that man does not obtain happiness by perpetually searching for boundless power, knowledge, or wealth, for unrestrained aspirations of this sort inevitably result in frustration and disillusionment. True happiness is the joy that accompanies realization of the limited goals compatible with one's natural abilities. Discipline is thus a necessary prerequisite for happiness and moral health.

Despite his high estimation of the advantages of the disciplined life, Durkheim recognizes that asceticism is not a good in and of itself. Discipline may well become excessive and, thus, a new source of psychological tyranny. It may also inhibit the child from adapting to and criticizing his ever-changing social milieu. Hence, it is important that "morality not be internalized in such a way as to be beyond criticism and reflection, the agents par excellence of all change." In other words, it does not follow from Durkheim's belief in the need for discipline that self-control necessarily involves blind and slavish submission. "Moral rules must be invested with that authority without which they would be ineffective," but they must be "sufficiently flexible to change gradually as proves necessary."[16]

Autonomy. "Self-determination" or "autonomy" is the second major moral character trait discussed by Durkheim. To act morally, it is not enough to discipline oneself to regulate one's behavior in accordance with rules not of one's own making. Conscience protests such conformity. "We do not regard an act as completely moral except when we perform it freely without coercion of any sort. We are not free if the law by which we regulate our behavior is imposed on us, if we have not freely desired it." If this is true, how is autonomy to be reconciled with disciplined obedience? Durkheim replies by identifying autonomy with rational understanding on the supposition that "thought is the liberator of the will." If we understand the raison d'être of moral rules,

15. *Ibid.,* pp. 44-45.
16. *Ibid.,* p. 52.

autonomy is assured. Hence, this second "element of morality is the understanding of it."[17]

Moral education fosters this second type of morality when the teacher explains and the child understands the reasons why the rules prescribing certain forms of behavior should be "freely desired," that is to say, "willingly accepted" by virtue of "enlightened assent."

For to teach morality is neither to preach nor to indoctrinate; it is to explain. If we refuse the child all explanation of this sort, if we do not try to help him understand the reasons for the rules he should abide by, we would be condemning him to an incomplete and inferior morality.[18]

Such instruction, obviously difficult, is nonetheless necessary.

Attachment. Durkheim's treatment of this third aspect of moral education varied in the course of his career. In *Moral Education,* moral attachment is defined in terms of devotion to social groups as well as to collectively shared ideals. The psychological predisposition that makes this devotion possible is said to be the child's "faculty of empathy," which is "another way of saying that the source of this aspect of moral life resides in the sum of those tendencies that we call altruistic and disinterested."[19] According to Durkheim, every child is born with a rudimentary ability to reproduce and therefore to share other people's sentiments, an aptitude for sympathizing with others which is the first form of genuine altruism. "Indeed, this is how a bond of constant communication is established between the consciousness of the child and others' consciousnesses. What happens in the latter reverberates in the former. He lives their lives, enjoys their pleasures, suffers their sorrows. He is thus naturally induced to act so as to prevent or soften others' sorrows . . . Just as he seeks to console others in the sorrow that he sees and shares, the child makes an effort to give them pleasure."[20] Initially, the child's ability to identify empathetically is limited by

17. *Ibid.,* pp. 112, 119, 120. In attempting to reconcile autonomy with obedience by defining the former as the "rational understanding" of obligatory rules, Durkheim is clearly following in Kant's footsteps. In *Formes élémentaires* (p. 387), Durkheim agrees with Kant that the cornerstone of personal autonomy is "the faculty of acting in conformity with reason, and the reason is that which is most impersonal within us." At the same time, Durkheim rejects Kant's concept of pure reason as autonomous in the sense of being independent of causal determination. For the mature Durkheim, reason itself is a product of collective representations; therefore, autonomy is a product of society.

18. Durkheim, *Moral Education,* pp. 120-121.

19. *Ibid.,* p. 207.

20. *Ibid.,* pp. 220-221.

several factors: his cognitive capacities are not sufficiently developed to enable him to identify with individuals or groups outside his immediate family;[21] the pressing biological needs arising from the child's organism result in the predominance of egoistic strivings over altruistic sentiments.[22] Hence, there is in the child more egotism than altruism, although he is not a stranger to the latter sentiment.

By building upon innate altruistic sentiments as well as upon the spontaneous growth of both cognitive and sympathetic abilities, the moral educator fosters that attachment to social groups which is the *sine qua non* of genuine moral devotion. Development of this propensity for collective altruism is especially favorable when the teacher gives the child a clear idea of the social groups to which he belongs. However, in order to attach the child to these groups, which is the final goal of moral education, it is not sufficient to merely give him an intellectual interpretation of them. In addition, it is important that the child vividly experience, by actively participating in the joys of collective life, the pleasures associated with saying "we."

To appreciate social life . . . , one must have developed the habit of acting and thinking in common. We must learn to cherish these social bonds that for the unsocial being are heavy chains. We must learn through experience how cold and pale the pleasures of solitary life are in comparison. The development of such a temperament, such a mental outlook, can only be formed through repeated practice, through perpetual conditioning.

At the same time, however, it is essential that the child also realize that such attachment never involves a narrow parochialism, but, rather, a devotion to institutions through which the ideal of humanity is realized.[23]

21. "No doubt his altruism is still rudimentary. We can see the principal reason for that. His mentality, generally speaking, is likewise rudimentary. Because his mind is in the process of formation, it does not reach far beyond his most immediate surroundings and consequently beyond a small number of human beings who are outside of himself: his family, his friends, objects familiar to him—they are all he knows. As a matter of fact, he conceives of everything else, because of its remoteness, only in uncertain and ephemeral fashion, in which the individuality of things is more or less attenuated." (*Ibid.*, p. 227.)

22. "He feels more vividly his own organism and its condition. Therefore, during the first years of his life, personal sensations—and none present themselves in that guise more than do organic sensations—play the preponderant part; they have the greatest bearing on his behavior; they are the center of gravity of child life, although from that moment on there are already urges of another type." (*Ibid.*)

23. *Ibid.*, pp. 233, 207.

Although Durkheim never explicitly abandoned the thesis of *Moral Education* that moral devotion involves a simultaneous attachment to society and to social ideals, his later writings, especially his article (1911) on "Education: Its Nature and Its Role," define moral attachment primarily in terms of devotion to collectively shared values. Society re-creates itself by inculcating in its members *an ideal image of what they ought to become.* Through education, society or, more accurately, specially designated agents of society mold younger members in accord with society's ideal image. "That is the task of education," says Durkheim, "and one can readily appreciate its grandeur. It is not limited to developing the individual in accordance with his nature, disclosing whatever hidden capacities lie there only seeking to be revealed. Education creates in man a new being."[24]

These pedagogical ideals, however, vary cross-culturally. Durkheim, accordingly, attacks those philosophers who, like Kant and J. S. Mill, held that one universal ideal of man could be discovered in the unchanging nature of man. "For Kant as for Mill, for Herbart as for Spencer, the aim of education was above all to develop in each individual the attributes distinctive of the human species in general while carrying them to their highest perfection."[25] Such concepts, says Durkheim, "stand in absolute contradiction to all that history teaches us; there is not a people, indeed, among whom it has ever been put into practice."[26] Far from there being one universally accepted goal of education, there are different goals in different societies.

Where the state of the social milieu inclines the public conscience toward asceticism, physical education will be spontaneously relegated to the background. Something of this sort took place in the schools of the Middle Ages. Similarly, following currents of opinion, this same education will be understood very differently . . . Thus, even those qualities which appear at first glance so spontaneously desirable, the individual seeks only when society invites him to, and he seeks them in the fashion that it prescribes for him.[27]

Evidently, these special pedagogical ideals build upon aptitudes inherent in human nature, but the direction in which the individual

24. Durkheim, "L'Education, sa nature et son rôle" (1911), in his *Education et sociologie* (Paris: Félix Alcan, 1938).

25. Durkheim, "Pédagogie et Sociologie," in *Education et sociologie*, p. 107.

26. *Ibid.*, p. 109.

27. Durkheim, "Pedagogy and Sociology," in *Education and Sociology,* pp. 127-128.

develops is determined by his social and moral milieu rather than by his inherited nature.

Western Pedagogical Ideals

Shortly after becoming convinced that pedagogical ideals were among the most important variables in moral education, Durkheim turned his attention to a historical analysis of the various ideals that have inspired pedagogical instruction in various periods of Western civilization. The results of this research are contained in his little-known but extremely important series of lectures on *L'Evolution pédagogique en France.*[28] Briefly, the thesis of this remarkable work is that an extremely broad historical perspective is necessary in order to properly evaluate the conflicting pedagogical ideals offered in one's own time. Durkheim thus writes on an extremely broad canvas. Starting with an analysis of Christian pedagogical ideals in the early Middle Ages, he traces these ideals through the High Middle Ages, the Renaissance, and the Enlightenment, to the modern period. In the process, Durkheim sketches not only the historical development of pedagogical ideals, but also the historical evolution of the differing concepts of man and his environment with which these ideals have been inexorably linked since the emergence of Western culture from the chrysalis of the Christian *Weltanschauung.*

Partly because *L'Evolution pédagogique en France* is one of Durkheim's most important theoretical works, but largely because it is extremely difficult to understand his conclusions concerning modern pedagogical ideals and practices in the absence of a thorough knowledge of this study, the following account of *L'Evolution pédagogique* attempts to preserve Durkheim's own complex and subtle analysis of Western intellectual history insofar as it bears upon his, and our, subject matter. Among the multiple themes to be traced, the following are worth noting here at the outset: the Christian *Weltanschauung* that emerged during the early Middle Ages was an intellectual synthesis *sui generis;* the concepts of man and his environment enshrined in this unique religious world view have decisively molded all Western moral values, including the secular moral concepts of contemporary culture; the history of Western pedagogical ideals cannot be understood apart from this cultural framework and historical variations within it, for pedagogical ideals invariably derive from fundamental beliefs regarding the nature of man and his environment; and, as new pedagogical ideals emerge from altered beliefs about man and nature, educational institu-

28. Originally entitled "l'Histoire et l'enseignement en France," these lectures were presented at the Sorbonne during the academic year 1904-1905.

tions and practices are created or altered in conformity with these ideological innovations. In short, the history of pedagogical ideals is inseparable from the history of comprehensive religious or philosophical beliefs and values.

In accord with his interest in origins, Durkheim begins *L'Evolution pédagogique* by showing that the Christian church was the first and most important educational institution in Western civilization, "the natural governess of the people she converted."[29] Because the church was the institutional means by which the German invaders were introduced to Christianity as well as to classical culture, the unique intellectual synthesis forged by the early medieval church provided Western culture with its most distinctive characteristics. Durkheim, accordingly, objects to the expression "the Middle Ages," because it suggests an intermediary period between the fall of the Roman Empire and the Renaissance. "Far from this [era] having been a simple period of transition, without originality, between two original and brilliant civilizations, it was, on the contrary, a time in which the deep germs of an entirely new civilization were elaborated." This distinctly new cultural synthesis was basically religious, but it contained, from the outset, two very different elements: "There was, on the one hand, the religious element, the Christian doctrine; on the other, ancient civilization and all that the church was compelled to borrow from it, that is to say, the secular element." Because Christianity contained these two elements within itself, the history of the Occident is in part the history of various attempts to unite and to divide the sacred and the profane, the secular and the religious.[30]

As a consequence of the emergence of the genuinely new cultural

29. Durkheim, *Evolution pédagogique en France,* I, 28. Several diverse factors are cited by Durkheim as having aided the church in its formidable task of instructing pagans in the first principles of Christianity. In the first place, the Christian message concerning the poor and the humble had an intrinsic appeal to the Germanic spirit which, like Christianity, was opposed to the elegant manners and high-minded ways of the Roman aristocrats. Secondly, the church carried in her bosom a superior culture that was destined, in the end, to triumph over the less complex cultural achievements of the invading tribes. Third, competition among monastic groups in the work of conversion, especially the vigorous rivalry between the Benedictines and the Irish monks, stimulated the educational activity of the missionary monks. Finally, the destruction of regional groups by successive waves of invasion paved the way for the emergence of the social and moral unity of Christendom. With the merging of diverse tribes and peoples within the perpetually moving kaleidoscope that was Western Europe during the early Middle Ages, Christianity increasingly became the sole civilization in which these culturally deprived societies could communicate. As a result of these several factors, the church eventually became the schoolmistress of Europe. (*Ibid.*, pp. 26-29.)

30. *Ibid.*, pp. 40, 33.

synthesis that was early medieval Christianity, the schools established around cathedrals and in monasteries were very different from those established in the Greco-Roman world. The new schools undoubtedly borrowed a great deal from pagan civilization, "but this material was elaborated in a totally new manner, and from this elaboration something entirely new resulted."[31] This "new element" was the fundamental Christian understanding of the school as a place for educating the total personality, a notion traced by Durkheim to the Christian conception of the unity and intrinsic moral value of the self.

Whereas the classical goal of education involved decorating the mind with bits of wisdom and the soul with particular habits, Durkheim contends that the goal of Christian education always involved directing the basic orientation of the self as a unified whole. For Christianity, it was not sufficient for the child to understand certain beliefs or rites or to develop several particular habits; the important thing was the general disposition of the mind and will of the whole personality.[32] In Durkheim's view, this fundamental Christian concept of training the total personality distinguishes the whole of Western pedagogical instruction, including modern secular education, from that of classical antiquity.

For us also, the principal goal of intellectual education is not to provide the child with more or less numerous bits of knowledge, but to form in him an interior and profound state, a sort of polarity of the soul which orients him in a definite direction not only during infancy, but for life. Undoubtedly, the aim of our educational system is not to form a Christian, since we have renounced the pursuit of confessional ends, but it is in order to make a man of him. For, just as in order to be a Christian it is necessary to acquire a Christian manner of thinking and sensing, so also, in order to become a man, it is not sufficient to have the intellect

31. *Ibid.*, p. 40.

32. "Christianity consists essentially in a certain attitude of the soul, a certain *habitus* of our moral being. To arouse this attitude in the child was the essential goal of education. This explains the appearance of an idea that antiquity had totally ignored and which, on the contrary, has played a considerable role in Christianity: this is the idea of conversion. In fact, a conversion, as Christianity understands it, is not adherence to certain particular concepts, to certain definite articles of faith. The true conversion is a profound movement by which the entire soul, by turning in a totally new direction, changes its position or posture and modifies, consequently, its conception of the world. It is so little a question of acquiring a certain number of truths that this movement may be realized instantaneously . . . This is what happens when, to employ sanctified terminology, the soul is suddenly touched by grace. Then, by a sort of about face, in an instant, it is turned toward totally new perspectives; unsuspected realities and previously ignored worlds are revealed to it; it sees and knows things of which it was formerly totally ignorant. But this same change can be produced slowly, under gradual and unknown pressure; and this is what happens through the effect of education." (*Ibid.*, pp. 37-38.)

stocked with a certain number of ideas, but it is necessary above all to have acquired a truly human manner of sensing and thinking. Our conception of the end has been secularized; hence, the means employed have to be changed; but the abstract schema of the educative process has not varied.

Thus, despite all the revolutionary changes through which the history of Western pedagogy has passed since the early Middle Ages, one essentially Christian goal of teaching has remained the same, namely, that of penetrating into the "depths of the soul which antiquity did not know."[33]

Despite this momentous pedagogical innovation of the medieval church, no elaborate system of education was possible during the early Middle Ages. The actual content of instruction was, to say the least, meager, and the schools culturally impoverished in comparison with those that preceded them in antiquity and succeeded them in Christendom. From the standpoint of formal instruction, then, this early formative era was indeed a dark age which prepared the way for, but did not realize, the latent potentialities contained within the emerging cultural synthesis.

In Durkheim's view, the reign of Charlemagne represents the first renaissance in the long series of renewals that dot the history of Western culture in general and of pedagogy in particular. At the heart of this renaissance was the new sense of transcendent moral devotion that followed the political unification of central Europe. Before Charlemagne, Durkheim states, "all Christian peoples had an obscure sentiment that they were part of the same whole, without this sentiment giving birth to a definite organ to express it." It was Charlemagne's great achievement to provide Western Europe with a stronger sense of solidarity by uniting formerly disparate feudal states in a new, broad-based, political unit. In him and through him, Christianity became a state. To be sure, Charlemagne did not draw this unity out of nothing; his achievement was to express and to organize the nascent unity that preceded his appearance on the stage of history. "But this organization was itself an innovation which involved other innovations: notably in that which concerns intellectual life."[34]

Among the various institutional and intellectual innovations introduced by Carolingian scholars, Durkheim attributes the greatest importance to the encyclopedic goal that inspired these pedagogical develop-

33. *Ibid.*, pp. 38-39.
34. *Ibid.*, p. 52.

ments. "A primary characteristic of this teaching was that it was or endeavored to be encyclopedic. Its goal was not to teach the student a certain number of facts, but the totality of human knowledge." This attempt to grasp the systematic coherence of knowledge is traced by Durkheim to two fundamental Christian beliefs. He contends that the encyclopedic vision of the Carolingian scholars stems, in part, from the Christian concept of the unity of truth:

> For it [Christianity], truth is not an abstract name given to a plurality, to a sum of particular truths. Truth is one in its essence; for it is the word of God, and God is one. Just as moral truth is entirely contained in a book, Scripture, it had to seem totally natural to the Christian scholar to believe that temporal, scientific truth must also have the same unity and find its expression in a book, in a breviary which would be in the profane order what Scriptures were in the sacred order.

In addition to this concept of the unity of truth and science, Durkheim finds another and more important cause underlying the encyclopedic interests of the Carolingian academicians—the Christian goal of developing the life of the spirt in its totality. "An incomplete instruction," Durkheim argues, "can only form incomplete thought; it cannot reach the roots of thought." For this goal to be attained, educational instruction cannot deal exclusively with particulars; it must envelop the total intellect by becoming encyclopedic. Because the humanities expressed the infinite worth of the human personality at the center of Christian morality, Durkheim further contends, these disciplines became the chief means employed in attempting to realize this encyclopedic goal.[35]

The period following Charlemagne's reign is described as an era of sorrowful anguish and general anxiety brought about by devastating invasions from without and by the internal collapse of the Carolingian Empire. Few scholars had either the leisure or the freedom to devote themselves to academic endeavors. Thus, no innovations of pedagogical significance were introduced.

By the beginning of the twelfth century, however, the conversion of the Scandinavians, the firm establishment of feudalism, and the emergence of the stable Capetian monarchy in Paris had set the stage for the second great renaissance within Western European history, the era of renewal that began in the twelfth century and ended in the fifteenth. This era is characterized by Durkheim as one of creative innovation, social reform, institutional effervescence, and intellectual stimulation. In Durkheim's view, it is one of the high points in Western history, a

35. *Ibid.*, pp. 58-59, 60.

creative period that gave birth to some of our greatest institutions, to magnificent scholarly achievements, and to new moral ideals.

The ideal that animated the renewal of scholarly life during this era was the Christian ideal of systematic or encyclopedic knowledge forged of faith and reason. "All the intellectual activity of the Middle Ages is, in fact, oriented toward the same end: to establish a science which would serve as a basis for faith." The dominant form of reasoning by which this goal was pursued by the scholastics was, of course, the dialectical method. Durkheim notes that the rediscovery of Aristotle was an important event in the emergence of the dialectical method within scholasticism, but denies that the latter was identical with the original Greek conception of this method. Whereas the Greeks viewed the dialectical method as a secular discipline, medieval scholars associated it with religious and moral values.

Now, closely tied to dogma, the dialectical method participated in the sentiments that dogma inspired. It was no longer something exterior and foreign to moral and religious education; it was the preparation for it. As a condition of the sacred par excellence, it was endowed with sanctity. Men have perhaps never had a higher concept of instruction and its moral value. From this derives the intellectual enthusiasm which, every year, brought about enormous migrations of students, moving from one part of Europe to another, despite the arduous and dangerous nature of the journey, in search of the truth. If, then, it is true that the Middle Ages borrowed its idea of teaching from antiquity, it infused it with a new spirit and, thereby, transformed it.

Thus, practice of the dialectical method was itself a religious and moral act, an act which directed the practitioner to the inestimable value of human consciousness.[36]

Durkheim admits that the resulting dialectical debates often degenerated, particularly during the waning years of the Middle Ages, into useless word games, but he denies the validity of the sharp critique leveled against it by scholars of the Renaissance and the Enlightenment. These criticisms were more often than not, he observes, based upon a caricature of the scholastic mind. Far from being a dry and useless pursuit, Durkheim maintains, the dialectical method was well suited to the intellectual temper and practical moral interests of the Middle Ages. Not only was this method particularly suited to an age in intellectual ferment and creativity, it was animated by an eminently practical and realistic spirit. By forming the mind of the student, in contrast with

36. *Ibid.*, pp. 210-212.

hanging virtuous ornaments on the nebulous Christmas tree of character depicted in classical humanism, scholasticism "formed the statesmen, the ecclesiastical dignitaries, and the administrators of the epoch."[37] Moreover, and this is a truly decisive point which casts considerable light upon Durkheim's own method, the dialectical method continues to remain a valid mode of inquiry. To be sure, modern men have discovered the empirical method, but the dialectical method remains indispensable in all those areas of knowledge that lie outside the experimental sciences.[38]

If scholasticism recognized a valid mode of rational inquiry, how did it fare with regard to morality? "Man," Durkheim maintains, "is not solely a thinking being"; in order for an individual to realize his potentiality as a moral being, "it is not sufficient to introduce him to the formal mechanisms of his thought and its normal functioning." As each individual is a single part of the wider universe, "in order for him to truly know himself, it is necessary that he acquires a knowledge of something other than himself. It is necessary that he looks around him in lieu of concentrating solely upon himself, that he makes an effort to comprehend this world that surrounds him and with which he is united, that he understands that its richness and complexity infinitely surpass the narrow framework of logical understanding." Did scholasticism foster this goal of transcendent attachment? In view of the clear evidence that it did, Durkheim's answer is curiously ambiguous.[39]

On the one hand, Durkheim's own analysis of scholasticism would seem to suggest that medieval scholars had a profound sense of trans-

37. *Ibid.*, II, 44.
38. Durkheim justifies continued use of the dialectical method in the following manner: "Pour pouvoir nous conduire d'une manière intelligente, il nous faut raisonner notre action, nous faire des choses sur lesquelles elle porte une idée réfléchie, et, puisque le raisonnement scientifique n'est pas applicable, il nous faut procéder comme nous pouvons, par voie d'analogie, de comparaison, de généralisation, de supposition, en un mot dialectiquement . . . Si donc les questions juridiques, morales, politiques restent le domaine de la discussion, c'est que la méthode expérimentale commence seulement à s'y introduire. Violà pourquoi, sur tous les sujets de cet ordre, il nous faut connaître non seulement des choses, mais des livres; c'est qu'en ces matières controversables, nous ne pouvons nous faire une opinion éclairée; il nous faut méditer, comparer les opinions de nos devanciers et les textes où elles sont consignées. Il n'en est pas de même dans les sciences physiques, naturelles; mais conçoit-on une éducation philosophique, juridique, sociologique même sans l'étude préalable des penseurs les plus réputés? Ainsi se justifie la place faite à l'étude des textes dans certains de nos examens. En un mot, si la science, à mesure qu'elle progresse, qu'elle arrive à des résultats plus précis et mieux démontrés, fait reculer la controverse, elle ne saurait cependant la chasser de ce monde. Il y a ainsi toujours une place pour la discussion dans la vie intellectuelle, et pour l'art de discuter dans l'enseignement." (*Ibid.*, I, 197-198.) Thus Durkheim, the so-called apostle of positivism, presents his defense of the method he is widely interpreted as denouncing.
39. *Ibid.*, I, 212.

cendent solidarity. If recognition of the infinite complexity of the universe beyond the self lies at the heart of the moral life, it would seem that the scholastic fusion of faith and reason vividly expressed precisely this sort of moral sensitivity. Yet Durkheim maintains, on the other hand, that the intellectualism of scholasticism failed to provide a sufficient sense of the transcendent. Reflection on the thinking self was stressed to the neglect of the sense of the self as a part of the universal whole. To be sure, Durkheim does not claim that a sense of participation in the wider universe was absent from medieval thought, but he does claim that "it belonged to the following ages to enlarge this first ideal and to enrich it with new elements."[40] As a historical interpretation, this contention is clearly untenable; medieval scholars clearly possessed a deeper sense of the participation of the self in the universal chain of being than most subsequent generations. But this misinterpretation of the scholastics is itself significant since it calls attention to the real affinity between Durkheim and the scholastics. Like them, Durkheim also sought to fuse a conception of transcendent attachment with dialectical reflection, albeit in a secularized mode.

The Renaissance of the sixteenth century constitutes the third major stage in the development of the intellectual history of the West and in the evolution of pedagogical goals. Without presuming to offer a complete analysis of the Renaissance, Durkheim distinguishes basic spiritual characteristics of the era. The first characteristic of the Renaissance temperament is broadly described as a taste for elegance, polish, grace, tact, finesse, and so forth.[41] This cultivation of refined tastes is traced to the fact that a considerable proportion of the nobility and the upper classes had managed, thanks to vastly improved economic conditions, to accrue considerable fortunes by the outset of the sixteenth century. As a result, these groups began to look upon the refined life, previously confined to a few wealthy courts, as a model of the good life. Once this

40. *Ibid.*, pp. 212-213.
41. Durkheim acknowledges with other scholars that these elegant Renaissance tastes emerged with an attempt to return to the classical spirit, but he rejects the uncritical assumption that this fundamental reorientation of values resulted from the recovery of new classical texts. Medieval scholars were well acquainted with much of this literature, he notes, but this acquaintance failed to evoke among scholastics the sentiments and ideals that characterized the Renaissance. "If therefore, everything changes in the sixteenth century, if suddenly people recognize an incomparable educational value in Greco-Roman art and literature, it is clearly because, at this moment, by virtue of an unexpected change in public mentality, logic lost its ancient prestige, whereas, on the contrary, people vividly sensed for the first time the need for a more refined, elegant and literary culture." (*Ibid.*, p. 215.) The scholars of the Renaissance did not acquire their penchant for elegant style and cultural refinement from newly discovered classical texts; they went back to these writings because they satisfied the refined tastes of the era.

ideal of the elegant life took root, there was a general reaction against the moral asceticism of the Middle Ages and, hence, against anything that restrained the desires, the needs, and the passions of men.

The second characteristic of the age is described by Durkheim as the spirit of criticism that followed the collapse of Christendom as a unified moral and social system. With the emergence of autonomous national states, Durkheim contends, a movement of individuation and differentiation began within the unified world of medieval Europe. This differentiation had a profound effect on the "world of ideas." Once the traditional beliefs associated with Christendom began to crumble, people began to "think and to believe in their own way" and to demand the right to deviate from earlier assumptions. This is the root cause, Durkheim maintains, not only of the Renaissance disparagement of scholasticism, but also of the Reformation.

Among the various currents of thought that arose during the Renaissance, Durkheim contends that the essentially aesthetic doctrine of man and of pedagogy advanced by Erasmus eventually triumphed over the cognitive conception of man and scientific instruction represented at the outset of the age by Rabelais. Man came to be viewed primarily as an "*objet d'art* to be polished and refined."[42] Undoubtedly, Renaissance scholars were not completely disinterested in scientific wisdom, but such knowledge was viewed as secondary to the adornment of the artistic faculty. Hence, the dominant pedagogical goal of the era stressed purely literary accomplishments at the expense of scientific knowledge. As a result, Durkheim contends, Renaissance pedagogy became increasingly detached from the serious issues of life as scholars and students alike devoted themselves exclusively to an unreal world of fantasy, imagination, pretense, and style. From this analysis, Durkheim concludes that the pedagogy of the Renaissance was, in the final analysis, far less realistic than that of scholasticism; the latter, in comparison, was eminently practical, relevant, and deeply concerned with genuine and important issues.

These several distinguishing characteristics of the Renaissance had profound consequences for the realm of morality. The typical Renaissance disparagement of the excessive severity associated with medieval asceticism led to a radical and, in Durkheim's view, unjustified rejection of the classical Christian idea of moral duty. "The ideal of the Christian life is duty performed because it is a duty, the rule obeyed because it is the rule; it is man rising above nature, breaking away from it, mastering

42. *Ibid.,* II, 73.

it, subjecting it to the laws of the spirit. It is, in a word, saintliness."[43] The ideal of the Renaissance, on the contrary, was the Greco-Roman concept of eudaemonism, albeit eudaemonism of a particular type. In place of the classical Greek definition of eudaemonism as activity in accordance with moral virtue, the Renaissance set personal honor and glory. This ideal, exemplified above all in the excessive desire of literary writers to have their names circulate in books, was based not upon personal integrity, but on the passing opinions of others.[44] It was also a class concept since "the higher the elevation of the class on the social ladder, the more valuable its honor."[45] Such an ideal, in Durkheim's view, represents a form of pure egotism incompatible with genuine social disinterestedness and devotion. Durkheim thus concludes his treatment of the Renaissance by describing it as an era of moral and pedagogical crisis during which men failed to adequately cope with genuine moral issues.

The fourth and last stage in Durkheim's history of the complex relationships between philosophical assumptions and pedagogical ideals begins with the emergence of the natural sciences in the eighteenth century. During this era, which stretches from the eighteenth to the twentieth centuries, humanistic ideals and values were retained, but a higher valuation was placed upon scientific knowledge and, consequently, upon scientific instruction.

Durkheim begins his analysis of this period by contrasting Western philosophical and pedagogical ideas with those of the ancient Greeks. The main thesis of this admittedly brief, but theoretically important, comparison is that Western scholars began with the study of man and then turned belatedly to the study of nature, whereas the Greeks proceeded in the inverse direction. Because the pre-Socratics began with nature, "it was not until Socrates, that is to say, only at a very late epoch, that the human spirit became an object of reflection and, consequently, of teaching." The explanation advanced to explain this striking difference demonstrates the extent to which religious views have influenced the fundamental philosophical assumptions upon which pedagogical ideals rest.

43. *Ibid.*, p. 47.
44. "Ce qui fait l'honneur, en effet, c'est l'estime et la considération dont nous jouissons, c'est l'opinion qu'autrui a de nous; or, la gloire, elle aussi, est affaire d'opinion. L'honneur, c'est le diminutif de la renommée. La renommée, la gloire ont pour base l'opinion que tous les hommes en général ont de nous, à quelque société, à quelque condition sociale qu'ils appartiennent; l'honneur, c'est plutôt l'opinion des hommes qui font partie de notre milieu immédiat." (*Ibid.*, p. 56.)
45. *Ibid.*, p. 57.

If Greek reflection was first and exclusively directed toward the world, this was because the world was then, in the esteem of public opinion, an excellent and holy thing. The world, in fact, was considered as divine, or rather the domain of the gods. The gods were not outside the world, they were in things, and there was nothing in which they did not reside: πάντα πλήρη θεῶν. It is man, the human spirit, which was then considered as profane and of little value; this is what Socrates himself teaches and it is upon this profane character that he lays claim to the right to speculate with complete independence; here, he says, thought ought to be expressed with complete liberty, for it does not risk encroaching upon the domain of the gods. For Christianity, on the contrary, it is the mind, the consciousness of man, that is the sacred and peerless thing: for the soul, the principle of our interior life, is a direct emanation of the deity . . . Between the mind and things, there is all the difference which separates the spiritual from the temporal. Thus God has disdainfully abandoned the world to the free utilization of men, *tradidit mundum hominum disputationi.*[46]

According to most post-Durkheimian theories of secularization, this association of the human mind with the sacred in Christianity would be interpreted as inhibiting rational inspection and analysis of human consciousness. Durkheim, however, explicitly rejects such an interpretation. It is precisely because the human mind was endowed with sacred qualities that Christian scholars first focused their attention upon it.

To adore the gods of antiquity was to provide for their material life with the aid of offerings and sacrifices, because the life of this world depended on their life; the God of the Christians desires to be adored, as the formula puts it, in spirit and in truth. For him, to be is to be believed, to be thought, and to be loved. Everything then inclines the Christian to turn his thought toward himself, since it is in himself that the source of life is found, I mean genuine life, that which counts most in his eyes, spiritual life. The details of the cult itself makes this concentration on oneself a necessity. The most ordinary rite is prayer, and prayer is an interior meditation. Since, for the Christian, virtue or piety does not consist in physical maneuvers, but in the interior state of the soul, he is bound to exercise a perpetual surveillance on himself. As he is obliged to perpetually examine his conscience, it is necessary that he learn to interrogate himself, to analyze himself, to scrutinize his intensions, in a word, to reflect upon himself.

Thus, it was around man "that the reflection of Christian societies had to gravitate, and, consequently, their system of instruction."[47]

46. *Ibid.*, pp. 138-139.
47. *Ibid.*, p. 140.

What, then, accounts for the remarkable emergence of the natural sciences in the eighteenth century and in later centuries? In his earlier writings Durkheim had more or less implied that science began with the eclipse of religion and the subsequent liberation of the sciences from their earlier tutelage to religion. While this thesis is maintained in *L'Evolution pédagogique* to the extent that secularization continues to be recognized as an important phenomenon in the modern history of the West, Durkheim now traces the roots of scientific development and secularization to none other than Martin Luther! Durkheim thus independently propounds the famous thesis associated with his great contemporary, Max Weber, during the academic year that Weber published *Die protestantische Ethik und der Geist des Kapitalismus* in the *Archiv für Sozialwissenschaft und Sozialpolitik* (1904-1905). The religious legitimation of the secular world in Protestantism and the subsequent reevaluation of temporal pursuits is the principal causal factor responsible for the emergence of Western science:

there was a sense of secular society and of its temporal interests in Protestantism that Catholicism did not and could not have. If Luther demanded schools, it was, he said himself, in order "to outwardly maintain the state of temporal things, *den weltlichen Stand,* so that men could better govern the country and so that women could better raise their child and maintain their homes." He did not wish to maintain the ancient system.[48]

This legitimation of the secular world explains, Durkheim further contends, why Protestant countries have led in the development of scientific instruction and why traditionally Catholic and humanistic countries, like France, have often lagged behind by as much as a hundred years.

Yet, Durkheim also observes that scientists, once freed from their former tutelage to religion and to metaphysics, immediately proceeded to advance views that conflicted with the mainstream of Western thought and morality. Because the first scientists devoted themselves almost exclusively to the study of the physical world, a materialistic bias colored their conception of the whole of reality, including man. Subsequently, and for understandable reasons, a vigorous conflict ensued between scientists and traditionalists over the nature of man, as well as over pedagogical goals. Scientists joined other scientists in disparaging spiritualistic concepts and idealistic values; Christians lined up with their former opponents, secular humanists, in defending tradi-

48. *Ibid.,* p. 144.

tional views against the new concepts and propositions advanced by scientists. As a result, scientists abandoned the lofty idealism of Western culture, while the foremost representatives of the fundamental values of Western civilization lost touch with the scientific temper of the age.

In Durkheim's view, the idealist-materialist terms in which the resulting intellectual skirmishes were fought permitted no adequate resolution of the basic issues at stake. For as long as scientists were committed to various forms of materialism,

not only for every Christian, but also for whosoever had a sense of what is truly and specifically human in man, what characterizes him and gives him his distinctive physiognomy in the midst of other beings, to form the child exclusively in the school of the sciences was to materialize him, to profane him, to hinder the development of his true nature.[49]

The history of pedagogy in the nineteenth century was thus largely a history of conflict, rather than of creative innovation, precisely because neither humanists nor scientists were in a position to successfully grapple with the age-old question: What is the nature of man? Humanists correctly clung to the earlier, more adequate theory of human nature, but failed to wrestle with the problems posed by the new scientific *Weltanschauung.* Scientists realized the necessity of the new perspective, but failed to relate it to the valid insights of Christianity and secular humanism.

Despite the failure of both groups to adequately resolve their differences, Durkheim, nevertheless, discerns several new and potentially significant lines of thought within the conflicting currents of nineteenth-century scholarship. Taken together, these provide a way out of the idealist-materialist impasse. Among these new doctrines, Durkheim cites fresh views regarding the nature of man, as well as innovations vis-à-vis the pedagogical and moral role of scientific instruction. As these fresh insights seemed, in 1904, to be converging toward a new *Weltanschauung,* Durkheim predicts that they will, by constituting the foundational perspective of twentieth-century philosophy, yield new pedagogical ideals.

Durkheim concludes that the old humanistic concept of man is in the last stages of an unstable gyration that will conclude with its final ejection from its prominent place in contemporary thought. The high valuation placed upon man, and enriching his consciousness, will be

49. *Ibid.,* p. 176.

continued, even strengthened, but the old notion that human nature is always and everywhere identical will be rejected. The principal reason for this is that the venerable concept of "man in general" is no longer tenable in view of the accumulated sociological evidence against it. In place of this ancient concept of "man in general," a new concept will emerge—it has in fact already emerged in the social and historical sciences—from the "spontaneous and progressive movement of ideas." This is the basic notion that human nature is extremely diverse. With respect to both mental processes and moral qualitites, scientifically informed men are increasingly realizing that humanity, far from being uniform and invariable, is extraordinarily rich in its variations and incredibly supple, flexible, and malleable. To use Durkheim's words, man is increasingly being viewed "not as a system of definite and numberable elements, but as an immensely flexible and proteiform force capable of assuming the most diverse forms under the pressure of ever new circumstances."[50] This new concept of man emphasizes not what man is, but what he may become by actualizing the diverse qualities and immense potentialities that lie dormant in the depth of his being as man.[51] It is thus not a narrower, but an enlarged and enriched, portrait of the being that is man.

This fresh conception of man implies a new form of instruction designed to acquaint students with the infinite moral worth of the rich diversity that is man. This goal can be achieved, Durkheim claims, in much the same way that classical humanists achieved their ideals, that is, by introducing students to the great literary works of the human spirit. This literature will not now be utilized to acquaint students with the abstract and general man of the past, but, rather, to apprise students of the immense variability and rich complexity of human nature. In realizing this goal, the insights of the historical and social sciences will be as indispensable as those of literature.

50. *Ibid.*, p. 199. The adverb "infiniment" in this passage is ambiguous. It may mean "infinitely," "immensely," or "extremely" flexible. In light of Durkheim's claim on page 198 that there is something "constant . . . dans l'humanite," the translation "immensely flexible" is more accurate than "infinitely flexible."

51.This understanding of the potentialities that lie within human nature, Durkheim contends, is more compatible with liberal social action than the older, more narrowly circumscribed concept of "universal man." The latter often served to inhibit realization of significant social and pedagogical reforms. Yet, this new concept also limits realization of the manifold possibilities that lie within the human breast by virtue of its emphasis upon the historical continuity of man's social environment. It is thus a concept which is compatible with reform without being revolutionary, a notion which stresses the historical continuity of social existence without being conservative. (*Ibid.*, pp. 200-201.) This liberal dialectical resolution of conservative and radical positions provides a typical example of Durkheim's basic approach to most social and political issues.

In addition to the emergence of a new conception of human nature in the disciplines associated with the humanities, Durkheim also discerns the emergence of a new pedagogical and moral role for the natural sciences. The basic goal of these sciences, declares Durkheim, is merging with that of the humanities, namely, "to cultivate man, to develop the germs of humanity which are in us." Only the means utilized to reach this moral end are different. Whereas the humanities direct man's attention to himself and other men, the natural sciences provide him with an appreciation of his place in the natural order. In so doing, however, the sciences also contribute immeasurably to human self-understanding. Since man is a part of nature, Durkheim contends, he cannot be abstracted from the natural world without mutilating his nature. Man is not a self-sufficient creature, but a part of the natural order within which he functions. He cannot adequately know himself if he does not have some idea of the natural world which surrounds him and on which he depends. This is why, Durkheim proposes, "even the most idealistic religions, even those which have the highest idea of thought and spirit, even those which endow thought and spirit with inestimable worth, are not without a certain cosmology. They do not limit themselves to teaching man about his diversity; they also inculcate in him a certain way of conceiving the world and, consequently, of situating himself in it."[52]

The goal of scientific pedagogy is thus to teach man about nature in order that he may formulate an adequate appreciation of his own relationship with, and attachment to, the realm of the natural. From this point of view, the teaching of science takes on a new significance. The role of the natural sciences is not simply to teach abstract theorems of geometry, laws of physics, and so forth. More important than these details is the formation of a general attitude toward, and an appreciation of, man's status as a creature in nature. There is a second major way in which the natural sciences complement the humanities. The natural sciences not only inform us about the physical, biological, and geographical features of our universe, they also intensify our moral respect for man by revealing "human reason in action." The seminal works of scientists thus stand alongside great moral, religious, and aesthetic treatises as examples of the highest achievements of the human spirit. Taken together, these scientific works represent a sort of résumé of human experience across centuries of thought. Thus, scientific literature contributes no less than moral, religious, and aesthetic literature to

52. *Ibid.*, p. 211.

the basic goal of appreciating the varied world of the human spirit. In a word, the natural sciences not only serve the basic humanistic values of Western civilization by informing man of his status in the world of nature, they complement our knowledge of man by providing a model of exquisitely human achievements.

The moral reward of this emerging form of instruction, in Durkheim's opinion, will be increased respect for the infinite worth of human personality, an ideal which dates back to the founding of Christianity and dominates the entire moral constitution of the Western world. For modern, secularized man, this respect has lost its supernatural foundations, but humanistic values are not, for that reason, any less sacred. Quite the contrary, man himself is now the holy of holies.

If the mind emancipated from dogma cannot admit that there exists in us a supernatural principle, an emanation of the deity, it remains true, nonetheless, . . . that human consciousness is for us an eminent thing of incomparable value, to which everything else ought to be referred . . . [53]

Children are to be taught, therefore, to honor rules respecting human rights, to appreciate the autonomy that man alone enjoys, and to devote themselves to genuinely humanistic goals.

This analysis of moral education arises from Durkheim's basic observation that education is the means, spontaneous or formal, by which societies develop in children culturally appropriate physical, intellectual, and moral attributes. Moral education in particular is understood by Durkheim as being primarily concerned with the formation of three basic character traits, each made possible by innate predispositions: a taste for discipline, a sense of individual autonomy, and devotion to collectively shared goals.

In his lectures on the history of pedagogy, Durkheim traces historical variations in Western culture regarding the third of these aspects of moral education, namely, differing concepts of the ideals governing educational theory and practice. These ideals are found to be intimately related to fundamental beliefs about the nature of man and his environment. Especially important in this connection is the Christian ideal of educating the general disposition of the mind and will of the total personality in a truly humanistic direction. This pedagogical ideal has not been essentially altered during the historical evolution of Western

53. *Ibid.*, p. 210.

civilization. What has changed, and is changing, is the concept of man and nature associated with this goal. Whereas Western philosophers have traditionally regarded man as a universal, abstract entity, modern scholars are beginning to appreciate the rich diversity and potentiality of the human spirit. The pedagogical goal that is emerging from modern, scientific culture stresses the immense variability of man as a procreative creature and his status as a creation not of God, but of the physical, biological, and social milieux in which, to use ecclesiastical language, he lives, moves, and has his being. Knowledge of the natural and anthropological sciences is now an indispensable pedagogical adjunct in training modern man to appreciate the infinite worth of human personality, a value which remains the polestar of secular moral education.

No critical assessment of Durkheim's moral pedagogy would be adequate that did not begin by acknowledging the profound perspicacity and deep ethical concern that permeate his writings in this area. As Piaget observes in this context,

we cannot enter upon a discussion of a work so sincere, so lofty in inspiration as that which we have just summarized without a feeling of profound respect for the memory of its author. But such is the seriousness of the questions at stake, that we must not hesitate to examine these theories of Durkheim's in detail and in a spirit of complete freedom. The greatest tribute we can pay to his vigorous scientific spirit is to forget for a moment his immense authority.[54]

With this sage advice in mind, a consideration of the merits and demerits of Durkheim's theory of moral education follows.

Durkheim's sociological perspective on moral education has the merit of fixing our attention on an aspect of moralization not previously granted the attention it clearly deserves. When one turns from the pedagogical theories of Durkheim's predecessors to his studies on moral pedagogy, one sees first of all that social conditioning is a central aspect of moral development. As post-Durkheimian studies have clearly verified, societies tend to select specific character traits for development. Yet, Durkheim does not fail to observe that "the child has a nature of its own," and that "we must, if we are to work effectively upon it, begin by trying to know it."[55] Durkheim also recognizes the importance of discipline in the moral training of young children: "The spirit of discipline, it must be agreed, constitutes the starting-point of all

54. Piaget, *Moral Judgment of the Child*, p. 360.
55. Durkheim, *Education morale*, p. 147.

moral life. There must be, not only a certain regularity of behavior, but rules, and rules clothed with sufficient authority. No one will seriously deny that this is the price to be paid for the development of personality."[56] In addition, Durkheim correctly stresses the importance of both autonomy and social devotion. How, indeed, can we foster moral autonomy in our children? How are we to lead children from egocentricity to a concern for humanistic ideals like universal solidarity, equality, and justice?

Yet there are several difficulties with Durkheim's sociological approach to moral education that cannot be ignored. One is the peculiar conception of moral man that emerges from focusing primarily upon socialization. The individual appears as an animal who is what he is as a moral being primarily because he has been molded by society to conform to customary rules and ideals. The trouble with this portrait is that it more or less implies that moral development is automatic given a certain degree of social constraint and the alluring nature of societal goals. To be sure, Durkheim somewhat modifies this portrait insofar as he acknowledges that each individual understands society in his own way, but the strong impression that societies can mold moral man in almost any direction remains. Social conditioning can do a great deal to channel moral development, but not everything; there appear to be limits set by the nature of man that go beyond the capacities recognized by Durkheim.

The following limits are noteworthy. Children as well as adults are capable of rejecting at least some of the moral principles in their surroundings. "The child as well as the adult sometimes hears rules formulated at which he is content to smile, or which even cause his moral judgment to revolt. How is such a phenomenon, in which sociologists will claim to see the clash of heterogeneous constraints, psychologically possible?"[57] Durkheim's answer is that individuals accept only those rules emanating from respected persons, but this simply pushes the problem a step further: How is it possible to reject commandments emanating from respected authorities unless individuals have an innate or developed ability to decide among the standards perpetrated around them? Studies by Piaget, Kohlberg, and MacRae suggest that rules and values are increasingly subjected to the test of consistency as the child matures.[58] This research clearly indicates that older children and adults

56. Piaget, *Moral Judgment of the Child*, p. 361.
57. *Ibid.*, p. 374.
58. For a brief, but useful summary of research findings relating to the test of consistency in moral judgment, see Roger Brown, *Social Psychology* (New York: Free Press, 1965; London: Collier-Macmillan, Ltd., 1965), pp. 403-411, *passim*.

develop an ability to judge conventional moral opinion in terms of logically consistent abstract principles. Moral opinion, then, frequently is not the unprocessed reflection of conventional morality that Durkheim's theory implies; the individual works over what he receives in quest of consistent generalizations.

Another difficulty with Durkheim's moral pedagogy derives from his concept of autonomy. Autonomy, as defined by Durkheim, means rational consent. As a corollary, it follows that autonomy is realized when the teacher correctly explains and the child understands the raison d'être of collective standards. The trouble with this definition and its pedagogical corollary is Durkheim's failure to recognize that autonomy is not limited to rational assent or even rational self-control. Autonomy also involves willful exploration, spontaneous initiative, competent mastery, and creative self-actualization.[59] We cannot, therefore, agree with Durkheim that autonomy is achieved by imposing rationally supported beliefs upon children. Autonomy does not exist unless the child is allowed to express initiative in spontaneous activity. This is not to say that children should be allowed to do whatever they like, or that consistent rules are undesirable. For children to mature, there must be, as Durkheim realized, an organized social life. But the foundations of genuine autonomy cannot be laid by means of external imposition, even when that imposition is rationally justified. The child must also be encouraged to exercise his own will, initiative, and creativity.

A further difficulty with Durkheim's moral pedagogy is his failure to distinguish, as he did in *The Division of Labor,* among differing types of social rules and respect for authority. According to the mature Durkheim, the rules of every group are accorded the respectful obedience the young child displays in relationship to parental authority. The work of Piaget, however, conclusively demonstrates that there are at least two types of rules. Those mutually agreed upon by fair-minded companions in a game of marbles are very different from those enforced by authority figures.

59. I am basing this definition of autonomy on recent developments in ego psychology. See, for example, Erik H. Erikson, *Childhood and Society,* 2nd ed. (New York: W. W. Norton & Company, 1963); Erik H. Erikson, *Identity, Youth and Crisis* (New York: W. W. Norton & Company, 1968); Heinz Hartmann, *Essays on Ego Psychology* (New York: International Universities Press, 1964); Ives Hendrik, "Work and the Pleasure Principle," *Psychoanalytic Quarterly,* XII (1943), 314-315; Robert White, "Competence and the Psychosexual Stages of Development," *Nebraska Symposium on Motivation,* VIII (1960).

And these two types of rules lead to opposite results. The rule of constraint, which is bound up with unilateral respect, is regarded as sacred and produces in the child's mind feelings that are analogous to those which characterize the compulsory conformity of primitive communities. But this rule of constraint remains external to the child's spirit and does not lead to as effective an obedience as the adult would wish. Rules due to mutual agreement and cooperation, on the contrary, take root inside the child's mind and result in an effective observance in the measure in which they are incorporated in an autonomous will.[60]

If Piaget is correct in this characterization of two extreme types of rules and of respect, his conclusion that social constraint is not the best way of developing morally autonomous individuals clearly follows. "It is obvious," Piaget observes,

that our results are . . . unfavorable to the method of authority . . . It is, as we said in connection with Durkheim, absurd and even immoral to wish to impose upon the child a fully worked-out system of discipline when the social life of children amongst themselves is sufficiently developed to give rise to a discipline infinitely nearer to that inner submission which is the mark of adult morality. It is idle, again, to try and transform the child's mind from outside, when his own taste for active research and his desire for cooperation suffice to ensure a normal intellectual development. The adult must therefore be a collaborator and not a master, from this double point of view, moral and rational.[61]

In short, it is impossible, in light of recent research, to accept Durkheim's contention that social constraint or discipline is the principal or best means of fostering morality.

Finally, several problems are raised by some of the claims introduced by Durkheim in support of secular moral education as a substitute for religious instruction. Today, there can be little doubt that Durkhiem was correct in believing that secular moral education is both possible and desirable. He was also correct in noting the gradual secularization of moral instruction in Western societies. He was probably further correct in asserting that traditional ways of viewing man and his supernatural environment are being eroded through popularization of new concepts emanating from the several sciences. But Durkheim is less than convincing when he predicts, on evolutionary grounds, that traditional religions are destined to be replaced by the new cult of man because they conflict with the modern scientific *Weltanschauung*. Durkheim, to

60. Piaget, *Moral Judgment of the Child*, p. 362.
61. *Ibid.*, p. 404.

be sure, does not expect religion to disappear; unlike other post-Enlightenment secular scientists, he appreciates the importance of non-rational dimensions of human existence. As he observes in *The Elementary Forms*, "there is something eternal in religion, namely, the faith and the cult."[62] But he also maintains that traditional religious beliefs will be transformed into the new, and yet very old, faith in, and cult of, man. In light of the decades of theological and ecclesiastical vitality that have followed Durkheim's era, this verdict is dubious at best. Twentieth-century theologians have not only responded in a creative way to the intellectual challenges posed by the sciences, they have found new ways of using traditional religious language to speak meaningfully to the human condition in this world.[63] In so doing, however, theologians and churchmen have unwittingly confirmed another dimension of Durkheim's thought, namely, his conviction that there are depths of reality lying beyond rational conceptualization that science will never be able to grasp. For this reason, Durkheim states, "even the most rational and secularized religions cannot and never will be able to dispense with a very particular form of speculation which . . . cannot really be scientific."[64]

62. Durkheim, *Formes élémentaires*, p. 615.
63. For an analysis of twentieth-century theological responses to the various challenges posed by the several sciences, see Roger Johnson, Ernest Wallwork, *et al.*, "Critical Issues in Modern Religion" (Englewood Cliffs, N.J.: Prentice-Hall, forthcoming).
64. Durkheim, *Formes élémentaires*, p. 615.

VI

Ethical Theory

Preceding chapters have dealt primarily with the scientific side of Durkheim's moral philosophy: What factors account for the nature of moral experience? How do socially engendered moral standards vary historically and within the diverse groups of advanced societies? How do we come to be moral both developmentally and pedagogically? Little or no attention has been given to strictly ethical questions: What things are good? What actions are right? How does one justify normative proposals?

Unraveling the ethical views of a moral philosopher as complex as Durkheim is always difficult. His writings contain a multiplicity of ethical assertions, yet no single work is devoted exclusively to philosophical ethics. Extracting a consistent ethical theory from Durkheim's works requires moving back and forth among a variety of publications while remaining sensitive to modifications in Durkheim's ethical views over time. This chapter begins with Durkheim's critique of other ethicians, followed by a detailed exploration of the historical development of his own metaethical and normative theories, because this approach appears to be the best way of obtaining a clear and unambiguous perspective on his entire ethical writings.

Rival Theories

Durkheim's perspicacity as a moral philosopher is nowhere more clearly evident than in his early critique of the dominant ethical theories of his era. In this critique one discovers a number of the major objections that have subsequently been raised by philosophical ethicians to refute Kant's categorical imperative, self-realization theories, psychological hedonism, and some forms of utilitarianism. Here, too, one finds implicitly stated the criteria by which Durkheim believed every ethical theory, including his own, should be tested, criteria still widely respected. Durkheim's refutation of rival philosophies thus provides the natural entrée into his own position in ethics.

In view of Durkheim's indebtedness to Kant, it is scarcely surprising that he felt compelled to develop several specific criticisms of the

Kantian ethic. As might be expected, it is not the German philosopher's respect for moral law or his recognition of human dignity that brings about Durkheim's critical reaction. It is, rather, Kant's failure to avoid several logical inconsistencies in defending his categorical and practical imperatives that disturbs Durkheim's typically French passion for rational clarity.

An initial grasp of Durkheim's critique of Kant can be obtained by beginning with the German philosopher's central thesis that a maxim is moral if, and only if, it can be universalized without rational inconsistency. In Durkheim's view, this so-called "categorical imperative" not only justifies the benevolent acts Kant intended it to cover, but it leaves open the possibility that egoistic maxims will also be justified. Kant, of course, thought his categorical imperative precluded the latter possibility for the following reasons cited by Durkheim:

We act morally only when the maxim of our action can be universalized. Consequently, to be moral in refusing assistance to our fellowmen when they are in need, we would have to be able to make the egoistic maxim a law applying to all cases without exception. We cannot generalize to this point without contradicting ourselves; for, in fact, every time we are in distress we wish to be assisted. Charity is then a general duty of humanity, since egoism is irrational.[1]

The difficulty with this line of reasoning, Durkheim observes (and most contemporary philosophers agree), is that a consistent and systematic egoist could universalize a purely egoistic maxim without self-contradiction. He could, to use Durkheim's words,

apply to himself the rule that he applies to others by formulating a law which would require nothing from others. The egoistic maxim is no more difficult to universalize than the other; it is sufficient to practice it with all its implied consequences. This logical rigor will be especially easy for men who feel themselves capable of being self-sufficient in all circumstances, and who are quite prepared to continually do without others provided others will always do without them.[2]

This criticism of Kant, it should be noted, does not imply that "universalizability," "rationality," and "consistency" are not among the valid reasons a philosopher or anyone else might offer in justifying a moral judgment. But it does suggest that universalizability, rationality, and

1. Durkheim, *Division du travail*, p. 6.
2. *Ibid.*

consistency are insufficient arguments when the justification of a moral judgment is at stake.

Equally unsatisfactory, in Durkheim's view, is Kant's hypothetical imperative which involves treating man as an end in himself and a member of a "Kingdom of Ends." As Kant formulates this second aspect of his ethical theory,

man, and in general every rational being, *exists* as an end in himself, *not merely as a means* for arbitrary use by this or that will: he must in all his actions, whether they are directed to himself or to some other rational being, always be viewed *at the same time as an end . . . Rational nature exists as an end in itself . . .* The practical imperative will therefore be as follows: *Act in such a way that you always treat humanity, whether in your own person or in the person of any other, never simply as a means, but always at the same time as an end.*[3]

Without contesting the fundamental humanistic values enshrined in this passage, Durkheim questions whether it justifies anything more than an inferior form of benevolence. True love, Durkheim writes,

which consists in self-giving, necessarily implies that I subordinate my person to an end transcending it. I wish this end to be other human beings; but I can exalt the humanity of others only by virtue of humiliating myself, lowering myself to the role of means. Such acts would then be deprived of all positive moral value, since, if, on the one hand, they conform to the law, they violate it on the other. Acts of this sort are neither exceptional nor rare; life is full of them, because otherwise it would be impossible. For example, does not conjugal society presuppose that husband and wife give themselves mutually and wholly to one another? Nothing is more lamentable than the way in which Kant deduces the constitutive rules of marriage. In his view, the sacrificial act by which one spouse consents to be an instrument of pleasure for the other is in itself immoral, and loses this quality only if it is compensated for by a similar and reciprocal sacrifice on the part of the other.[4]

In brief, Kant's practical imperative fails to justify deeply rooted and widespread moral sentiments, such as sacrificial love and disinterested benevolence.

In addition to directing these specific criticisms against Kant, Durkheim raises several fundamental and far-reaching questions regarding the philosophical enterprise of deducing ethical principles from assump-

3. Immanuel Kant, *The Moral Law*, tr. H. J. Paton (New York: Barnes and Noble, 1950), pp. 95-96.
4. Durkheim, *Division du travail*, p. 7.

tions about "the essential nature of man." Although these criticisms are applied to Kant, they are most carefully delineated in Durkheim's critique of self-realization theories. Fully cognizant of the fact that many Western ethicians since Aristotle have assumed that the good for man consists in that form of activity which most fully realizes the distinctive moral potentialities of human nature, Durkheim raises the basic question whether self-realization in and of itself constitutes an ethical principle. Self-realization clearly entails the realization of something, but this "something" varies from philosopher to philosopher.

The differences distinguishing the doctrines derive solely from the fact that man is not everywhere conceived in the same manner. Some endow him with pure will; others grant more or less room to the emotions; some see an autonomous creature made for solitude; others, an essentially social being. For some, man is so constituted that he cannot live without a law which surpasses and dominates him, which is imposed upon him with an imperative authority. Others, on the contrary, are more impressed by everything that man spontaneously and freely does naturally; they conclude from this that the ideal must have an attraction which stimulates desire.[5]

These conflicting definitions of man encouraged Durkheim not only to question the value of this entire speculative enterprise but also to raise several logical, ethical, and empirical objections against ethical theories of the self-realization variety.

   Logically, Durkheim notes that at least some self-realization theorists are guilty of committing the fallacy of deriving ethical statements from factual assertions. Here the problem is simply that an ethical conclusion cannot be logically induced or deduced from nonethical premises. Janet's contention that man is essentially a social being destined to realize himself in a community represents one example of this logical confusion. Whatever this solidarity may be, Durkheim states,

it can only be presented as a *fact,* and that is not sufficient to establish it as a *duty.* The observation that man is not in fact entirely his own master is not sufficient to justify the conclusion that he should not try to master himself. Undoubtedly we are dependent upon our neighbors, our ancestors, and our past; many of our beliefs, sentiments, and actions do not originate with us, but come to us from without. But where is the proof that this dependence is a good thing? What endows it with a moral value? Why should it not be, on the contrary, a yoke from

5. *Ibid.,* pp. 18-1y.

which we ought to seek to free ourselves? Why should duty not consist in a complete emancipation? . . . It [solidarity] may be inevitable, but it does not follow that it is moral.[6]

One basic difficulty with self-realization theories is thus the tendency to beg precisely the question which is at issue when one moves from the "is" to the "ought," namely, what is morally acceptable or justifiable self-development?

Another difficulty raised by Durkheim with respect to self-realization theories derives from his own critical premise that a tenable ethical theory must be compatible with generally accepted principles of morality. Unless the principles deduced from the nature of man are consonant with the moral judgments which men actually make, Durkheim contends, philosophical subtleties cannot remove the inadequacies of the proposed formulas. The trouble with most self-realization theories is their tendency to stress the morality of realizing states of the self at the expense of other-regarding activities. Consequently, formulas of this sort not only generally fail to justify altruistic activities, but they easily degenerate into pure egotism. If the self-perfectionist remains consistent with himself, Durkheim observes, "he will have to practice the most intractable moral egotism. People will in vain call attention to sympathy, familial instincts, patriotic sentiments, considered among our natural, even our most noble, propensities, and ask, for this reason, that they be cultivated. The duties that the self-perfectionist will be able to deduce exclusively from his assumptions do not at all resemble those really binding us to our fellow men; for the latter consist of obligations to serve others, and not to make them serve our personal perfection."[7]

To be sure, altruistic activities may also contribute indirectly to self-realization, but there is an important difference between seeking fulfillment through activities directed toward the realization of subjective states and finding fulfillment in activities directed toward objects beyond the self. The latter activities require justification, in Durkheim's view, if the concept of self-realization is to be compatible with generally recognized moral obligations.

A further difficulty introduced by Durkheim in refutation of self-realization theories is strictly scientific in nature. The various concepts of man underlying the moral deductions of philosophers, Durkheim

6. *Ibid.*, pp. 8-9.
7. *Ibid.*, p. 8.

contends, have not been elaborated through application of the empirical method of science by which statements of fact alone can be verified. In fact, the concepts of man, "serving as the basis of all these deductions, cannot be the product of a scientific elaboration, methodically conducted; for science is not in a position to provide precise information on this matter. We are beginning to know some of the elements which constitute man, but we are ignorant of a great many of them, and we have only a very confused notion of the whole that they form. There is every reason to fear, then, that the moralist determines his concept of man in accordance with his own beliefs and personal aspirations."[8]

Years later, Durkheim went even further and suggested, as previously observed, that men vary historically under the pressure of changes within their social milieux. Thus, far from there being "one human nature, the forms and properties of which are determinable once and for all," the nature of "man is eminently plastic."[9] If this contention is true, however, all ethical theories based upon nonplastic, essentialist definitions of human nature are untenable.

Finally, Durkheim criticizes several specific self-realization theorists for their inability to justify, with their abstract rules designed for ideal beings, the highly specific maxims that govern our day-to-day domestic, occupational, political, and educational activities.[10] The latter are difficult for ethical theories that emphasize the realization of abstract human virtues to justify precisely because they call for the concentration of human activities on specific, limited tasks. As Durkheim sees it, the harmonious development of all human faculties "is indeed necessary and desirable," but it is no less true that we are called upon to concentrate on specific, functional responsibilities: "We cannot and we must not all be devoted to the same kind of life; we have, according to our aptitudes, different functions to fulfill, and we must adapt ourselves to what we must do. We are not all made for reflection; there is need for men of feeling and of action. Conversely, there is need of those whose job is thinking."[11] To contend, as Renouvier did, that

8. *Ibid.,* p. 19.

9. Durkheim, *Education and Sociology,* pp. 115, 118. It is noteworthy that Durkheim uses the adverb "eminently" rather than "infinitely" in this context. Unlike W. G. Sumner, with whom he is often erroneously compared, Durkheim does not claim that man is infinitely and predictably plastic or variable. His point is rather that the nature of man is such as to allow for considerable variation. "There is," he writes, "a man in general, but this is not the whole man. Man is always similar, identical with himself, and always different." (Durkheim, "Introduction à la morale," p. 89.)

10. Durkheim, *Division du travail,* pp. 9-10.

11. Durkheim, *Education and Sociology,* p. 62.

these specialized activities are inferior in comparison with the cultivation of the abstract qualities associated with mankind in general, says Durkheim, is to go against the grain of human experience. For it entails relegating to a morally inferior status domestic responsibilities, vocational duties, and other activities of "unquestioned morality."[12]

Equally unsatisfactory is the utilitarian alternative to self-realization theories. Especially repugnant to Durkheim is the hedonistic psychological premise which, until the end of the nineteenth century, was widely accepted by those utilitarians who argued that the rightness or wrongness of an act should be judged in terms of its utility in the production of happiness.[13] In rejecting psychological hedonism, Durkheim appeals to introspection, particularly to the phenomenological distinction between desiring pleasure and finding an object pleasant. "There is," Durkheim notes in this context, "an inclination whose object is pleasure," but it is not "the prototype of all inclinations."[14] For there are, in addition to "the love of pleasure," disinterested tendencies which aim not at pleasurable states of consciousness but the good of some object or person other than the self. Pleasure often accompanies altruistic acts, but pleasure is not the object sought. Pleasurable states of consciousness, rather, follow the pursuit of desirable ends beyond the self. A case in point is maternal selflessness. "The mother sacrifices herself for her child with joy. Still it is quite clear that what she seeks in the sacrifice is the health of the child and not the joy of sacrifice. The joy comes as an addition. It facilitates the sacrifice, makes it a blissful experience. It is neither the determining cause nor the object of it."[15] Not only do we often make this phenomenological distinction, says Durkheim, but we generally feel that there is a moral danger in the love of pleasure, a danger which most moralists have appreciated. "We feel that there is something morbid in setting pleasure as an end in itself, to seek it out for itself, when it should only be a consequence, a corollary, or a concomitant state."[16] Pleasure is not, then, the only thing which is valuable or which deserves to be sought.

To say that psychological hedonism is untenable is one thing; to question the ethical thesis of utilitarianism is quite a different matter. Acknowledging this distinction, Durkheim denies the tenability of that form of "social utilitarianism" advanced by Wiart, Ihering, Post, and Schaeffle. According to this type of utilitarianism, an act or institution

12. Durkheim, *Division du travail*, p. 10.
13. *Ibid.*, p. 11.
14. Durkheim, *Moral Education*, p. 213.
15. *Ibid.*, p. 211.
16. *Ibid.*, p. 213.

is right if and only if it contributes to the survival of society. Three principle arguments are introduced by Durkheim to repudiate this claim. First, "a good number of things are useful or even necessary to society which are not moral."[17] For example, a well-equipped army or a great industrial complex may be profitable to society, but the possession of cannons and steam engines scarcely renders a people moral. Second, "there are a good number of moral practices no less obligatory than others which apparently do not render any particular service to the community."[18] For instance, modern societies support a large number of individuals, like the incurably ill, who make no contribution to society, yet the prolongation of their lives is considered a moral obligation. Finally, Durkheim objects to the obscurity of the utilitarian criterion, although he is somewhat obscure himself regarding a constructive alternative.

To summarize the main points raised by Durkheim in this admittedly incomplete critique of other ethical views is to discover the criteria by which Durkheim felt ethical theories should be tested. The first criterion is clearly rational consistency since Durkheim obviously believes that he has made a telling point in uncovering logical inconsistencies in Kant, Janet, Ihering, and others. The second criterion is summarized as: an ethical theory must be compatible with all the principles or standards "the moral nature of which is undisputed."[19] This test is not simply the implicit criterion employed in refuting Kant's hypothetical imperative, theories of self-realization, and social utilitarianism; it is the principal criterion explicitly mentioned by Durkheim at the outset of the introduction to the first edition of *The Division of Labor*. Here Durkheim quotes Janet to the effect that moralists must continually refer to the moral consciousness of mankind:

"If a close examination is undertaken," Janet justly says, "one will observe that theories of moral obligation appeal much more to the conscience of men and to their innate or acquired idea of their duties than to this or that abstract principle... The proof of this is that in arguments against false ethical systems people always draw their examples, and arguments based upon them, from duties which they assume to be acknowledged on all sides... In short, every science must rest on facts. Now, the facts which constitute the foundations for ethics are generally acknowledged duties."[20]

17. Durkheim, *Division du travail*, p. 11.
18. *Ibid.*, p. 12.
19. *Ibid.*, p. 5.
20. *Ibid.*

Closely related to this second criterion is Durkheim's final assumption that an ethical theory must be compatible with the facts about man and society discovered by science.

Early Ethical Theory, 1885-1893

The task of reconstructing Durkheim's own ethical theory is made difficult by a number of factors, and the difficulties lie with the author as well as with the reconstruction of his position in ethics. Although Durkheim wrote no single work dedicated explicitly to philosphical ethics, his entire work is concerned with it. It is not always clear, however, precisely how Durkheim himself related the various ethical assertions contained in his writings. Particularly serious are difficulties posed by the presence of seemingly contradictory statements in his work. In the absence of a definitive ethical treatise from Durkheim himself, it is not always possible to ascertain whether one of several conflicting views should be accorded more weight than another. There is also the problem of determining whether Durkheim altered his ethical views in the course of his intellectual development. Had Durkheim completed his proposed volume on *La Morale* before his untimely death in 1917, this question as to possible differences of doctrine between his early and mature periods might have been easier to resolve. I believe that there are two very different ethical theories embedded in Durkheim's work. The first is contained in the works written between 1885 and 1893; the second gradually emerges in the works written between 1893 and 1917. Presumably this final position, which was not clarified until the last decade of his life, would have been developed in greater detail, and possibly modified, in Durkheim's unfinished manuscript.

An initial grip on the young Durkheim's ethical theory can be obtained by distinguishing between the two traditional areas explored by philosophical ethicists, currently differentiated by the terms "normative ethics" and "metaethics." Normative ethics is concerned with the explication and defense of fundamental ethical principles, that is, norms and values. We might call this area of ethics the criticism and justification of the basic principles of ethics and the examination of the ethical foundations of the major institutions of society.[21] Metaethics is concerned with the meaning of the ethical terms employed in normative ethics and with the "kind of reasoning or evidence [that] constitutes a valid 'defense' or 'justification' of ethical principles," meaning

21. Richard Brandt, *Ethical Theory* (Englewood Cliffs, N.J.: Prentice-Hall, Inc., 1959), p. 6.

"how can we show that some particular kind of reasoning is a valid defense or justification."[22] Both areas may be illustrated by selections from John Stuart Mill. In his now classic work on *Utilitarianism,* Mill sets forth the following normative proposition: "happiness is desirable, and the only thing desirable, as an end; all other things being only desirable as means to that end."[23] This normative proposal is founded on the metacritical assumption that "the sole evidence it is possible to produce that anything is desirable is that people do actually desire it."[24] The desirable or the good is, therefore, that which is desired.

Inasmuch as metaethical issues logically precede normative problems, the analysis of Durkheim begins with the metaethical assertions contained in his early writings. It is important to note at the outset of this discussion, however, that Durkheim was at one with his contemporaries in concentrating primarily upon normative issues. Thus, metaethical issues are not explicitly recognized by Durkheim as distinct from normative proposals. Equally noteworthy is his lack of concern with the contemporary problem of deciding what is meant by saying that something is good, right, and so forth. Insofar as Durkheim has a metaethical theory, it is one that deals almost exclusively with the second metacritical question: what kind of evidence constitutes a valid defense of ethical principles?

In order to understand Durkheim's initial metacritical position, it is important to remember that he was a student of Wundt. What Wundt taught Durkheim is what he teaches anyone who reads his *Ethics* with care, namely, the principle that the test of truth is universal consent. Socrates was right, Wundt states in a passage that could have been penned by the young Durkheim, "in beginning his search for an ethical principle by trying to find out what all men thought on the subject, . . . [for] we shall never obtain a higher test of truth than that of universal consent. What every normal consciousness, under conditions of sufficient enlightenment, recognizes as self-evident, we call certain."[25] Hence, the first problem in the search for valid ethical principles is to answer the question: What moral standards are universally, or at least widely, recognized as moral? It is this approach that underlies not only Durkheim's critique of other ethicians for neglecting generally

22. *Ibid.,* p. 7.
23. John Stuart Mill, *Utilitarianism,* 4th ed. (London: Longmans, Green, Reader, and Dyer, 1871), p. 52.
24. *Ibid.,* pp. 52-53.
25. Wilhelm Wundt, *Ethics,* III, p. 76. Durkheim's early epistemological assumption that "only the universal is rational" clearly favored his acceptance of Wundt's "test of truth." See Durkheim, *Division du travail,* p. 321.

recognized moral phenomena, but his positive assertions that various principles are right because they are "undisputed,"[26] "everywhere" acknowledged,[27] "generally considered to be moral,"[28] "common to all moralities."[29]

Durkheim's metaethical theory is thus a form of ethical naturalism, where by "naturalistic theory" is meant "the proposal that ethical standards can, after all, be confirmed, ethical questions answered, by observation and inductive reasoning of the very sort that we use to confirm statements in the empirical sciences."[30] The obvious reason for this classification is that Durkheim's concept of the validation of ethical principles calls for an empirical inquiry directed toward eliciting "generally accepted" or "undoubted" moral assertions. The task of the ethician is twofold: he must consider the various phenomena generally considered moral by various peoples, and he must attempt to elicit the universal phenomena embedded in these assertions. "The method is 'positive' in the sense that the ideals are not to be laid down a priori, but to be 'disengaged' from the 'facts' of the moral life."[31]

It should be noted that a naturalistic theory of this sort does not commit the logical fallacy of deriving ethical statements from factual assertions, for it is a statement concerning the validity of moral proposals. The premises within the following syllogism may be unacceptable for a variety of reasons, but the conclusion is a justified inference from the premises:

Ethical premise: An ethical duty is right if and only if it is a universally recognized standard of morality.

Scientific premise: "It is a fundamental duty everywhere to assure the existence of the fatherland."[32]

Conclusion: Therefore, it would not be ethically right to regard "practices as moral which would be subversive of the societies observing them."[33]

No less logically impeccable is the following example of syllogistic reasoning contained in several of Durkheim's later publications:

26. Durkheim, *Division du travail*, p. 5; his "Morale en Allemagne," p. 130.
27. *Ibid.*, p. 21.
28. *Ibid.*, p. 65.
29. *Ibid.*, p. 179.
30. Brandt, *Ethical Theory*, p. 152.
31. Morris Ginsberg, "Durkheim's Ethical Theory," in Nisbet, *Emile Durkheim*, p. 142.
32. Durkheim, *Division du travail*, p. 21.
33. *Ibid.*

Ethical premise:	An act cannot be considered morally right if it has never been so regarded.
Scientific premise:	"No act has ever been regarded as moral which is *oriented exclusively* to the preservation of the individual."[34]
Conclusion:	Therefore, acts directed solely toward self-preservation cannot be considered moral.[35]

Durkheim, to be sure, frequently fails to explicitly express his ethical premises, but when the suppressed premises are made explicit, as they are from time to time, no logical fallacy is involved. The only question remaining is whether the premises are true.

One might ask, when Durkheim suggests that we shall never obtain a higher test of truth than universal consent, which of the following various meanings of the term "consent" he presupposes. If it is taken as being synonymous with desiring, J. S. Mill's widely discredited thesis that the good is that which is everywhere desired would be implied. A second possibility is Wundt's proposal that universal consent refers to what "every normal consciousness, under conditions of sufficient enlightenment, recognizes as self-evident." Still another possibility is that a principle of morality is universally acknowleged if it is found in all known social codes.

In his early writings Durkheim vacillates among these several possible interpretations of universal consent. In two passages in *The Division of Labor*, for example, he suggests that something is good if it is everywhere desired or preferred:

The only experimental fact proving that life is generally *good* is that the vast majority of men *prefer* it to death.[36] [Italics mine.]

[Science] does not command. That is true. Science merely tells us what is necessary for life. But clearly, *the supposition, man wishes to live,* a very simple assumption, immediately transforms the laws that science establishes into imperative rules of conduct.[37]

The obvious difficulty with this line of reasoning is that a desire, preference, or wish does not necessarily make something good if we recognize, as Durkheim does, the existence of amoral and immoral desires. For example the fact that "the vast majority of men" desire wealth scarcely makes money an intrinsic good or avarice a moral virtue. The

34. Durkheim, "Determination of Moral Facts," p. 50.
35. *Ibid.*
36. Durkheim, *Division du travail*, p. 269.
37. *Ibid.*, p. v.

things men desire, then, cannot be considered synonymous with the things that they consider good. True, the term "good" may be synonymous with "desirable," but the latter term suggests the impersonal quality we normally ascribe to the ethically good. It was, in fact, precisely because Durkheim recognized the impersonal sense in which we use terms like "good" and "desirable" that he eventually dropped the terms "desire," "prefer," and "wish" from his ethical vocabulary.

With respect to the important question whether universal consent refers to what every sufficiently enlightened moral conscience recognizes as right and good or to the common principles sanctioned by the moral codes of various societies, Durkheim's early position is somewhat equivocal. On the one hand, Durkheim appeals to "common knowledge" and to the views of philosophers (who, in this context, are presumably enlightened moral judges) to support many of his own contentions. This is the time-honored method of ethics utilized by Plato, Aristotle, and Kant, a method which presupposes "that in all the main theories, no less than in the views of the plain man, there is much that is true, and that even when theories are in broad opposition to each other, each is probably erring only by overstatement or mis-statement of something that is profoundly true."[38] On the other hand, Durkheim frequently refers to the common moral consciousness of humanity as revealed in the moral codes of various societies, especially when stressing his empirical evidence for asserting that an act or rule is universally recognized. Presumably, Durkheim felt both appeals were legitimate inasmuch as the moral conscience of mankind finds its objective expression in the common prescriptions of right and wrong contained within philosophical works and diverse moral codes.

In making a case for the foregoing interpretation of Durkheim's early naturalism, I do not wish to slight the importance of the strong current of relativism in his early writings. This current is exemplified, above all, in his claim that moral rules not only vary "in fact, but by right (*droit*)."[39] Fundamental to the present interpretation, however, is the thesis that Durkheim was initially a cultural, not an ethical, relativist. That Durkheim was a cultural relativist can scarcely be doubted since he obviously was convinced that most moral rules systematically vary from

38. Sir W. David Ross, *Foundations of Ethics* (Oxford, Eng.: Clarendon Press, 1939), p. 2.

39. Durkheim, *Division du travail,* p. 22. The use of the term "droit" in this context is ambiguous, since it connotes "law" as well as "right." Durkheim seems to be implying that it is "right" that ethical rules vary cross-culturally, although he may simply be noting that the ethical rules codified in "law" vary. The latter interpretation is implied by George Simpson's translation. See *The Division of Labor* (New York: Macmillan Company, 1933), p. 423.

society to society. The young Durkheim was also an ethical relativist if by this term one simply means that conflicting ethical opinions may be justified, for it was his contention that moral rules may be valid in one society that are not valid in another. But this latter claim rests upon the nonrelativist assertion that universally acknowledged values and states of affairs permit the justification of conflicting rules. In other words, Durkheim began by accepting the nonrelativist assumption that there are universally valid ethical principles.

If the young Durkheim's metaethical thesis states that ethical opinions are justified if and only if they contain principles universally acknowledged by the moral consciousness of mankind, how did he treat the major questions of normative ethics, that is, questions like: What things are good? What rules and acts are right? The first of these questions calls for proposals about phenomena that are worthwhile in themselves, or, to use the technical philosophical term, intrinsically desirable. The second question seeks to determine obligatory rules, right conduct, moral duty; in short, the acts we ought to perform.

Although Durkheim nowhere sets forth a comprehensive list of fundamental moral standards in his early writings, the following passages indicate the moral principles which he initially assumed were universally approved by the moral conscience of mankind:

—*Order, harmony, and social solidarity* are generally considered to be moral.[40]
—It is a fundamental duty everywhere to assure *the existence of the fatherland.*[41]
—The supreme law of every society is *the welfare of its members.*[42]
—*Life* is generally good.[43]
—For societies as for individuals, *health* is good and desirable; disease, on the contrary, is bad and ought to be avoided.[44]
—There is no doubt . . . that conscience confers a certain moral character on actions undertaken on behalf of one's fellow man. In a general sense, *altruistic conduct* is universally considered as morally praiseworthy.[45]

40. Durkheim, *Division du travail*, p. 65.
41. *Ibid.*, p. 21.
42. Durkheim, "Montesquieu's Contribution to Social Science," p. 17.
43. Durkheim, *Division du travail*, p. 269. In "La Philosophie dans les universités allemandes," Durkheim states that "life is the most extraordinary thing in the world, nothing surpasses it" (p. 436).
44. Durkheim, *Règles*, p. 61. This claim is justified by the argument that health is "commonly understood as a state generally preferable to disease." (*Ibid.*, p. 73.)
45. Durkheim, *Moral Education*, p. 81. Although this passage comes from a later work, it clearly expresses an opinion less succinctly presented in Durkheim's early writings. See, for example, *Division du travail*, pp. 55-56, 448.

—If there is one rule common to all . . . moralities, it is certainly that which *prohibits attacks against the person*.[46] [All italics mine.]

Durkheim's early normative theory thus includes a plurality of moral standards, including social order and solidarity, patriotism, welfare, life, health, benevolence, and not harming others. In addition, justice and promise-keeping are frequently treated as if they were also universally acknowledged moral rules and thus essential components of a truly comprehensive normative theory.[47]

When Durkheim turns to practical issues, as he does at the conclusion of *The Division of Labor*, his approach is the traditional casuistic one of combining the ethical principles thus justified with the facts uncovered by scientific exploration. For example, the fundamental practical problem in *The Division of Labor* is whether or not occupational specialization is a desirable development within modern societies. If so, is it a moral duty to become a functional specialist rather than a man of *culture générale?* Before one can respond to these practical questions, Durkheim notes in the introduction, it is first necessary to study the effects of the division of labor and to compare these effects with other recognized moral phenomena. "If we find that the division of labor plays a role similar to some other practice whose moral . . . character is undisputed . . . , we shall be able to conclude that it must be classified among the latter."[48] Having demonstrated in the main body of the book that the main effect of the division of labor is not increased economic output but increased social solidarity, Durkheim concludes that the division of labor must be recognized as morally desirable since order, harmony, and social solidarity are universally considered valuable. With this proposition in hand, Durkheim goes on to argue not only that we have a moral duty to engage in specialized occupations but also that we must train students differently in light of the specialized functions they will be called upon to fulfill.[49] This is not to say that modern men should eschew cultivation of *culture générale;* it is to say, given the morally desirable consequences of occupational specialization, that men should be taught to recognize the moral value of performing the circumscribed tasks necessary for the maintenance of solidarity in advanced societies.

46. Durkheim, *Division du travail*, pp. 179-180.
47. *Ibid.*, pp. 52, 250-251, 424-425, 434, 458.
48. *Ibid.*, p. 43.
49. *Ibid.*, p. 452, n1.

Mature Ethical Theory, 1893-1917

Durkheim's mature ethical writings are marked by several major developments both on the normative and metaethical levels of moral discourse. Revisions in Durkheim's normative theory will be considered first, primarily because his mature metaethical position chronologically follows, and reaches out from, alterations in his normative theory.

In the process of clarifying and simplifying his initial list of moral principles, Durkheim lays increasingly heavy stress upon the good or the desirable. This is true to such a degree, in fact, that the question of the good or the desirable gradually becomes the central issue in Durkheim's normative theory. All questions of morally correct rules of conduct are increasingly considered in relation to the goodness of their consequences; rules of conduct are considered right if they engender desirable results. The principal reason for this increasing stress upon the good derives from Durkheim's early conviction that rules vary cross-culturally, whereas at least some morally desirable ends are invariant. Hence, worthwhile ends alone seemed capable of being justified by universal approbation.

In reflecting on universally acknowledged intrinsic goods, Durkheim gradually abandoned his early pluralistic theory of moral standards in favor of the monistic thesis that society is the only intrinsically desirable end of moral conduct. The principal justification of this shift rests upon an appeal to "contemporary moral consciousness" and "the moralities of all known peoples."[50] If a systematic investigation of the moral conscience of humanity were undertaken, Durkheim argues, one would discover that "the qualification 'moral' has never been given to an act which has individual interests, or the perfection of the individual from a purely egotistic point of view, as its object."[51] If moral value is never predicated of acts directed toward purely personal ends, it logically follows that the personal ends of other individuals are of no greater value than those of the actor. As for taking the sum total of individual interests as a moral end, "the sum of zeros is, and can only be, equal to zero."[52] For "if a particular interest, whether mine or someone else's, is amoral, several such particular interests must also be amoral."[53] From this, Durkheim concludes that morality "can only have as object the group formed by the associated individuals—that is to say, society, *with*

50. Durkheim, "Determination of Moral Facts," p. 37.
51. *Ibid.*
52. Durkheim, *Moral Education*, p. 59.
53. *Ibid.*

*the condition that society be always considered as qualitatively differ-
ent from the individual beings that compose it.* "⁵⁴

If society is regarded as desirable in and of itself, does this debase our
ordinary concern with self-realization and altruistic devotion to the
service of others? Durkheim holds that this conclusion does not follow.
For society is not only desirable in itself, but it makes self-realization
and benevolence possible. Self-realization, for example, is only possible
through devotion to society since man "is not truly himself, he does
not fully realize his own nature, except on the condition that he is
involved in society."⁵⁵ Society, as the repository of all the riches of
civilization without which man would fall to the level of an animal,
contributes all that is of value in human nature. Man cannot cultivate
the best part of himself, then, without attaching himself to the social
source of that which enriches his being. Benevolence, too, is only realiz-
able through service of, and devotion to, society. For it is primarily
through being committed to a group that one is psychologically bound
"to the people who compose it and through whom it comes into being.
For although society is something other than the individual, although it
is not completely in any one of us, there is nonetheless no one in whom
it is not reflected. As a result, it is altogether natural that the sentiments we have for it are borne back upon those in whom society is
partially embodied."⁵⁶

If society is the supreme good and the end of all morally worthwhile
conduct, moral rules must obviously be justified by their social consequences. A conventional rule, like respect for the dignity of others, is

54. Durkheim, "Determination of Moral Facts," p. 37. In repudiating these
arguments, Morris Ginsberg rightly observes: "It is truly remarkable that Durkheim could have believed that these dialectical arguments could claim the support
of experience. He offers no evidence that no people has ever regarded the efforts
of an individual to develop his personality at the cost of immediate satisfaction as
morally praiseworthy. Again, it is simply not true that we deny moral quality to
acts which are directed at the relief of suffering or the promotion of good will
between individuals . . . Patriotism may be a virtue, but it is surely to fly in the
face of all the evidence to say that it is the only virtue. Nor is it at all clear that
patriotism implies the attribution to society of a personality which is qualitatively
different from the members which compose it. This is a conclusion which Durkheim may or may not be justified in reaching on other grounds. But that such a
view is implied in the moral judgments of our own or any other society he has
certainly not succeeded in showing." (Ginsberg, "Durkheim's Ethical Theory," in
Nisbet, *Emile Durkheim*. pp. 144-145.
55. Durkheim, *Moral Education*, p. 68.
56. *Ibid.*, p. 82. These arguments seem to imply that self-realization and
benevolence are also intrinsically desirable, society being the means by which
these ends are actualized. Durkheim, however, denies this conclusion. See *ibid.*,
pp. 55-59, and "Determination of Moral Facts," p. 37.

thus justified, in Durkheim's scheme, by its function in preserving social solidarity within society as a whole. If most people did not adhere to the rule regarding the dignity of man, there would not be sufficient assurance concerning the future behavior of others, and social cooperation, with all its benefits, would collapse.

Justificatory arguments of this sort sound strikingly similar to the social utilitarianism Durkheim initially criticized and subsequently rejected for justifying practices, such as warfare, which, while necessary for the survival of society, are not usually considered moral. The question, therefore, arises as to whether Durkheim held that a practice, rule, or institution is justified by its social utility, where by social utility is meant the survival of society. A number of passages scattered throughout Durkheim's mature writings superficially suggest an affirmative answer to this question. In attempting to justify moral discipline in secondary schools, for example, Durkheim explicitly refers to its "social utility."[57] On the whole, however, Durkheim analyzes moral rules in a way that presupposes their participation in, and contribution to, the intrinsic value of specifically moral relationships among men. Conventional rules and institutions are not "useful" in the sense of social survival at any cost but because they must exist if a group is to be more than a pack of isolated individuals in perpetual conflict. Conventional rules are justified insofar as the peaceful solidarity made possible by the rules has intrinsic value. In other words, rules are justified if and only if they share in the intrinsic value of social solidarity, assuming that solidarity includes peace, trust, mutuality, and cooperation. Durkheim's justificatory scheme does not extend, therefore, to those customs, like the dog-eat-dog ethic of nineteenth-century capitalism, which are detrimental to peaceful coexistence.

Precisely how this justification of conventional rules is employed by Durkheim may be illustrated by his arguments in defense of individual rights in "L'Individualisme et les intellectuels." In this essay, written at the height of the Dreyfus controversy, Durkheim contends, against anti-Dreyfusards, that the rights of man enshrined in the French constitution cannot be suspended in the interests of national security. The principal reason set forth by Durkheim in refusing to accept the suspension of natural rights advocated by anti-Dreyfusards is that these rights "are the only system of beliefs which can assure the *moral unity* of the nation."[58] [Italics mine.] The neglect of Dreyfus' rights by the army is thus equated with an attack upon the "intellectual and moral commun-

57. Durkheim, *Moral Education,* ch. iii, *passim,* and *Règles,* ch. iii, *passim.*
58. Durkheim, "L'Individualisme et les intellectuels," p. 10.

ion" upon which the moral solidarity of the French nation, and that of other civilized countries, depends. "To consent to a temporary eclipse of these principles, in order not to trouble the functioning of a public administration, which everyone recognizes, in other respects, as indispensable to the security of the State," is equivalent to national "moral suicide."[59] Hence, Durkheim concludes that it would be worse for France even temporarily to renounce rules respecting "the value and dignity of life" than to fail to provide sufficient national security, for the rejection of these rights entails a repudiation of the very principles upon which moral solidarity in France is based.[60]

The similarity of this justification of conventional rules with contemporary forms of rule-utilitarianism is sufficiently striking to elicit special comment. As the term "rule-utilitarianism" itself suggests, proponents of this normative theory have attempted to mediate between deontologists and utilitarians by arguing that "acts are to be regarded as right only if they conform to rules that can be supported on utilitarian grounds."[61] Rule-utilitarians thus oppose classical act-utilitarianism on the grounds that we are not obliged to produce the best possible consequences of a particular act, but to abide by those rules that have the best consequences for the general welfare. Unlike earlier deontological theories, however, rules are justified on utilitarian grounds.

In a similar vein, Durkheim argues that we should decide particular

59. *Ibid.*, p. 12.

60. Additional examples of this functional justification of conventional rules may be found as follows: In "L'Enseignement philosophique et l'agrégation de philosophie," *RP*, XXXIX (1895), 121-147, and again in "L'Evolution et le role de l'enseignement secondaire en France," *RB*, Series 5, V (1906), 70-77, Durkheim argues that a coordinated university curriculum is necessary in order to realize the ethical goal of intellectual and moral communion, which communion is essential for national Solidarity. In "Le Divorce par consentement mutuel," *RP*, Series 5, V (1906), 549-554, Durkheim maintains that social rules regulating divorce must be evaluated in terms of their probable functional consequences, although other moral considerations enter into deciding particular cases of divorce. After analyzing the likely dysfunctional social consequences of divorce by mutual consent (as contrasted with divorce through legal channels), Durkheim concludes that this legal innovation would be ethically undesirable. By weakening the institution of marriage, which is one of "les conditions essentielles de la santé morale et du bonheur," divorce by mutual consent would further undermine the interpersonal solidarity made possible by this institution. In the second preface to *La Division du travail* (p. xv), Durkheim argues that rules regulating economic behavior are justified by their "common utility." It is noteworthy that Durkheim abandons his former distaste for the term "utility" in these and other works written during the middle of his career. Whereas "utility" is invariably used in a derogatory sense in his early publications, Durkheim freely employs the terms in these writings. He is careful to distinguish his own understanding of "common" or "public" utility, however, from the so-called "private utility" advocated by some British act-utilitarians.

61. David Lyons, *Forms and Limits of Utilitarianism* (Oxford, Eng.: Clarendon Press, 1965), p. vii.

cases by following general prescriptions, the rightness of these general prescriptions having been established by the intrinsic value of their being generally observed.[62] It should be noted, however, that Durkheim considers the consequences of rules in relation to society conceived as a reality *sui generis*, whereas many Anglo-Saxon rule-utilitarians concentrate, rather, upon the social utility of rules in relationship to the greatest good of the greatest number. Durkheim's unique form of rule-utilitarianism is thus closer to those contemporary structural functionalists who contend that rules should be evaluated in terms of their functional consequences for entire social systems, although he does differ in maintaining that the relevant functional consequences are the qualitative elements of trust, cooperation, and mutuality that characterize social interaction at its best rather than the survival of the system at any cost.

This interpretation of Durkheim's rule-utilitarianism, incidentally, is not rendered problematical by those passages in which Durkheim suggests that we ought to obey moral precepts out of respect for rules and for this reason alone. For passages of this sort apply not to the rightness and wrongness of rules, but to the goodness and badness of acts. When the rightness of rules is under consideration, Durkheim appeals to their collective functional consequences. When morally praiseworthy acts are under review, however, Durkheim stresses the desirability of obeying perceived commandments "simply because we ought to, regardless of the consequences our conduct may have for us."[63] This latter claim simply states the point that an act is morally praiseworthy if the actor obeys the rules inscribed in his own conscience. A claim of this sort is irrelevant vis-à-vis the justification of rules, since the latter are justified only if they engender desirable social consequences.[64]

62. It is noteworthy that Durkheim's begins "L'individualisme et les intellectuels" with a critique of utilitarians and deontologists which is strikingly similar to that perpetrated by contemporary rule-utilitarians. In repudiating act-utilitarianism, for example, Durkheim notes that "the greatest good of the greatest number" criterion can be employed to justify the suspension of fundamental rules, such as those respecting individual liberties (p. 8). Against deontologists, such as Kant and Rousseau, Durkheim argues that rules respecting political liberties are means, not ends; they have value only insofar as they serve desirable social aims (p. 12).

63. Durkheim, *Moral Education*, p. 30.

64. A clear example of this distinction between objectively justified practices and subjectively praiseworthy behavior is found in Durkheim's discussion of moral discipline in his 1902 lectures on *Moral Education*. In attempting to justify moral discipline in secondary schools, Durkheim argues that the institution of moral discipline is justified because it fosters peaceful coexistence. In other words, the institution of moral discipline is justified in terms of morally desirable values. Yet, Durkheim also notes in this context that we rightly praise a person when he obeys a moral precept simply because he feels obliged to do so. (See chs. ii, iii.)

If moral rules are justified insofar as they contribute to socially desirable states of affairs, when and under what conditions does an individual have a right to criticize and reject socially sanctioned moral standards? In responding to this question, Durkheim suggests several occasions when the critical rejection of socially approved moral rules is justified. First, dissent is justified when public opinion enforces traditional rules of conduct that no longer foster peaceful coexistence or solidarity. When public opinion, weighted down by the baggage of moral rules inherited from the past, enforces rules that no longer engender social cooperation, dissent is justified. Criticism of public opinion is also permissible when societies forget or reject moral rules or practices which, if reconstituted, would foster solidarity.[65] A case in point is Durkheim's own criticism of modern industrial societies for failing to reinstitute rules analogous to the guild regulations that once governed economic behavior. When societies suppress institutions or principles that continue to be required, individuals have a moral responsibility to demonstrate that these institutions or principles continue to be required in order to establish more intimate forms of social solidarity.[66] Finally, Durkheim argues that the critic of public opinion is justified if he possesses a deeper insight into the future state of society than public opinion. Socrates and Jesus were right, Durkheim notes in this context, because they expressed more faithfully than their critics the morality appropriate for the societies that were coming into being.[67] Hence, it does not follow from Durkheim's belief in the need for obligatory rules that morally correct behavior involves uncritical obedience to the status quo.

65. Durkheim, "Determination of Moral Facts," p. 60.
66. Durkheim, *Division du travail*, 2nd ed., pp. xxxiii-xxxvi.
67. Durkheim, *Règles*, pp. 88-89, *Moral Education*, p. 53, and "Determination of Moral Facts," pp. 64-65. In the absence of further clarification from Durkheim himself, this argument seems to confuse "more evolved" with "ethically better." As G. E. Moore observes regarding a similar confusion in Spencer, Durkheim "does not seem aware that to assert the one is . . . not the same thing as to assert the other. He argues at length that certain kinds of conduct are 'more evolved,' and then informs us that he has proved them to gain ethical sanction in proportion, without any warning that he has omitted the most essential step in such a proof. Surely this is sufficient evidence that he does not see how essential the step is." (Moore, *Principia Ethica* [Cambridge, Eng.: Cambridge University Press, 1929], p. 49.) In a somewhat similar vein, Imogene Seger contends that "Durkheim not only believed in progressive evolution and therefore always regarded the new as the better; he also, quite openly and explicitly, wanted to help evolution along in the direction he saw it taking, i.e., towards greater rationality, secularism, away from a religiously bound morality and towards a scientifically understood 'natural' order, i.e., an ethic and religion based on science." (Seger, *Durkheim and His Critics on the Sociology of Religion*, Monograph Series [New York: Columbia University Press, 1957], p. 65.) A sympathetic reading of Durkheim at this point might well lead to a different

This attempt on Durkheim's part to justify rules as well as dissent with respect to their functional consequences brings us to his now widely discredited concept of the normal, as distinct from the pathological, as the principal empirical method of ascertaining the value of social rules and institutions in society. According to this thesis, the normality of a social institution, rule, or practice constitutes the soundness identified with the well-being of a society.[68] In other words, demonstration of the normality of a social practice is an empirical means of assessing whether the particular practice is essential to the well-being or health of the society in which it occurs.[69] Two principal tests are offered as a means of ascertaining the normality and, hence, the desirability of a given social phenomenon. The first involves demonstrating the dependence of the phenomenon upon the conditions of social existence from which it derives.[70] The second entails demonstration of its useful social function.[71] Moral rules, like those respecting

conclusion, however, if one assumes that the phrase "the morality appropriate for the societies that were coming into being" refers to rules relatively better suited to peaceful coexistence and mutuality in advanced societies. For an assumption of this sort not only does not confuse "more evolved" and "ethically better," it explicitly states a criterion for establishing why the contributions of Socrates and Jesus were ethically superior to those perpetrated by their critics. It is the present writer's opinion that this latter reading is more in keeping with Durkheim's thought as a whole than the contention that he confused "more evolved" with "ethically better."

68. Georges Davy notes this association of normality with social well-being in his introduction to Durkheim, *Professional Ethics and Civic Morals,* p. xxii.

69. "In fact, for societies as for individuals, health is good and desirable; disease, on the contrary is bad and ought to be avoided. If, then, we find an objective criterion, inherent in the facts themselves, which enables us to scientifically distinguish health from illness in the diverse categories of social phenomena, science will be in a position to illuminate practical problems, while remaining faithful to its own method." (Durkheim, *Règles,* p. 61.)

70. *Ibid.,* pp. 74-80. This appeal to "conditions of social existence" modifies, but does not essentially alter, Durkheim's utilitarian justification of rules and practices. For Durkheim assumes that the fundamental conditions of social existence, as well as phenomena engendered by these conditions, are essential to collective well-being. "It would be incomprehensible," he states, "if the most widespread forms of organization would not also be, *at least on the whole,* the most advantageous." (*Ibid.,* p. 73.) It is noteworthy, however, that this criterion of normality does exclude some useful phenomena from being ethically justified, since the formula states that only those socially useful phenomena that are also necessitated by basic conditions of social existence are both normal and desirable. Thus, "if it is true that everything that is normal is useful . . . , it is not true that everything that is useful is normal." (*Ibid.,* p. 79.) Durkheim nowhere provides an example, however, of a social fact that is useful, but unrelated to fundamental conditions of social existence.

71. *Ibid.,* pp. 79-80. Although Durkheim states that a phenomenon may be normal without being useful if it is necessitated by social conditions, he assumes that all normal facts are essential to the optimum well-being of society. The first test of normality thus presupposes the second. "This is why, once the generality of the phenomenon has been established, one can, by demonstrating its utility, confirm the results of the first method."

private property, are justified, therefore, if they are shown to be so deeply rooted in the nature of a certain type of society at a specific phase of its development as to be essential for its optimum moral cohesion.

An illustration of a social practice justified in this manner is provided by Durkheim in *Suicide*. The ethical issue with which Durkheim wrestles in the conclusion of this study is whether or not, given the general increase in suicide rates, the rule prohibiting suicide is justified in advanced societies. In discussing this issue, Durkheim begins by arguing that no society, beyond the most primitive, is known "where the individual is unreservedly granted the right to kill himself."[72] Given such general reprobation, Durkheim continues, "an author must have great faith in the strength of his logic to venture . . . a revolt, in the name of a system, against the moral conscience of humanity; or, if he considers the prohibition of suicide founded on the past and advocates its abolition only for the immediate present, he should first prove that some profound change in the basic conditions of collective life has occurred recently."[73] Far from such a basic change in the conditions of modern societies having occurred, however, these conditions have tended to strengthen the prohibition by favoring sentiments respecting the sacred value of the human person. Under the general conditions prevailing in modern societies, any violation of the sacred life of man, such as suicide, denigrates "this cult of human personality on which all our morality rests."[74] Suicide, therefore, must be classified among immoral acts, "for in its main principle it denies this religion of humanity" which is the principal basis of solidarity in advanced societies.[75]

Several obvious methodological difficulties are raised by this attempt to define the desirability of social facts in terms of normality. In the first place, it is clearly impossible to specify with any degree of precision those rules, institutions, and practices that are both necessitated by social conditions and required for the moral integration of society. This principal difficulty is aggravated, Georges Davy rightly observes, "by the fact that each normal type is normal only to one definite society and not to human society in general. It is increased too by the fact that, to establish the existence of the normal type, there must be a classification of societies."[76] The danger that emerges from these methodo-

72. Durkheim, *Suicide*, p. 332.
73. *Ibid.*
74. *Ibid.*, p. 334.
75. *Ibid.*, p. 337.
76. Georges Davy, in the introduction to Durkheim, *Professional Ethics and Civic Morals*, p. xxii.

logical difficulties is that the selection of normal and, hence, desirable phenomena is, in the final analysis, fairly arbitrary. That Durkheim himself was at least partly aware of these difficulties seems indicated by his obvious difficulty in applying his criterion of normality without getting entangled in complex logical gymnastics.[77] In any case, it is a matter of record that Durkheim placed considerably less stress on the test of normality after 1897. Thereafter, he employed the broad rule-utilitarian position previously discussed until this position was also abandoned in favor of ethical relativism.

Thus far, society has been discussed as if it were one rather than many. Given the existence of various groups (families, unions, clubs, political parties, nations, and humanity), how are we to decide cases of conflicting loyalty? Once again, Durkheim finds a helpful reply in Wundt's *Ethics*. According to Wundt, there is a "hierarchy of moral ends . . . that decides the values of different ends and settles the question of precedence in the event of their mutual conflict."[78] In a similar vein, Durkheim argues that the social group to be preferred is the one that serves the larger social interests.[79] Secondary group loyalty is less valuable, according to this criterion, than patriotism; national loyalty less desirable than cosmopolitanism. Mankind, however, does not constitute a single society. How, then, can humanity provide a social orientation for moral behavior? Durkheim's response, as previously noted, involves a fusion of patriotism with cosmopolitanism. The only way of resolving conflicts between patriotism and cosmopolitanism, Durkheim declares, "is to seek the realization of the human ideal through the most highly developed groups that we know, through those closest to mankind as a whole," that is to say, through particular nations.[80]

77. This difficulty of applying the normality criterion is apparent in the final chapter of *Suicide*. Having previously justified the rule prohibiting suicide, Durkheim turns, in this chapter, to whether or not the *rate*, as distinguished from the norm against suicide, is both normal and desirable. Briefly, Durkheim's conclusion is that a moderate rise in the suicide rate in advanced societies is produced by conditions that also engender greater freedom and moral solidarity. In other words, a moderate rise in the suicide rate is normal. Durkheim does not wish to conclude, however, that any statistical rate of suicide is ethically desirable. Hence, he is forced to argue that a practice, like suicide, cannot be declared morally desirable if it conflicts with a justified rule to the contrary. This leads to the paradoxical conclusion stated in the first preface to *Les Règles* (p. vi) that a crime, like suicide, may be "normal, [but] it is nonetheless [morally] odious." What this conclusion demonstrates is the inadequacy of the normality criterion, since other criteria are clearly being employed in an attempt to avoid the logical conclusions of the normality test.

78. Wundt, *Ethics*, III, 139.

79. See Durkheim, *Moral Education*, pp. 73-81.

80. *Ibid.*, p. 77. If a state failed to concern itself with the general interests of humanity, this criterion would presumably justify civil disobedience.

An important application of this hierarchy of moral ends is contained in Durkheim's wartime pamphlet: "Germany above All." The thesis of this pamphlet is that Germany and her allies ignored and seriously jeopardized the interests of humanity. By initiating hostilities against other sovereign nations and by conducting the war in an inhuman manner in the name of the alleged superiority of the Germanic race, Durkheim contends, Germany opted for a nationalistic policy incompatible with the humanitarian moral code recognized by all civilized nations.

For morality to us, that is to say to all civilized nations, to all those who have been in the school of Christianity, has for its primary object the realization of humanity, its liberation from the servitudes that belittle it, its growth in loving-kindness and fraternity. To say that the state should be deaf to the great human interests is therefore to put it outside and above morality.[81]

No state can justify acts against humanity with jingoistic terms since human interests ethically transcend national interests. Durkheim concludes, therefore, by condemning Germany's imperialistic policy as patently immoral.

Turning from the normative arguments contained in Durkheim's mature writings to his final metaethical position, it is clear that his original metaethical thesis regarding universal approbation extends well into his mature writings. At numerous crucial points, at least, the mature Durkheim alleges that a moral principle is right because it is universally acknowledged by the moral conscience of mankind. These assertions are joined, however, with numerous statements that more or less imply ethical relativism, that is, the metaethical thesis that conflicting ethical standards are equally valid.

Three major developments apparently lead Durkheim in the direction of ethical relativism. As his thought matured, he became increasingly convinced that the relevant ends of moral action are collectively engendered values rather than social solidarity, harmony, well-being, and so forth. Since collective values were shown by Durkheim's own empirical studies, especially by *L'Evolution pédagogique en France,* to vary cross-culturally, ends seemed no more capable of being justified by the moral conscience of mankind than rules.[82] If there are no universally recognized rules or values, however, universal approbation obviously cannot function as a metaethical theory.

---

81. Durkheim, *Germany above All: The German Mental Attitude and the War,* Studies and Documents on the War (Paris: Armand Colin, 1915), pp. 20-21.
82. See, for example, Durkheim, "Introduction à la morale," pp. 83, 86.

Another of the developments in Durkheim's thought responsible for his final ethical relativism is his increased emphasis on the hyperspiritual and transcendent characteristics of social groups. The relevance of this development for Durkheim's ethical relativism is not to be found in the implications of this doctrine for his causal explanations of moral experience; it is located, rather, in the philosophical conclusions drawn regarding the justification of ethical statements. This metaethical conclusion states that the nature of society is such as to virtually guarantee that collectively formulated rules and values are right. In Durkheim's words, "society is qualified to play the part of legislator because in our eyes it is invested with a well-founded moral authority."[83] In describing those attributes that qualify society as a legitimate or well-founded moral authority, Durkheim states:

The term "moral authority" is opposed to material authority or physical supremacy. Moral authority is a psychic reality, a higher and richer conscience than our own, one upon which we feel that our own depends. I have shown how society presents this characteristic because it is the source and seat of all the intellectual benefits that constitute civilization. From society derive all the essentials of our mental life . . . It is to society that we owe the power over matter which is our glory. It is society that has freed us from nature. Is it not then to be expected that we think of it as a mental being higher than ourselves from which our mental powers emanate?[84]

In other words, collective rules and values are always or usually right because society is a higher, richer, and presumably more intelligent psychic reality than any single individual. Curiously, however, this seemingly relativist claim is justified by arguments that presuppose the absolute validity of several nonrelativist statements: the knowledge generated by civilization is good and the freedom made possible by social existence is desirable. In addition, Durkheim presupposes the validity of duties of gratitude insofar as he argues that we should obey society because we are indebted to it for the riches of civilization: "society is the benevolent and protecting power, the nourishing mother from which we gain the whole of our moral and intellectual substance and toward whom our wills turn in a spirit of love and gratitude."[85] These arguments in support of ethical relativism do not succeed, therefore, in avoiding nonrelativist assumptions.

The third, and chronologically the last, development responsible for

83. Durkheim, "Determination of Moral Facts: Replies to Objections," p. 73.
84. *Ibid.*
85. Durkheim, *Moral Education*, p. 92.

Durkheim's ethical relativism is the distinctive epistemological theory contained in his last major writings, especially "Value Judgments and Judgments of Reality' (1911) *The Elementary Forms of the Religious Life* (1912), and *Pragmatisme et sociologie* (1913-14). In these works, Durkheim argues that valid moral judgments, like scientific judgments, correspond to realities. The realities at the basis of value judgments, however, are different from the facts with which the empirical sciences deal. Whereas statements in the empirical sciences are valid if they faithfully represent facts, value judgments are valid if and only if they correctly express collective rules and ideals. These collective moral standards are real, but not in the same sense that empirical objects are real. For collective moral principles do not reside in things, but in the value society confers upon them. Unlike scientific judgments, conflicting value judgments may be equally valid since the test of ethical truth is correspondence with collectively shared ideals which systematically vary.

No critical evaluation of Durkheim's ethical theories that did not begin with a survey of his merits would do justice to his perspicacity as a philosophical ethicist. He was essentially correct in his critique of Kant's ethics, self-realization theories, psychological hedonism, and social survival forms of utilitarianism. He was further correct in holding that universal approbation is an important consideration in the determination of valid ethical standards. One need not accept universal approbation as a metaethical theory to acknowledge that the moral convictions of mankind are important considerations in deciding what is right or good. "Such convictions, we may assume, have been subject to and have withstood criticism over the years, especially by those who may have suffered from them; hence, the main moral convictions of . . . [humanity] may be expected to have strong reason on their side."[86] The young Durkheim was similarly justified in assuming that benevolence, justice, promise-keeping, and not harming others are ethically valid rules and that casuistic issues can only be solved by combining these and other valid moral standards with relevant factual information. Durkheim's own liberal and humanitarian conclusions are clearly well-taken, especially his great respect for the human person, the rights of man, and the interests of mankind.

Once these merits have been acknowledged, however, several critical objections to Durkheim's ethical theories must be raised. His early

86. Brandt, *Ethical Theories*, p. 58.

metaethical thesis was that universal approbation provides a sufficient justification of ethical statements. The importance of this criterion is the assumption that ethical conflicts can be resolved, ethical disagreements settled, because there is essential agreement concerning many fundamental normative principles. Traditional natural law theories to the contrary, however, the fact that most men acknowledge a certain principle as morally right does not necessarily establish its validity or correctness. For instance, the fact that most men consider life worthwhile in itself is not sufficient warrant for assuming that life is intrinsically good rather than a means to the realization of other intrinsic goods, such as knowledge and pleasure. Similarly, with regard to widely accepted moral prohibitions, most peoples prohibit sexual intercourse in public. Yet this widespread prohibition scarcely proves that public intercourse is morally wrong since it may be due to a universal emotional reaction or prejudice. If most men may be in error, universal approbation is obviously not a sufficient metaethical theory.

On the normative side, Durkheim's early assumption regarding justified moral standards suffers from a failure to formulate an adequate list of fundamental ethical rules, and a neglect of the customary distinction between intrinsic values and less central objects of interest. With respect to the first point, Durkheim implicitly recognizes the importance of promise-keeping, justice, benevolence, and not harming others, but neglects equally fundamental duties respecting truthfulness, reparation, gratitude, and self-improvement.[87] In his discussion of the second point regarding values, Durkheim fails to distinguish intrinsic goods from other objects of interest that hardly count as things of intrinsic worth. For example, Durkheim speaks of life, health, social harmony, and the existence of the fatherland as if they were intrinsic goods. Yet, many ethicians consider these as means to other intrinsically worthwhile values. Durkheim nowhere grapples with the philosophical issues involved in deciding whether or not a phenomenon is intrinsically worthwhile.

As for the mature Durkheim's monistic thesis that society is the only intrinsically worthwhile object, the arguments offered in support of this claim cannot be accepted. The argument by exclusion wherein society must be regarded as the sole end of moral devotion because poeple have never regarded acts of self-improvement or benevolence as morally praiseworthy is clearly untenable. Durkheim not only fails to offer any evidence for this contention, but the popular opinion to which he

87. For a persuasive list of fundamental ethical duties, see Sir David Ross, *The Right and the Good* (Oxford, Eng.: Clarendon Press, 1930), pp. 16-47.

appeals clearly concedes that acts of self-improvement as well as acts of benevolence are morally desirable.[88] His arguments for the intrinsic worth of society clearly invalidate his assertion that society is the sole intrinsic good. Society is said to have intrinsic worth because it is our sole source of knowledge, freedom, and peace as well as the sole means by which self-realization and benevolence are possible. If the principal reasons for the worth of society derive from its role in the genesis of other values (knowledge, freedom, peace) and its status as a means by which self-realization and benevolence are actualized, society is clearly to be valued primarily as a means rather than an end.

The rule-utilitarian theory contained in several works written around the turn of the century is suggestive, but finally unacceptable. In addition to the difficulties raised by claiming that social solidarity is the sole intrinsic good to be served by rules, several decisive objections to rule-utilitarianism as a type of normative theory have been advanced by contemporary ethicians.[89] The most important is that some rules, like justice and promise-keeping, are constitutive rather than consequential. In other words, some rules are right in themselves, not merely because of their utility. The following line of argument clearly indicates why it is necessary to hold out for constitutive principles other than utility.

Suppose we have two rules, R1 and R2, which cannot both be made a part of our morality. Suppose further that in the case of each rule we know the results of everyone's always acting in appropriate situations on that rule (in practice, of course, there would be great difficulties in knowing this) and that when we compute, as best we can, the values of those results, we find that the score is even—in both cases we obtain the same balance of good over evil in the long run for the universe as a whole. Then, the rule-utilitarian must say that R1 and R2 will serve equally well as principles of right and wrong and there is no basis for choosing between them. But it still may be that they distribute the amount of good realized in different ways: acting on R1 may give all of the good to a relatively small group of people without any merit on their part (to let merit count at this point is already to give up utilitarianism), while acting on R2 may spread the good more equally over a larger part of the population. In this case, it seems to me that we must and would say that R1 is an unjust rule and that R2 is morally preferable.[90]

88. See Raymond Aron, *Main Currents in Sociological Thought*, II, 93.
89. See William K. Frankena, *Ethics*, Foundations of Philosophy Series (Englewood Cliffs, N.J.: Prentice Hall, 1963), pp. 32-35; Lyons, *Forms and Limits of Utilitarianism*, pp. 161-197.
90. Frankena, *Ethics*, p. 33.

If it makes perfectly good sense to speak in this manner of justice overruling utility, "then the criterion for determining the rules of morality is not merely utility but also justice."[91] Consequently, rule-utilitarianism cannot be accepted as a sufficient normative theory.

Another difficulty with Durkheim's rule-utilitarianism is raised by his assumption that the social forces that produce rules and institutions virtually guarantee that these are the most desirable ones for the society in question. A "hidden order" is presumed to operate in the development of rules and institutions that generally assures that the status quo, or some future version of it, is, ethically, the most desirable arrangement. It is incorrect to assume, however, that it is usually better for generally accepted moral beliefs to be followed than less generally accepted convictions.[92] Durkheim, to be sure, attempts to extricate himself from the conservative implications of this position by arguing that disobedience to conventional opinion is justified if it either promotes solidarity or the society that is coming into being. It is simply not true, however, that all ethically justified forms of disobedience take one of these two forms. Some forms of disobedience necessarily lead to disruption rather than greater solidarity; others are based upon the conviction that alternative future possibilities should be chosen other than those implied by the most powerful social forces operating in the present. The major forces driving a society may, after all, be sufficiently corrupt to justify a thoroughgoing cultural and structural revolution.

The arguments educed by the mature Durkheim in favor of ethical relativism—the belief that conflicting moral opinions are equally valid—are also untenable. The principal reason offered in support of ethical relativism is that value judgments are valid if and only if they correctly represent changing collective ideals. The problem with this argument lies with the underlying assumption that the statement "x is right or good" means "x is approved by my society." These statements, however, are not synonymous, for it is one thing to say that murder is disapproved by my society, but it is quite a different thing to assert that murder is wrong for reasons that rational men will accept. As Sir David Ross notes in criticizing Durkheim on this point,

---

91. *Ibid.* Durkheim himself unwittingly acknowledges this conclusion in those passages in which he appeals to promise-keeping and justice as if these principles were independent of the utilitarian criterion. See *Division du travail,* 2nd ed., pp. xxxiii-iv, and *Germany above All,* p. 7.

92. For a succinct refutation of the assumption that hidden factors virtually assure that the status quo is the ethically most desirable arrangement for a society, see Brandt, *Ethical Theories,* pp. 60-61.

"right" does not mean "ordained by any given society." And it may be doubted whether even primitive men thought that it did. Their thoughts about what in particular was right were to a large extent limited by the customs and sanctions of their race and age. But this is not the same as to say that they thought that "right" just meant "what my race and age ordains." Moral progress has been possible just because there have been men in all ages who have seen the difference and have practiced, or at least, preached a morality in some respects higher than that of their race and age. And even the supporters of the lower morality held, we may suspect, that their laws and customs were in accordance with a "right" other than themselves. "It is the custom" has been accompanied by "the custom is right," or "the custom is ordained by some one who has the right to command."[93]

Durkheim's principal justification of ethical relativism must, therefore, be dismissed as unacceptable.

Once these critical points have been acknowledged, however, it must also be said that Durkheim was a far more sophisticated ethician than his sociological interpreters have previously acknowledged. Whatever the limitations of his metaethical and normative theories, his views were as, if not more, advanced than those of his contemporaries. It is thus quite unfair to dismiss Durkheim's lifelong quest for an adequate ethical theory as "misguided" and "curious, a question for the sociology of knowledge."[94] What should interest the sociologist of knowledge is not why Durkheim was interested in ethical issues, but why his beliefs have been so burlesqued and camouflaged that it is difficult to understand how a scholar trained in classical philosophy could ever have believed in them or excited the sympathetic interest of similarly trained students.

93. Ross, *Right and the Good,* p. 12.
94. Richter, "Durkheim's Politics and Political Theory," in *Emile Durkheim,* ed. Wolff, p. 171.

VII

Retrospective Analysis

In developing the various themes of this study, the classical problems of moral philosophy have been used as a means of gaining access to Durkheim's thought and also as a touchstone for evaluating his contributions to scholarship. At the same time it has been argued that the traditional issues of moral philosophy stimulated many of Durkheim's sociological studies. Central to this discussion has been the claim that Durkheim's sociological discoveries were a by-product of his concern with moral issues.

This thesis may be stated in a slightly different form by referring to Durkheim's definition of "scientific philosophy."[1] For Durkheim, the task of philosophy was to reflect upon both the fundamental premises of the sciences and the new materials offered for philosophical speculation by empirical research. Philosophy and science were thus closely joined in his mind and work. Like other eminent scientists before him, he philosophized about science and submitted philosophical problems to scientific scrutiny. Hence, his treatment of the classical questions of moral philosophy was at once a philosophical and scientific enterprise.

The time has now come to return to the question posed in the introduction: What is the lasting significance and value of Durkheim's moral philosophy? Should his work in this area be summarily dismissed as merely the rather quaint means by which he launched contemporary sociology, an issue of interest primarily to the historian and the sociologist of knowledge, or does this work deserve to be seriously considered for insights vis-à-vis still current issues? Arguing that Durkheim's moral philosophy contains still valid elements requires an analysis of several fundamental aspects of his work from the standpoint of contemporary philosophy and social science, indicating at the same time where Durkheim's legacy endures today.

1. Durkheim defines "scientific philosophy" in "Philosophie dans les universités allemandes," pp. 332-333, and in "Enseignement philosophique et l'agrégation de philosophie," pp. 121-147, esp. p. 131. Both articles contain clear statements to the effect that scientific philosophy is compatible with metaphysics.

No aspect of Durkheim's thought is more important than philosophical naturalism. It is the basis of his attempt to explain moral experience, the root of his theory of society as a reality with a structure and a character of its own, the foundation of his doctrine of moral development, and the metaethical basis of his normative theories. Hence, the credibility of his most characteristic assertions depends in large part upon the plausibility of naturalistic perspectives on these issues.

That Durkheim's naturalistic approach to moral and religious experience has been confirmed by the mainstream of twentieth-century philosophy and science can scarcely be gainsaid. In marked contrast to the hostility that greeted Durkheim's utilization of this approach during his thesis defense of *The Division of Labor*,[2] twentieth-century scholarship has been overwhelmingly naturalistic in its basic approach to moral phenomena. In the writings of John Dewey and G. H. Mead, to mention only two influencial twentieth-century philosophers, naturalistic interpretations of morality received profound legitimation. As the human sciences gained recognition and stature, it no longer became necessary to engage in the noisy battles and polemical refutations of the nineteenth century in defense of the naturalistic, and, hence, scientific study of human experience. This widespread acceptance of naturalistic interpretations of morality has been largely due to the success, however limited, of those seminal scholars around the turn of the century, who, like Durkheim, demonstrated that the human sciences could provide insight into man's moral nature. In this respect, Durkheim's early prediction that naturalism would be confirmed not by philosophical argumentation but by the success of the human sciences has been impressively confirmed.

The phenomenal success of naturalism has also been assisted by the emergence of the new form of naturalism described at the outset of this study as neonaturalism. Unlike crude forms of materialism and biologism, proponents of neonaturalism have attempted to do justice to the richness of phenomenological experience while eschewing simplistic forms of reductionism. On this fresh philosophical ground, the insights of idealists and other phenomenologists of the inner life have been joined with the basic tenets of science. Durkheim clearly advanced

---

2. Marcel Mauss ("Introduction," *Socialisme,* pp. vii-viii) and Célestin Bouglé ("Quelques Souvenirs," in Bouglé *et al.,* "Oeuvre sociologique d'Emile Durkheim," p. 281) state that Durkheim's scientific treatment of morality in the *Division of Labor* enraged the "touchy moralists," like Paul Janet, on his thesis committee. "As a result of conflicts of this kind," Mauss observes, "he was excluded from professorships in Paris."

widespread adoption of this innovative naturalistic perspective through his now classic sociological studies.

Durkheim himself, to be sure, eventually fell victim to reductionism in the new sociological form. As his career progressed, he increasingly argued not only that society is the sole source of all higher mental processes (moral, religious, even intellectual), but that the unconscious referent of moral and religious beliefs is social. Fortunately, these claims are now largely outmoded, at least among leading social scientists. It is now widely recognized that moral, religious, and rational experiences are simply too complex to be attributed either to a single cause or to exclusively psychological or sociological causal factors. Also, the fundamental distinction between the cause of a phenomenon and its validity has impressed most prominent scholars. In refuting the genetic fallacy of confusing the origin of a belief with its validity, Gordon Allport has written a particularly eloquent critique of psychological reductionism that applies to all similar efforts.

Were we to gauge our evaluations by origins we would disparage the eloquence of Demosthenes because his oratory served as a compensation for his tendency to stammer. We would depreciate Schumann's music because it may have been touched by his psychosis. The rationalism of Kant's philosophy would be invalid because it represented at the outset his protest against the hypochondria induced by his sunken chest. Longfellow's benignant outlook on life would be discredited since it served to rationalize his comfortable Victorian existence. Quakerism with its inner voice of guidance would be worthless because the founder of Quakerism, George Fox, suffered severe hallucinations. St. Paul's vision on the road to Damascus would have no significance because it may have been epileptoid in character. And the fact that many psychologists take up their science because of personal maladjustments would make psychology worthless.[3]

This distinction between knowing the causal factors influencing beliefs and knowing whether they are correct does not mean, Allport to the contrary, that causal theories have no relevance vis-à-vis their verification. Causal theories may occasionally undermine a justificatory argument, but unless explanatory theories demonstrate that the causal factors involved represent genuine instances of knowing, they cannot establish validity.[4]

3. Gordon Allport, *The Individual and His Religion* (New York: Macmillan Company, 1950), pp. 109-110.
4. Causal theories can be used to undermine either a particular belief or a justificatory argument. With respect to invalidating a particular belief, Sir David Ross observes: "if any one can show that A holds actions of type B to be wrong

Durkheim's own reductionistic tendencies to the contrary, there is an aspect of his sociological interpretation of morality and religion which is at variance with his own manifest intentions. This countercurrent to reductionism is implicit in his use of rich symbols, like God and the sacred, to convey what he means by society. When meaningful symbols like these are found to be necessary to describe the underlying phenomena responsible for the genesis of other symbols and beliefs, it is implicitly being confessed that scientific language cannot adequately convey the meaning intended by the word "society." Hence, the use of the language of poetry and religion. If religious language is necessary to convey the meaning of society, however, it appears that the symbols of religion have their own integrity and meaning which cannot be conveyed in any other way. An admission of this sort, however, really sounds the death knell of reductionism.

The question of reductionism aside, Durkheim not only promoted a new form of naturalism, but he began the task of describing and explaining moral facts that has subsequently been pursued by scientists in various fields of study. In psychology, sociology, and anthropology, many of Durkheim's basic insights and hypotheses have been subsequently confirmed. This is especially true of his description of morality and some of his leading explanatory hypotheses, although neither his descriptive nor his explanatory work is as sophisticated as that currently being undertaken within social psychology. But, then, Durkheim never expected the science of morality to terminate with his initial endeavors. As he confessed several years before his death, "it cannot be said at present how far these explanations are capable of being extended, and whether or not they are of a nature to resolve all the problems. But is is equally impossible to mark in advance a limit beyond which they can go. What must be done is to try the hypothesis and submit it as methodically as possible to the control of facts. That is

---

simply because (for instance) he knows such actions to be forbidden by the society he lives in, he shows that *A* has no real reason for believing that such actions have the specific quality of wrongness, since between being forbidden by the community and being wrong there is no necessary connexion. He does not, indeed, show the belief to be untrue, but he shows that *A* has no sufficient reason for holding it true; and in this sense he undermines its validity." (Ross, *Right and the Good,* p. 14.) Causal theories can also undermine the plausibility of justificatory arguments in favor of metaethical theories like intuitionism. As Richard Brandt notes in this context, "it is awkward to say that ethical insight into what is fitting in particular situations is somehow an 'intuitive apprehension of an objective fact,' and at the same time to admit that some psychologists are right in supposing that one's particular 'insights' derive from the values of one's father and are a result of 'identification' with him (and would have been quite different if one's father's values had happened to be different)." (Brandt, *Ethical Theory,* p. 115.)

what we have attempted to do."[5] In retrospect, Durkheim's fundamental "hypothesis" that sociology could clarify the nature and genesis
of morality has been eminently substantiated.

Turning from Durkheim's naturalistic interpretation of morality to
his concept of nature, it is retrospectively apparent that his basic
assumptions in this area are also in the vanguard of twentieth-century
philosophy. For Durkheim, as for most contemporary philosophers,
nature is neither permeated by mind as in ancient Greek philosophy nor
organized like a machine as in Renaissance cosmology.[6] Nature is,
rather, an ever-changing process which continually engenders higher
orders or systems of increasing complexity. Each emergent system is a
reality *sui generis*, which can neither be reduced to nor explained by
the less complex phenomena out of which it emerged. In an early
explication of this fundamental thesis of the doctrine subsequently
referred to as emergent evolution, Durkheim declares:

It is quite certain that there are only molecules of raw matter in the
living cell. But they are associated and this association is the cause of
those new phenomena which characterize life, the germ of which cannot possibly be found in any of the associated elements. A whole is not
identical with the sum of its parts. It is something new, and its properties differ from those of its component parts. Association is not, as has
sometimes been believed, an unproductive phenomenon, consisting
merely in bringing into external relation established facts and constituted properties. On the contrary, it is the source of all the innovations
which have occurred successively in the course of the general evolution
of things. What difference is there between the lower organisms and
others, between organized living things and simple protoplasm, between
the latter and the inorganic molecules that compose it, if not different
forms of association? In the last analysis, all these beings may be reduced to elements of the same kind, but these elements are here juxta-
posed, there associated, here associated in one way, there in another.[7]

In short, biological life has emerged out of matter, psychological
occurrences out of life, and society out of psychological interaction.

This fundamental concept of nature as a process of emergent evolution, R. W. Collingwood convincingly argues in *The Idea of Nature*,
represents the culmination of the new view of nature that began to
appear in eighteenth-century historicism and nineteenth-century biology, but it did not gain philosophical exposition until the late nine-

5. Durkheim, *Formes élémentaires*, p. 638.
6. For a discussion of Greek, Renaissance, and modern concepts of nature, see
Collingwood, *Idea of Nature*.
7. Durkheim, *Règles*, pp. 126-127.

teenth century. In comparison with the amateurish attempts of other nineteenth-century scholars, like Spencer, to explicate this modern concept of nature, Durkheim's position represents one of the more articulate expositions of his era. Since the turn of the century, this modern concept of nature has been systematically developed far beyond anything Durkheim attempted in the process philosophies of Alexander, Whitehead, and Hartshorne. Yet, it is noteworthy that Durkheim's basic idea of nature represents an early formulation of this significant movement within twentieth-century philosophy.

Durkheim presents a somewhat unique form of emergent evolution insofar as he argues in favor of society as the most complex entity in the emerging cosmos. There are really two fundamental ideas at the heart of this claim, which may be distinguished by the terms "complexity" and "equilibrium." "Complexity" refers to Durkheim's characteristic assertion that a society is the most powerful compound of physical and moral forces in nature, the richest combination of diverse materials, and the highest form of intellectual and moral life. For the reasons stated in the conclusion of the third chapter, this doctrine of social realism is unacceptable partly because it rests upon a faulty rationale but largely because it isolates psychosocial phenomena that are not existentially separable. Yet, once this has been said, it must also be conceded that, as so often happens in intellectual history, Durkheim won a recognized place for the social sciences, as well as recognition of the structural and cultural aspects of society, by virtue of his exaggerated claims. Just as historically successful political movements have had to overestimate the importance of their aims in order to gain public recognition, so, too, cultural heroes have often had to inflate the value of their insights in order to make an impact upon intellectual history. From this perspective, Durkheim's social realism stands beside Darwin's survival of the fittest, Marx's class conflict, and Freud's unconscious as a heuristically valuable concept that revealed hitherto neglected aspects of existence, albeit in terms that subsequently required considerable modification.

The "equilibrium" aspect of Durkheim's concept of society as an emergent reality refers to his underlying assumption that a society, like every lower form of organization, is an equilibrium system. His fundamental image of society is that of a network of interactions among component "forces limiting and constraining each other and forming an equilibrium."[8] The source of this image is the biological concept of the

8. Durkheim, *Formes élémentaires*, p. 291.

organic system, a derivation which Durkheim explicitly acknowledges in his lecture of 1887 on structural functional analysis.[9] Contrary to some of his critics, Durkheim's structural functionalism does not deny the existence of conflicts and tensions within society. In *The Division of Labor, Leçons de sociologie,* and *L'Evolution pédagogique en France,* Durkheim explicitly acknowledges both the existence and the functional value of moderate competition and interinstitutional tension.[10] But Durkheim's structural functionalism, like other variants of this contemporary social theory, stresses order, stability, and equilibrium at the expense of conflict. Consequently, the existence of conflict, along with its value for the social system as a whole and for the realization of ethically desirable goals, is unjustifiably muted. Contemporary conflict theorists are thus quite correct in arguing that the merits of structural functionalism need to be supplemented by a strong dose of Marx.

Closely related to Durkheim's concept of society as an emergent system of nature is his concept of social evolution. For Durkheim, social evolution is a process of increasing differentiation and complexity of social organization. This process of differentiation includes the formation of secondary groups in society, each of which develops its own system of morality. Historical and cross-cultural moral diversity is a product of the evolutionary stage of the society as a whole as well as the stages achieved by the secondary groups within society. In critically evaluating this evolutionary interpretation in the conclusion of the fourth chapter, it was suggested that Durkheim's historical framework was governed in part by his desire to mediate between conservative organic social theories on the one hand and the natural rights tradition on the other. By relating the emergence of the cult of man and the rights associated with it to social differentiation, Durkheim attempted to root the rights of man in a metaphysics of history. When this theme is related to the other aspects of Durkheim's moral philosophy analyzed in this study, his affinity with the great tradition of

9. See Durkheim, *Cours de science social,* pp. 43-44. The young Durkheim criticized the extensive use of biological concepts and theories by nineteenth-century sociologists, like Lilienfeld and Spencer, but he also argued that biology presented sociologists with heuristically valuable conceptual tools.

10. In *Division du travail* (p. 409), Durkheim observes that "it is neither necessary nor even possible for social life to be without conflicts. The role of solidarity is not to suppress competition, but to moderate it." In *Professional Ethics and Civic Morals* (p. 93), Durkheim emphasizes the historical importance of interinstitutional conflicts in the emergence of individual liberties. "It is out of this conflict of social forces," he writes, "that individual liberties are born." In *Evolution pédagogique en France,* I (47-48), Durkheim refers to the eufunctional consequences of intellectual conflicts.

natural law and natural right is even closer than this initial observation suggests.

Despite his sharp critique of natural law assumptions about the nature of man and society, Durkheim accepted the classical natural law belief that uniformities exist among the diversity of moral phenomena. In this spirit, he began his career by arguing in favor of innate sympathetic instincts. At the same time, he initiated his lifelong search for an inclusive definition of morality that would do justice to the essential nature of the diverse phenomena in question. During this early period, Durkheim also adopted the traditional ethical doctrine of natural law theorists that moral concepts are right if approved by the conscience of mankind. In scattered places throughout his early writings, he repeatedly employs universal approbation in defense of normative principles like benevolence, health, patriotism, and social solidarity.

As Durkheim's study of morality progressed, this search for uniformities increasingly took the form of describing the formal characteristics of moral obligation and valuation. Apparently, his historical studies convinced him that most moral standards systematically vary from society to society. Yet, he continued to maintain that there are culturally universal forms of moral experience underlying this variation in moral content. This eventually led Durkheim to argue, in *Moral Education,* that the essential form of morality is culturally invariant because social authority and solidarity are ubiquitous. This claim underlies his pedagogical assumption that moral education invariably involves formation of a sense of obligation and a sense of attachment to social groups. Even during the middle part of his career, however, Durkheim continued to maintain that moral solidarity and the common good are universally recognized values. Indeed, as late as his wartime pamphlets, he continued to utilize a form of rule-utilitarianism involving the justification of rules in terms of their promotion of universally approved social solidarity and well-being.

Though Durkheim was eventually seduced by ethical relativism, his final relativism is modified by the uniformities contained within his theory of social evolution. The ethical relativist thesis that "x is valid if and only if it is approved by society" is qualified by the evolutionary thesis, based upon the research that went into his lectures on the history of various groups, that societies do not arbitrarily create fundamental moral rules and ideals. The only moral standards compatible with the fundamental conditions of modern social existence are those that respect the sanctity of man and promote universal well-being. In fact, this respect for the human person is pushed back to the beginning of time in *The Elementary Forms of the Religious Life*, where the sacredness of man is said to be recognized wherever men exist in societies.[11] Even the notion of international solidarity is found in germinal form in the relationships that primitive peoples sustain with other societies:

There are neither people nor states which are not involved with another society, more or less unlimited, which includes all the people and states with which the first are directly or indirectly in relationship. All forms of national life are dominated by a collective life of an international nature. In proportion as we advance in history, these international groups become more important and extensive.[12]

In other words, Durkheim's final ethical relativism is joined with invariant moral beliefs vis-à-vis the sacredness of man, human rights, and international solidarity.

Today, Durkheim's evolutionary theory appears overly simplified in light of subsequent research. Yet, his search for constancies amidst the flux of moral phenomena and ethical opinion is very much alive in the social sciences and psychology. In the social sciences, Linton, Kluckhohn, and others have attempted to find universally approved moral standards and practices. In psychology, the search for cross-cultural similarities in moral judgment continues, especially within the Piagetian tradition. The partial results of the latter quest indicate that there are various modes of moral judgment rather than the single mode described by Durkheim.[13] Yet, his description of moral obligations, in terms of obedience to socially sanctioned, order-maintaining rules, is generally recognized as an extremely common mode of moral judgment among adults in various societies.

Durkheim's search for a naturalistic ethical theory is also alive and well in philosophical ethics; indeed, ethical naturalism is rapidly becoming, if it has not already become, the dominant metaethical option. As previously stated, a naturalistic metaethical theory holds that ethical statements are cognitive judgments that can be confirmed by observation and inductive reasoning of the sort used to confirm scientific statements.[14] This central claim distinguishes naturalism from the other two major metaethical options, namely, nonnaturalism and noncognitivism.

11. Durkheim, *Formes élémentaires*, pp. 189-190, n2, 325.
12. *Ibid.*, p. 609.
13. See Kohlberg, "From Is to Ought."
14. For a careful refutation of the popular belief that metaethical naturalism rests upon a logical fallacy, see William K. Frankena, "The Naturalistic Fallacy," *Mind,*XLVIII (1939), 464-477.

Naturalistic theories agree with the nonnaturalistic argument that ethical statements are true or false, but they contest the central nonnaturalistic contention that ethical terms refer to nonnatural, indefinable properties perceived as self-evident or apprehended through intuition. In rejecting this claim, naturalists observe that intuitionism is difficult to square with psychosocial interpretations of moral experience. Naturalists also note, in critizing nonnaturalism, that intuitionists have generally failed to convincingly demonstrate how veridical intuitions are to be distinguished from pseudointuitions. Naturalistic theories also contest the noncognitive or emotivist thesis that ethical statements are neither true nor false, but, rather, expressions of feelings, attitudes, recommendations, prescriptions, and the like. In challenging noncognitivist theories, naturalists observe that emotivists, like Stevenson and Hare, have failed to explain why people think ethical judgments are true or false and refer to facts in explaining their ethical positions.[15]

While a thorough analysis of twentieth-century metaethical naturalism would require a lengthy monograph, Roderick Firth's recent reformulation of earlier naturalistic theories is worth mentioning in the present context because it represents a plausible modern alternative to Durkheim's early doctrine of universal approbation. According to Firth, "x is right" means "if anyone were, with respect to x, fully informed and vividly imaginative, impartial, dispassionate, consistent, and otherwise normal, he would be disposed to approve of x."[16] Ethical statements are justified, the theory states, if the decision maker is "fully informed and vividly aware" of all relevant nonethical facts, "impartial" with respect to the special interests of the particular individuals and groups involved, "dispassionate" in the sense of being relatively free of such distracting emotional states as jealousy, fear, and hatred, "consistent," and "normal," that is to say, beyond childhood, mentally healthy, and so forth. Like all naturalistic theories, Firth's definition assumes that the truth of ethical statements can be tested by observation of the sort explicated by the conditions set forth by the theory. The theory is absolutist since it holds that ethical statements are true or false without special reference to the individuals or groups who happen to express them.

Superficially, Firth's theory seems far removed from Durkheim's

15. For further discussion and critical evaluation of metaethical naturalism, nonnaturalism, and noncognitivism, see Brandt, *Ethical Theory*, chs. vii-x; Frankena, *Ethics*, ch. vi.

16. Roderick Firth, "Ethical Absolutism and the Ideal Observer," *Philosophy and Phenomenological Research*, XII (1952), 317-345. For a critical evaluation of Firth's theory, see Brandt, *Ethical Theory*, pp. 173-176.

early universal approbative test, but close inspection of the latter test indicates that this is not the case. Wundt, from whom Durkheim initially borrowed this early metaethical theory, defined universal consent in terms of what every "normal conscience," under sufficient conditions of "enlightenment," recognizes as morally valid. Apparently, "normal conscience" and "enlightenment" in this definition describe characteristics further specified by Firth. Although Durkheim is somewhat equivocal about the precise meaning of universal consent, he nevertheless implies that moral opinions held over time are a product of vast experience, rational deliberation, and impartiality. These factors more or less assure the validity of widely held beliefs. Accordingly, Durkheim writes that "an author must have great faith in the strength of his logic to venture . . . a revolt, in the name of a system, against the moral conscience of humanity."[17] As in the case of Wundt, the young Durkheim appears to have attributed some of the characteristics to the moral conscience of humanity that Firth includes among the optimal criteria for correct moral decision making.

In a similar vein, the mature Durkheim attempts to support his final social approbation theory by attributing to society qualities that virtually guarantee that collective beliefs are correct. The collective conscience is increasingly endowed by Durkheim with a superior wisdom and impartiality surpassing that of any single individual, precisely because qualities of this sort are necessary in order to argue that collective moral beliefs are generally valid. The obvious problem with this line of reasoning is that collective beliefs frequently fail to exhibit either these characteristics or those specified by Firth. Some collective beliefs, like racism, are, in fact, patently immoral. Hence, Durkheim's final ethical position is now widely discredited.

On balance, Durkheim's naturalistic moral philosophy contains a mixture of tenable and untenable elements, plausible and implausible arguments. On the positive side, Durkheim succeeded in formulating a new form of naturalism involving respect for the phenomenological facts of moral experience, recognition of social conditioning in the genesis of morality, appreciation of the functional role of moral standards in achieving social consensus, and acknowledgment of both cross-cultural moral diversity and similarity. Many of his basic philosophical assumptions have become part of twentieth-century philosophy and science; more than a few of his empirical insights and theoretical hypotheses are now widely accepted. With respect to these achievements, at least,

17. Durkheim, *Suicide*, p. 332.

Durkheim's contributions to moral philosophy must be ranked as seminal, even though these achievements are combined with unwarranted assumptions vis-à-vis social realism, sociological reductionism, and ethical relativism.

From another standpoint, Durkheim's naturalistic moral philosophy represents a crucial transitional stage in the history of moral philosophy. Like Plato, Aquinas, and Kant, Durkheim attempted to treat all the great issues in a comprehensive and systematic way. At the same time, by formulating a naturalistic philosophy calling for specialized scientific investigation of specific issues, Durkheim helped inaugurate the new era that has emerged since his death, an era during which the interrelated issues of moral philosophy have been divided among several different disciplines. The irony of Durkheim's role in history is that he unwittingly destroyed the integrity of moral philosophy by thus assisting in its fragmentation.

Despite the fragmentation of moral philosophy in the twentieth century, several recent developments suggest that a new naturalistic philosophy—similar in some respect to, but different from, Durkheim's work in this area—may be emerging from specialized studies in several different contemporary disciplines. Recent cross-cultural studies indicate that many basic moral principles are recognized in all cultures.[18] By rendering implausible the cultural relativist claim that basic moral principles systematically vary from society to society, these findings call into question the principal argument against metaethical theories, namely, that moral variation is so great that there is, in principle, no objectively valid way of rationally justifying ethical standards to everyone's satisfaction. And, several studies of moral discourse in various cultures indicate that adult moral judgments are cognitive evaluations rather then emotional reactions.[19] These findings tend to weaken the plausibility of the emotivist thesis that ethical judgments can be exhaustively characterized by reference to subjective feelings, emotions, and the like. At the same time, studies of moral cognition further weaken the intuitionist interpretation of morality by explaining the formation of moral judgment as a natural process. Scientific results like these clearly do not establish the validity of any metaethical proposals, but they tend to support the metaethical naturalist claim that ethical statements are based upon cognitive judgments. Since an adequate metaethical theory of what moral judgment ought to be must be compatible

18. For a summary of recent research on universal moral principles, see Kohlberg, "From Is to Ought."
19. *Ibid.*

with scientific accounts of what it is, these results further strengthen the already strong hand of metaethical naturalists. A fully adequate naturalistic metaethical theory has yet to be formulated, but recent proposals of Firth, Brandt, and Rawls constitute important steps in this direction.[20] Thus, Durkheim's lifelong quest for a naturalistic moral philosophy is being vigorously pursued today. Recent developments indicate that his dream may be realized in the final quarter of the twentieth century by the convergence of contemporary trends within both the human sciences and philosophy.

20. See Firth, "Ethical Absolutism and the Ideal Observer;" Brandt, *Ethical Theory*, ch. x; John Rawls, "Justice as Fairness," *Philosophical Review*, LXVII (1958), 164-194; John Rawls, *A Theory of Justice* (Cambridge, Mass.: Harvard University Press, 1971).

Bibliography

The Works of Emile Durkheim
(lectures published posthumously are listed by the year
in which they were first completed)

1883 "Discours aux Lycéens de Sens." *Cahiers internationaux de sociologie,* XLIII (1967), 25-32. An address delivered at the end of Durkheim's first year at the Lycée de Sens.

1885 "Schaeffle, A., *Bau und Leben des Sozialem Körpers: Erster Band."* *RP,* XIX, 84-101.
"Fouillée, A., *La Propriété sociale et la démocratie. RP,* XIX, 446-453.
"Gumplowicz, Ludwig, *Grundriss der Sociologie."* *RP,* XX, 627-634.

1886 "Les Études de science sociale." *RP,* XXII, 61-80.
"DeGreef, Guillaume, *Introduction à la sociologie."* *RP,* XXII, 658-663.

1887 "La Philosophie dans les universités allemandes." *RIE,* XIII, 313-338, 423-440.
"Guyau, M., *L'Irréligion de l'avenir."* *RP,* XXIII, 299-311.
"La Science positive de la morale en Allemagne." *RP,* XXIV, 33-58, 113-142, 275-284.

1888 "Cours de science sociale: Leçon d'ouverture." *RIE,* XV, 23-48.
"Le Programme économique de M. Schäffle." *Revue d'économie politique,* II, 3-7.
"Introduction à la sociologie de la famille." *Annales de la faculté des lettres de Bordeaux,* pp. 257-281.
"Suicide et natalité: Etude de statistique morale." *RP,* XXVI, 446-463.

1889 "Lutoslawski, W., *Erhaltung und Untergang des Staatsverfassungen nach Plato, Aristoteles und Machiavelli."* *RP,* XXVIII, 317-319.
"Tönnies, F., *Gemeinschaft und Gesellschaft."* *RP,* XXVII, 416-422.

1890 "Les Principes de 1789 et la sociologie." *RIE,* XIX, 450-456.

1892 *Quid Secundatus politicae scientiae instituendae contulerit.* Bordeaux: Gounouilhou. "Montesquieu's Contribution to the Rise of Social Science," in *Montesquieu and Rousseau: Forerunners of Sociology.* Translated by Ralph Manheim. Ann Arbor, Mich.: University of Michigan Press, 1960.

195

"La Famille conjugale: Conclusion du cours sur la famille." *RP*, XCI (1921), 1-14. The last of seventeen lectures on the family given by Durkheim at the University of Bordeaux in 1892.

1893   "Richard, Gaston, *Essai sur l'origine de l'idée de droit*." *RP*, XXXV, 290-296.

De la division du travail social: Etude sur l'organisation des sociétés supérieures. Paris: Félix Alcan. *The Division of Labor in Society*. Translated by George Simpson. New York: Macmillan Company, 1933.

"Note sur la définition du socialisme." *RP*, XXXVI, 506-512.

1895   *Les Règles de la méthode sociologique*. Paris: Félix Alcan. *The Rules of the Sociological Method*. Translated by Sarah A. Solovay and John H. Mueller, edited by George E. G. Catlin. Chicago: University of Chicago Press, 1938.

"L'Enseignement philosophique et l'agrégation de philosophie." *RP*, XXXIX, 121-147.

"Crime et santé sociale." *RP*, XXXIX, 518-523.

"L'Origine du mariage dans l'espèce humaine, d'après Westermarck." *RP*, XL, 606-623.

1896   *Le Socialisme: Sa définition, ses débuts, la doctrine Saint-Simonienne*. Edited by M. Mauss. Paris: Félix Alcan, 1928. A course of lectures delivered at the University of Bordeaux during the academic year 1895-1896. *Socialism and Saint-Simon*. Translated by Charlotte Sattler, edited and with an introduction by Alvin W. Gouldner. Yellow Springs, Ohio: Antioch Press, 1958.

1897   *Le Suicide: Etude de sociologie*. Paris: Félix Alcan. *Suicide: A Study in Sociology*. Translated by John A. Spaulding and George Simpson, edited and with an introduction by George Simpson. Glencoe, Ill.: Free Press, 1951.

"Richard, Gaston, *Le Socialisme et la science sociale*." *RP*, XLIV, 200-205.

"Labriola, Antonio, "Essais sur la conception matérialiste de l'histoire." *RP*, XLIV, 645-651.

"Preface." *AS*, I, i-vii.

"La Prohibition de l'inceste et ses origines." *AS*, I, 1-70.

Book reviews on the family, marriage, punishment, social organization, etc. *AS*, I, *passim*.

1898   "Représentations individuelles et représentations collectives." RMM, VI, 273-302. "Individual and Collective Representations," in *Sociology and Philosophy*. Translated by D. F. Pocock. London: Cohen and West, Ltd., 1953.

"L'Individualisme et les intellectuels." *RB*, Series 4, X, 7-13.

"Préface." *AS*, II, i-vi.

"De la définition des phénomènes religieux." *AS*, II, 1-28.

"Note sur la morphologie sociale." *AS*, II, 520-521.

Book reviews on cults, mores, family, sexual morality, marriage, property rights, penal law, etc. *AS*, II, *passim*.

1899 "Enquête sur la guerre et le militarisme." *L'Humanité nouvelle*, numéro sup-militarisme, 50-52.

Book reviews on social organization, family, marriage, contracts, etc. *AS*, III, *passim*.

1900 *Leçons de sociologie: Physique des moeurs et du droit.* Foreward by H. Nail Kubali, introduction by Georges Davy. "Publications de l'Université, Faculté de Droit," No. 111. Istanbul: l'Université d'Istanbul, 1950; Paris: Presses Universitaires de France, 1950. *Professional Ethics and Civic Morals.* Translated by Cornelia Brookfield. London: Routledge and Kegan Paul, 1957. The final draft (November 1898 to June 1900) of a course of lectures given by Durkheim between 1890 and 1900 at Bordeaux and repeated at the Sorbonne in 1904 and again in 1912.

"La Sociologie en France au XIXe siècle." *RB*, Series 4, XIII, 609-613, 647-652.

"Deux lois de l'évolution pénale." *AS*, IV, 65-95.

"Introduction à la section de sociologie criminelle et statistique morale." *AS*, IV, 433-436.

Book reviews on the mentality of groups, social, political and domestic organization, law of property, etc. *AS*, IV, passim.

1901 "Le Contrat social de Rousseau." *RMM*, XXV (1918), 1-23, 129-161. A lecture presented at the University of Bordeaux around 1901 and published posthumously by Xavier Leon.

"Rousseau's Social Contract," in *Montesquieu and Rousseau: Forerunners of Sociology.* Translated by Ralph Manheim. Ann Arbor: University of Michigan Press, 1960.

"Sur le totémisme." *AS*, V, 82-123.

Book reviews on the subject matter and method of sociology, social philosophy, juridical and moral sociology, domestic organization, social morphology, etc. *AS*, V, *passim*.

1902 *De la Division du travail social*, 2nd Ed., with a new preface entitled "Quelques remarques sur les groupements professionels. Paris: Félix Alcan.

"Pédagogie et sociologie." *RMM*, XI (1903), 37-54. Reprinted in *Education et sociologie.* Paris: Félix Alcan, 1922. "Pedagogy and sociology," in *Education and Sociology.* Translated, with an introduction, by Sherwood D. Fox. Glencoe, Ill.: Free Press, 1956.

"De quelques formes primitives de classification: Contribution à l'étude des représentations collectives." *AS*, VI, 1-72. With Marcel Mauss. *Primitive Classifications.* Translated, edited, with an introduction by Rodney Needham. Chicago: University of Chicago Press, 1963.

Book reviews on the subject matter and method of sociology, the mentality of groups and collective ethology, social, domestic, and political organization, statistics of domestic and conjugal life, social morphology, etc. *AS*, VI, *passim*.

1903   *L'Education morale.* Paris: Félix Alcan, 1925. *Moral Education.* Translated by Everett K. Wilson and Herman Schnurer, edited with an introduction by Everett K. Wilson. New York: Free Press of Glencoe, Inc., 1961. A course of lectures offered at the Sorbonne in 1902-1903.

      Book reviews on social, domestic, and political organization, general theories of law and ethics, crime and the criminal, social morphology, education, etc. *AS,* VII, *passim.*

1904   "L'Elite intellectuelle et la démocratie." *RB,* Series 5, I, 705-706.

      "Sociologie et sciences sociales." *RP,* LV, 465-497. With Fauconnet.

      "Sur l'organisation matrimoniale des sociétés australiennes." *AS,* VIII, 118-147.

      Book reviews on juridical systems, domestic and political organization, penal law, social morphology, etc. *AS,* VIII, *passim.*

1905   *L'Evolution pédagogique en France,* 2 vols. Paris: Félix Alcan, 1938. A course of lectures delivered at the Sorbonne during the academic year 1904-05.

      "Réponse à une enquête sur la morale sans Dieu." *La Revue,* LIX, 306-308.

      Discussion of "Sur la séparation des eglises et de l'etat." *Libres entretiens,* I, 317-377, 453-508, *passim.*

      "L'Evolution et le rôle de l'enseignement secondaire en France." *RB,* Series 5, V (1906), 70-77. Reprinted in *Education et sociologie.* Paris: Félix Alcan, 1922. "The Evolution and the Role of Secondary Education in France," in *Education and Sociology.* Translated, with an introduction by Sherwood D. Fox. Glencoe, Ill.: Free Press, 1956. The opening lecture for a course organized for the candidates for the *agrégations* in secondary education, and presented in November 1905.

      Book reviews on methodology, social philosophy, group psychology, social, political and domestic organization, law of property, domestic and matrimonial institutions, etc. *AS,* IX, *passim.*

1906   "La Détermination du fait moral." *Bulletin de la société française de philosophie,* VI. Reprinted in *Sociologie et philosophie.* Paris: Félix Alcan, 1924. "The Determination of Moral Facts," in *Sociology and Philosophy.* Translated by D. F. Pocock. London: Cohen and West, Ltd., 1953.

      "Le Divorce par consentement mutuel." *RB,* Series 5, V, 549-554,

      Book reviews on the general conception of sociology, law and ethics, social, political, and domestic organization, juridical and moral systems, etc. *AS,* X, *passim.*

1907   Discussion of "Pacifisme et patriotisme." Séance du 30 décembre 1907, *Bulletin de la société française de philosophie,* VIII (1908), 31-70, *passim.*

1908 Discussion of "La Morale positive: Examen de quelques diffi-
cultés." Séance du 26 mars 1908. *Bulletin de la société française
de philosophie,* VIII, 161-211, *passim.*
Discussion of "L'Inconnu et l'inconscient en histoire." Séance
du 28 mai, 1908. *Bulletin de la société française de philosophie,*
VIII, 217-247, *passim.*
Discussion of "Science et Religion." Séance du 19 nov. 1908.
Bulletin de la société française de philosophie, IX, 19-74, esp.
56-60.

1909 "Note sur la spécialisation des Facultés des Lettres et l'agrégation de philosophie." *RIE,* LVII, 159-161.
"Examen critique des systèmes classiques sur les origines de la
pensée religieuse." *RP,* LXVII, 1-28, 142-162.
"Sociologie religieuse et théorie de la connaissance." *RMM,*
XVII, 733-758.
Discussion of "L'Efficacité des doctrines morales." Séance du
20 mai, 1909. *Bulletin de la société française de philosophie,* IX,
193-231, *passim.*
Discussion of "La Notion d'égalité sociale." Séance du 30
decembre, 1909. *Bulletin de la société française de philosophie,*
X, 53-80, *passim.*
"Préface." *AS,* XI, i-iii.
"Note sur les systèmes religieux des sociétés inférieures." *AS,*
XI, 75-76.
Book reviews on social philosophy, sociological conditions of
knowledge, domestic and matrimonial organization, suicide, etc.
AS, XI, *passim.*

1911 "Jugements de valeur et jugements de réalité." *RMM,* XIX,
437-453. Reprinted in *Sociologie et philosophie.* Paris: Félix
Alcan, 1924. "Value Judgments and Judgments of Reality," in
Sociology and Philosophy. Translated by D. F. Pocock. Lon-
don: Cohen and West, Ltd., 1953.
Discussion of "L'Education sexuelle." Séance du 28 fevrier,
1911. *Bulletin de la société française de philosophie,* XI, 29-52,
passim.
"Education." "Pédagogie." *Nouveau dictionnaire de pédagogie
et d'instruction primaire.* Published under the direction of F.
Buisson. Paris: Hachette. Reprinted in *Education et sociologie.*
Paris: Félix Alcan, 1922. "Education: Its Nature and Its Role"
and "The Nature and Method of Pedagogy," in *Education and
Sociology.* Translated, with an introduction by Sherwood D.
Fox. Glencoe, Ill.: Free Press, 1956.
"Préface." Hamelin, Octave. *Le Système de Descartes.* Paris:
Félix Alcan.

1912 *Les Formes élémentaires de la vie religieuse: Le système
totémique en Australie.* Paris: Félix Alcan. *The Elementary
Forms of the Religious Life.* Translated by Joseph Ward Swain.
London: George Allen and Unwin, 1915.

"Note sur la notion de civilisation." *AS*, XII, 46-50. With Mauss.
"Note sur les systèmes religieux des sociétés inférieures." *AS*, XII, 90-91.
"Note sur les systèmes juridiques." *AS*, XII, 365-366.
Book reviews on methodology, collective psychology, sociological conditions of knowledge, ethics, juridical systems, domestic and matrimonial organization, geographic bases of social life, etc. *AS*, XII, *passim.*

1914 *Pragmatisme et sociologie.* Paris: J. Vrin, 1955. Lectures delivered at the Sorbonne in 1913-1914, and reconstructed from student notes by Armand Cuvillier.
"Le Dualisme de la nature humaine et ses conditions sociales." *Scientia*, XV, 206-221. "The Dualism of Human Nature and Its Social Conditions." Translated by Charles Blend. In *Emile Durkheim, 1858-1917.* Edited by Kurt H. Wolff. Columbus, Ohio: Ohio State University Press, 1960.

1915 "La Sociologie." *La Science française*, Vol. I. Paris: Librairie Larousse.
Qui a voulu la guerre?: Les origines de la guerre d'après les documents diplomatiques. Paris: Armand Colin. With E. Denis. *Who Wanted War? The Origin of the War according to Diplomatic Documents.* Translated by A. M. Wilson-Garinei. Studies and Documents on the War. Paris: Armand Colin.
"L'Allemagne au-dessus de tout": La mentalité allemande et la guerre. Paris: Armand Colin. *"Germany above All": The German Mental Attitude and the War.* Translated by J.S. Studies and Documents on the War. Paris: Armand Colin.

1917 "Introduction à la morale." *RP*, LXXXIX (1920), 79-97. Written between March and September 1917;
"La 'Pédagogie' de Rousseau." *RMM*, XXVI (1919), 153-180.

Reference Works

Aimand, Guy. *Durkheim et la science economique.* Paris: Presses Universitaires de France, 1962.

Alpert, Harry. *Emile Durkheim and His Sociology.* New York: Columbia University Press, 1939.

————— "Emile Durkheim and Sociologismic Psychology." *American Journal of Sociology*, XLV (1939), 64-70.

————— "Emile Durkheim: A Perspective and Appreciation." *American Sociological Review*, XXIV (1959), 462-465.

————— "Emile Durkheim: Enemy of Fixed Psychological Elements." *American Journal of Sociology*, LXII (1958), 662-664.

Angell, Robert Cooley. *Free Society and Moral Crisis.* Ann Arbor: University of Michigan Press, 1965.

Anton, John P. *Naturalism and Historical Understanding.* Albany: State University of New York Press, 1967.

Aron, Raymond. *German Sociology.* Glencoe, Ill.: Free Press, 1964.

———— *Main Currents in Sociological Thought*, 2 vols. New York: Basic Books, Inc., 1965.

Bacon, Francis. *The New Organon and Related Writings*. Indianapolis, Ind.: The Bobbs-Merrill Company, Inc., 1960.

Barker, Ernest. *Principles of Social and Political Theory*. London: Oxford University Press, 1961.

Barnes, Harry Elmer, ed. *An Introduction to the History of Sociology*. Chicago: University of Chicago Press, 1948.

———— "Durkheim's Contribution to the Reconstruction of Political Theory," *Political Science Quarterly*, XXXV (1920), 236-254.

Baur, E. Jackson. "Public Opinion and the Primary Group." *American Sociological Review*, XXV (1960), 208-219.

Becker, Howard, and Harry Elmer Barnes. *Social Thought from Lore to Science*, 3 vols., 3rd ed. New York: Dover Publications, Inc., 1961.

Bellah, Robert N. *Beyond Belief*. New York: Harper and Row, 1970.

Belot, Gustave. "Emile Durkheim: *L'Année sociologique*." *RP*, XLV (1898), 649-657.

———— "Sur la definition du socialism." *RP*, XXXVI (1893), 182-189.

Bendix, Reinhard. *Max Weber*. Garden City, N.Y.: Doubleday and Company, Inc., 1962.

Benedict, Ruth. *Patterns of Culture*. New York: New American Library of World Literature, Inc., 1946.

Benoît-Smullyan, Emile. "The Development of French Sociologistic Theory and Its Critics in France. Unpublished Ph.D. dissertation, Harvard University, 1937.

Benrubi, Issak. *Les Sources et les courants de la philosophie contemporaine en France*, 2 vols. Paris: Félix Alcan, 1933.

Berger, Peter L. *Invitation to Sociology: A Humanistic Perspective*. Garden City, N.Y.: Doubleday and Company, Inc., 1963.

———— and Thomas Luckmann. *The Social Construction of Reality*. Garden City, N.Y.: Doubleday and Company, Inc., 1967.

Bergson, Henri. *The Two Sources of Morality*. Translated by R. Ashley Audra and Cloudesley Brereton. Garden City, N.Y.: Doubleday and Company, Inc., 1935.

Bernard, L. I. "The Conditions of Social Progress." *The American Journal of Sociology*, XXVIII (1922), 21-48.

Bertocci, Peter A., and Richard M. Millard. *Personality and the Good*. New York: David McKay Company, Inc., 1963.

Bierstedt, Robert. *Emile Durkheim*. London: Weidenfeld and Nicolson, 1966.

———— "The Means-End Schema in Sociological Theory." *American Sociological Review*, III (1938), 665-671.

Binet, Alfred. *The Mind and the Brain*. London: Kegan Paul, Trench, Trübner and Company, Ltd., 1907.

Binkley, Luther J. *Contemporary Ethical Theories*. New York: Citadel Press, 1961.

Black, Max, ed. *The Social Theories of Talcott Parsons*. Englewood Cliffs, N.J.: Prentice-Hall, 1961.

Blau, Peter M. "Structural Effects." *American Sociological Review,* XXV (1960), 178-193.

Bloch, Herbert A. "Methodological Presuppositions for the Evaluation of Social and Sociological Theory." *American Journal of Sociology,* L (1944), 29-37.

Bosserman, Phillip. *Dialectical Sociology.* Boston: Porter Sargent, Publisher, 1968.

Bouglé, Célestin. *Bilan de la sociologie française contemporaine.* Paris: Félix Alcan, 1938.

_____ *The Evolution of Values.* Translated by Helen S. Sellars, with an introduction by Roy Wood Sellars. New York: Henry Holt and Company, 1926.

_____ *The French Conception of "Culture Générale" and Its Influence upon Instruction.* New York: Bureau of Publications, Teachers College, Columbia University, 1938.

_____ *Qu'est-ce que la sociologie?* Paris: Félix Alcan, 1932.

_____ Georges Davy, Marcel Granet, Raymond Lenoir, and René Maublanc. "L'Oeuvre sociologique d'Emile Durkheim." *Europe,* XXII (1930), 281-304.

Bourgeois, Emile. "M. Fustel de Coulanges." *RIE,* XIX (1890), 121-151.

Boutroux, Emile. "Du rapport de la philosophie aux sciences." *RMM* (1911).

Bradley, F. H. *Ethical Studies.* Indianapolis, Ind.: Bobbs Merrill Company, Inc., 1951.

Bramson, Leon. *The Political Context of Sociology.* Princeton, N.J.: Princeton University Press, 1961.

Brandt, Richard B. *Ethical Theory.* Englewood Cliffs, N.J.: Prentice-Hall, Inc., 1959.

_____ ed. *Social Justice.* Englewood Cliffs, N.J.: Prentice-Hall, Inc., 1962.

_____ ed. *Value and Obligation.* New York: Harcourt, Brace and World, Inc., 1961.

Braybrooke, David. *Philosophical Problems of the Social Sciences.* New York: Macmillan Company, 1965.

Brogan, D. W. *The Development of Modern France 1870-1939,* Vol. I. New York: Harper and Row, 1966.

Brown, Roger. *Social Psychology.* New York: Free Press, 1965.

_____ and Eric H. Lenneberg. "A Study in Language and Cognition." *Journal of Abnormal and Social Psychology,* XXXXIX (1954), 454-462.

Bruner, Jerome S. *The Progress of Education.* Cambridge, Mass.: Harvard University Press, 1960.

Carritt, E. F. *Morals and Politics.* Oxford, Eng.: Clarendon Press, 1935.

Casserley, J. V. Langmead. *The Christian in Philosophy.* London: Faber and Faber, Ltd., 1949.

Clark, Terry N. "Emile Durkheim and the Institutionalization of Sociology in the French University System." *Archives européennes de sociologie,* IX, 37-71.

———— "The Structure and Functions of a Research Institute: *The Année sociologique,*" *Archives européennes de sociologie,* IX, 72-91.

Clausen, John A., ed. *Socialization and Society.* Boston: Little, Brown and Company, 1968.

Cobban, Alfred. *A History of Modern France,* 3 vols. Baltimore: Penguin Books, 1961.

Cohen, Morris R., and Ernest Nagel. *An Introduction to Logic and Scientific Method.* New York: Harcourt, Brace and Company, 1934.

Collingwood, Robin George. *The Idea of Nature.* Oxford, Eng.: Clarendon Press, 1945.

Collins, James. *A History of Modern European Philosophy.* Milwaukee, Wisc.: Bruce Publishing Co., 1954.

Comte, Auguste. *A General View of Positivism.* Translated by J. H. Bridges, London: Trubner and Company, 1865.

———— *The Positive Philosophy.* Freely translated and condensed by Harriet Martineau. New York: Calvin Blanchard, 1858.

Copleston, Frederick. *A History of Philosophy,* Vols. IV, VI, VII, VIII. Garden City, N.Y.: Doubleday and Company, Inc., 1967.

Coser, Lewis. *The Functions of Social Conflict.* New York: Free Press, 1956.

Coser, Rose L., ed. *The Family: Its Structure and Functions.* New York: St. Martin's Press, 1964.

Coulanges, Fustel de. *The Ancient City.* Garden City, N.Y.: Doubleday and Company, Inc., 1955.

Crawford, Lucy Shepard. *The Philosophy of Emile Boutroux.* New York: Longmans, Green and Company, 1924.

Curtins, Ernst Robert. *The Civilization of France.* Translated by Olive Wyon. Vintage Books. New York: Alfred A. Knopf and Random House, 1962.

Cuvillier, Armand. *Ou va la sociologie française?* Paris: Marcel Rivière et cie, 1953.

Dahrendorf, Ralf. *Essays in the Theory of Society.* Stanford, Calif.: Stanford University Press, 1968.

Davy, Georges. *Emile Durkheim.* Paris: Louis-Michaud, 1912.

———— "Emile Durkheim." *Revue française de sociologie,* I (1960), 3-24.

———— "Emile Durkheim." *RMM,* XXVI (1919), 181-198; XXVII (1920), 71-112.

———— "La sociologie de M. Durkheim." *RP,* LXXXII (1911), 47-71, 160-185.

———— *Sociologues d'hier et d'aujourd'hui.* Paris: Félix Alcan, 1931.

DeGeorge, Richard T., ed. *Ethics and Society.* Garden City, N.Y.: Doubleday and Company, Inc., 1966.

DeGré, Gerard. *Society and Ideology.* New York: Hamilton Press, 1943.

Dennes, William Ray. *The Methods and Presuppositions of Group Psychology.* University of California Publications in Philosophy, No. 6. Berkeley and Los Angeles: University of California Press, 1924.

Deploige, Simon. *Le Conflit de la morale et de la sociologie.* Louvain and Paris: Félix Alcan, 1912.

Dohrenwend, Bruce. "Egoitism, Altruism, Anomie: A Conceptual Analysis of Durkheim's Types." *American Sociological Review* (1959), 466-472.

Dollard John. "Culture, Society, Impulse and Socialization." *American Journal of Sociology,* XLV (1939), 50-63.

Douglas, Jack D. *The Social Meanings of Suicide.* Princeton, N.J.: Princeton University Press, 1967.

Dray, William H. *Philosophy of History.* Englewood Cliffs, N.J.: Prentice-Hall, Inc., 1964.

Duncker, Karl. "Ethical Relativity." *Mind,* XLVIII (1939), 39-57.

Duprat, Guillaume L. *Science sociale et démocratie.* Paris: V. Giard and E. Brière, 1900.

Dyck, Arthur. "A Gestalt Analysis of the Moral Data and Certain of Its Implications for Ethical Theory. Unpublished Ph.D. dissertation, Harvard University, 1965.

Edel, Abraham. "Anthropology and Ethics in Common Focus." *Journal of the Royal Anthropological Institute of Great Britain,* LXXXXII, Part I (1962), 55-72.

————*Ethical Judgment.* Glencoe, Ill.: Free Press, 1955.

Edman, Irwin. "Naturalism." *Encyclopaedia of the Social Sciences,* Vol XI, ed. Edwin A. A. Seligman and Alvin Johnson. New York: Macmillan Company, 1933.

Edwards, Paul. *The Logic of Moral Discourse.* New York: Free Press, 1955.

Eisenstadt, S. N., ed. *The Protestant Ethic and Modernization.* New York: Basic Books, Inc., 1968.

Emmet, Dorothy. *Rules, Roles and Relations.* New York: St. Martin's Press, 1966.

Engels, Friederich. *The Origins of the Family, Private Property and the State in light of the researches of Lewis H. Morgan.* New York: International Publishers, 1942.

Essertier, Daniel. *Philosophes et savants française du XXe siècle.* Paris: Félix Alcan, 1930.

———— *Psychologie et sociologie: Essai de bibliographie critique.* Paris: Félix Alcan, 1927.

Etzioni, Amitai. *Modern Organizations.* Englewood Cliffs, N.J.: Prentice-Hall, Inc., 1964.

Evans-Pritchard, E. E. *Social Anthropology and Other Essays.* Glencoe, Ill.: Free Press, 1962.

Faris, Ellsworth. "Emile Durkheim on the Division of Labor in Society." *American Journal of Sociology,* XXXX (1934), 376-377.

Fauconnet, Paul. "The Pedagogical Work of Emile Durkheim." *American Journal of Sociology,* XXVII (1923), 529-553.

———— "The Durkheimian School in France." *Sociological Review,* XIX (1927), 15-20.

———— and Marcel Mauss. "Sociologie." *Grande encyclopédie,* XXX, 165-176.

Finney, Ross L. *A Sociological Philosophy of Education.* New York: Macmillan Company, 1928.

Firth, Raymond. *Human Types.* New York: New American Library, 1958.

——— *We, the Tikopia.* Boston: Beacon Press, 1963.

Firth, Roderick. "Ethical Absolutism and the Ideal Observer." *Philosophy and Phenomenological Research,* XII (1952), 317-345.

Frankena, William K. *Ethics.* Englewood Cliffs, N.J.: Prentice-Hall, Inc., 1963.

——— "The Naturalistic Fallacy." *Mind,* XLVIII (1939), 464-477.

Freund, Julien. *The Sociology of Max Weber.* New York: Random House, 1968.

Friedmann, Georges. "La Thèse de Durkheim et les formes contemporaines de la division du travail," *Cahiers internationaux de sociologie,* XIX (1955), 45-58.

Friedrich, Carl J., ed. *The Public Interest. Nomos V.* Yearbook of the American Society for Political and Legal Philosophy. New York: Atherton Press, 1966.

Garnett, A. Campbell. *Ethics.* New York: Ronald Press Company, 1960.

Gerth, Hans, and C. Wright Mills. *Character and Social Structure.* New York: Harcourt, Brace and World, Inc., 1953.

——— *From Max Weber: Essays in Sociology.* New York: Oxford University Press, 1958.

Gehlke, C. E. *Emile Durkheim's Contributions to Sociological Theory.* New York: Columbia University Press, 1915.

Gierke, Otto von. *Natural Law and the Theory of Society 1500-1800.* Translated with an introduction by Ernest Barker. Cambridge, Eng.: Cambridge University Press, 1934.

——— *Political Theories of the Middle Ages.* Translated with an introduction by Frederic Maitland. Cambridge, Eng.: Cambridge University Press, 1900.

Gold, Martin. "Suicide, Homicide, and the Socialization of Aggression," *American Journal of Sociology,* LXII (1958), 651-661.

Goldenweiser, Alexander A. "Religion and Society: A Critique of Durkheim's Theory of the Origin and Nature of Religion," in *Reader in Comparative Religion,* 2nd ed. Edited by William A. Lessa and Evon Z. Vogt. New York: Harper and Row, 1958.

Goodsell, Willystine. *The Conflict of Naturalism and Humanism.* New York: Teachers College, Columbia University, 1910.

Gouldner, Alvin W. *Patterns of Industrial Bureaucracy.* Glencoe, Ill.: Free Press, 1954.

——— "The Norm of Reciprocity: A Preliminary Statement." *American Sociological Review,* XXV (1960), 161-178.

Greef, Guillaume de. *Introduction à la sociologie,* Vols. I and II. Brussels: Gustave Mayolez, 1886; Paris: Félix Alcan, 1886.

Grice, Russell. *The Grounds of Moral Judgment.* Cambridge, Eng.: Cambridge University Press, 1967.

Gunn, John A. *Modern French Philosophy: A Study of the Development since Comte.* London: T. Fisher Unwin, 1922.

Gurvitch, Georges. *Essais de sociologie.* Paris: Librairie du Recueil Sirey, 1938.

──────── *Morale théorique et science des moeurs.* Paris: Presses Universitaires de France, 1961.

────────ed. *Traité de sociologie.* Paris: Presses Universitaires de France, 1958.

──────── and Wilbert E. Moore, eds. *Twentieth Century Sociology.* New York: Philosophical Library, Inc., 1945.

Halasz, Nicholas. *Captain Dreyfus.* New York: Simon and Schuster, 1955.

Halbwachs, Maurice. "La Doctrine d'Emile Durkheim." *RP,* LXXXV (1918), 353-411.

──────── "Individual Psychology and Collective Psychology." *American Sociological Review,* III (1938), 615-623.

Hamelin, Octave. *Le Système de Renouvier.* Paris: J. Vrin, 1927.

Heider, Fritz. *The Psychology of Interpersonal Relations.* New York: John Wiley and Sons, Inc., 1958.

Heimann, Eduard. *Reason and Faith in Modern Society.* Middletown, Conn.: Wesleyan University Press, 1961.

Henderson, Stella Van Petten. *Introduction to Philosophy of Education.* Chicago: University of Chicago Press, 1947.

Hollander, E. P., and Raymond Hunt, eds. *Current Perspectives in Social Psychology.* New York: Oxford University Press, 1963.

Homans, George Caspar. *Social Behavior: Its Elementary Forms.* New York: Harcourt, Brace and World, Inc., 1961.

──────── *The Human Group.* New York: Harcourt, Brace and Company, 1950.

──────── *The Nature of Social Science.* New York: Harcourt, Brace and World, Inc., 1967.

Horowitz, Irving, ed. *The New Sociology.* New York: Oxford University Press, 1965.

Hughes, H. Stuart. *Consciousness and Society.* Vintage Books. New York: Random House, 1958.

Janet, Paul. *The Theory of Morals.* New York: Charles Scribners Sons, 1883.

Jaspers, Karl. *Kant.* Edited by H. Arendt and translated by Ralph Manheim. New York: Harcourt, Brace and World, Inc., 1957.

Jensen, Howard E. "Sociology as a Science: Autonomous or Natural?" *Sociology and Social Research,* XVIII (1934), 503-510.

Joad, C. E. M. *Guide to Philosophy.* New York: Dover Publications, 1936.

Jones, Richard M., ed. *Contemporary Educational Psychology.* New York: Harper and Row, 1967.

Jones, W. T. *The Sciences and the Humanities.* Berkeley: University of California Press, 1967.

Kant, Immanuel. *Critique of Pure Reason.* Translated by Norman Kemp Smith. New York: Modern Library, 1958.

———————*Education.* Ann Arbor: University of Michigan Press, 1960.

——————— *The Moral Law.* Translated by H. J. Paton. New York: Barnes and Noble, 1950.

——————— *Perpetual Peace.* Indianapolis, Ind.: Bobbs-Merrill Company, Inc., 1957.

Kardiner, Abram and Edward Preble. *They Studied Man.* Cleveland, Ohio: World Publishing Company, 1965.

Kaufman, Felix. *Methodology of the Social Sciences.* New York: Oxford University Press, 1944.

Kluckhohn, Clyde. *Culture and Behavior.* New York: Free Press, 1962.

——————— "Ethical Relativity: Sic et Non." *Journal of Philosophy*, LII (1955), 663-677.

Kohlberg, Lawrence. "The Development of Children's Orientations Toward a Moral Order: I. Sequence in the Development of Moral Thought." *Vita Humana,* VI (1963).

——————— "From Is to Ought: How to Commit the Naturalistic Fallacy and Get Away with it in the Study of Moral Development." *Cognitive Development and Epistemology.* Edited by Theodore Mischel. New York: Academic Press, 1971 (in press).

——————— "Moral Development and Identification." *Child Psychology.* Sixty-Second Yearbook of the National Society for the Study of Education. Chicago: University of Chicago Press, 1963.

——————— "On Moral Education." Paper presented at the Conference on the Role of Religion in Public Education. Cambridge, Mass., May 19 and 20, 1966.

Köhler, Wolfgang. *Gestalt Psychology.* New York: Liveright Publishing Corporation, 1947.

Körner, Stephan. *Kant.* Middlesex, Eng.: Penguin Books, Ltd., 1955.

Krikorian, Yervant H., ed. *Naturalism and the Human Spirit.* New York: Columbia University Press, 1944.

Kuhn, Thomas S. *The Structure of Scientific Revolutions.* Chicago: University of Chicago Press, 1962.

Lachelier, Henri. "Les Lois psychologiques dans l'école de Wundt." *RP,* XIX (1885), 121-146.

Lacombe, Roger. *La Méthode sociologique de Durkheim, Étude critique.* Paris: Félix Alcan, 1926.

Lalande, André. "Philosophy in France." *Philosophical Review,* XIV (1905), 429-454.

Laski, Harold J. *Authority in the Modern State.* New Haven: Yale University Press, 1919.

——————— *The State in Theory and Practice.* London: George Allen and Unwin, Ltd., 1935.

Lazarsfeld, Paul F., William H. Sewell and Harold L. Wilensky, eds. *The Uses of Sociology.* New York: Basic Books, Inc., 1967.

LeBon, Gustave. *The Crowd.* New York: The Viking Press, 1960.

Lerner, Daniel, ed. *The Human Meaning of the Social Sciences.* Cleveland, Ohio: World Publishing Company, 1959.

Levine, George, and Owen Thomas, eds. *The Scientist vs. the Humanist.* New York: W. W. Norton and Company, Inc., 1963.

Lévy-Bruhl, Lucien. *History of Modern Philosophy in France.* London: Kegan Paul, Trench, Trübner and Co., Ltd., 1899.

_____ *How Natives Think.* New York: Washington Square Press, 1966.

Lindsay, A. D. *The Modern Democratic State.* New York: Oxford University Press, 1962.

Loewenstein, Karl. *Max Weber's Political Ideas in the Perspective of our Time.* Boston: University of Massachusetts Press, 1966.

Long, Wilbur H. "The Philosophy of Charles Renouvier and Its Influence on William James." Unpublished Ph.D. dissertation, Harvard University, 1925.

Loomis, Charles P., and Zona K. Loomis. *Modern Social Theories,* 2nd ed. Princeton, N.J.: D. Van Nostrand Company, Inc., 1965.

Lovejoy, Arthur O. *The Revolt Against Dualism,* 2nd ed. LaSalle, Ill.: Open Court Publishing Company, 1960.

Luethy, Herbert. *France against Herself.* Translated by Eric Mosbacher. New York: Meridian Books, Inc., 1957.

Lyons, David. *Forms and Limits of Utilitarianism.* Oxford: Clarendon Press, 1965.

MacRae, Duncan, Jr. "A Test of Piaget's Theories of Moral Development." *The Journal of Abnormal and Social Psychology,* XLIX (1954), 14-18.

_____ "The Development of Moral Judgment in Children." Unpublished Ph.D. dissertation, Harvard University, 1950.

Madge, John. *The Origins of Scientific Sociology.* New York: Free Press, 1962.

Maine, Henry Sumner. *Ancient Law.* Boston: Beacon Press, 1963.

Malinowski, Bronislaw. *Crime and Custom in Savage Society.* Paterson, N.J.: Littlefield, Adams and Co., 1964.

_____ *Magic, Science and Religion.* Garden City, N.Y.: Doubleday and Company, Inc., 1948.

_____ *Man and Culture.* New York: Harper and Row, 1964.

Mandelbaum, Maurice. "Societal Facts." *British Journal of Sociology,* VI (1955), 305-317.

_____ *The Phenomenology of Moral Experience.* Glencoe, Ill.: Free Press, 1955.

_____ *The Problem of Historical Knowledge.* New York: Harper and Row, 1967.

_____ Francis W. Gramlich, and Alan R. Anderson, eds. *Philosophic Problems.* New York: Macmillan Company, 1957.

Manuel, Frank E. *The Prophets of Paris.* Cambridge, Mass.: Harvard University Press, 1962.

Margenau, Henry. *Ethics and Science.* Princeton, N.J.: D. Van Nostrand Company, Inc., 1964.

Marjolm, Robert. "French Sociology—Comte and Durkheim." Translated by Alice P. and Hugh D. Duncan. *American Journal of Sociology,* XLII (1937), 693-704.

Martindale, Don, ed. *Functionalism in the Social Sciences.* Monograph

5 in a series sponsored by the American Academy of Political and Social Science. Philadelphia, February 1965.

Martineau, James. *Types of Ethical Theory,* Vols. I and II. Oxford, Eng.: Clarendon Press, 1886.

Maus, Heinz. *A Short History of Sociology.* London: Routledge and Kegan Paul, 1962.

Mauss, Marcel. "In Memoriam: l'oeuvre inédit de Durkheim et de ses collaborateurs." *Année sociologique,* New Series, I (1923), 7-29.

———— *Sociologie et anthropologie.* Paris: Presses Universitaires de France, 1950.

Mayer, Jacob P. *Political Thought in France from the Revolution to the Fifth Republic.* London: Routledge and Kegan Paul, Ltd., 1961.

Meiklejohn, Alexander. *Education between Two Worlds.* New York: Atherton Press, 1966.

Melden, A. I., ed. *Essays in Moral Philosophy.* Seattle: University of Washington Press, 1958.

Merton, Robert. "Durkheim's *Division of Labor in Society." American Journal of Sociology,* XL (1934), 319-328.

———— "Social Structure and Anomie." *American Sociological Review,* III (1938), 672-682.

———— *Social Theory and Social Structure.* Glencoe, Ill.: Free Press, 1957.

———— Leonard Broom, and Leonard S. Cottrell, eds. *Sociology Today.* New York: Basic Books, 1959.

Messner, Johannes. *Social Ethics: Natural Law in the Modern World.* Translated by J. J. Doherty. St. Louis and London: B. Herder Books, 1949.

Michels, Roberto. *First Lectures in Political Sociology.* Translated with an introduction by Alfred de Grazia. Minneapolis: University of Minnesota Press, 1949.

Mihanovich, Clement S. *Social Theorists.* Milwaukee, Wisc.: Bruce Publishing Company, 1953.

Mill, John Stuart. *Auguste Comte and Positivism.* Ann Arbor: University of Michigan Press, 1965.

———— *A System of Logic.* New York: Harper and Brothers, 1859.

———— *Utilitarianism,* 4th ed. London: Longmans, Green, Reader, and Dyer, 1871.

Miller, Hugh. *An Historical Introduction to Modern Philosophy.* New York: Macmillan Company, 1947.

Mills, C. Wright. *The Sociological Imagination.* Oxford, Eng.: Oxford University Press, 1959.

Mitchell, M. Marion. "Emile Durkheim and the Philosophy of Nationalism." *Political Science Quarterly,* XLVI (1931).

Montesquieu, Baron de. *The Spirit of the Laws.* New York: Hafuer Publishing Company, 1949.

Moore, G. E. *Principia Ethica.* Cambridge, Eng.: Cambridge University Press, 1929.

Moore, Wilbert E. *Social Change.* Englewood Cliffs, N.J.: Prentice-Hall, Inc., 1963.

Morgan, Lewis Henry. *Ancient Society*. Cleveland, Ohio: World Publishing Company, 1963

Muelder, Walter G. *Moral Law in Christian Social Ethics*. Richmond, Va.: John Knox Press, 1966.

Mueller, Iris Wessel. *John Stuart Mill and French Thought*. Urbana: University of Illinois Press, 1956.

Naegele, K. D. "Attachment and Alienation: Complementary Aspects of the Work of Durkheim and Simmel." *American Journal of Sociology*, LXIII (1958), 580-589.

Nisbet, Robert A. "Conservatism and Sociology." *American Journal of Sociology*, LVIII (1952).

_____ *Emile Durkheim*. Englewood Cliffs, N.J.: Prentice-Hall, Inc., 1965.

_____ *The Sociological Tradition*. New York: Basic Books, 1966.

Northrop, F. S. C. *The Complexity of Legal and Ethical Experience*. Boston: Little, Brown and Company, 1959.

Nowell-Smith, P. H. *Ethics*. Baltimore: Penguin Books, 1954.

O'Connor, William T. *Naturalism and the Pioneers of American Sociology*. Catholic University of America Studies in Sociology, Vol. VII. Washington, D.C.: Catholic University of America Press, 1942.

O'Dea, Thomas F. *The Sociology of Religion*. Englewood Cliffs, N.J.: Prentice-Hall, Inc., 1966.

Olafson, Frederick A. *Justice and Social Policy*. Englewood Cliffs, N.J.: Prentice-Hall, Inc., 1961.

_____ *Society, Law and Morality*. Englewood Cliffs, N.J.: Prentice-Hall, Inc., 1961.

Ottaway, A. K. C. "The Educational Sociology of Emile Durkheim." *British Journal of Sociology*, VI (1955), 213-227.

Painter, Georges S. "The Idea of Progress." *American Journal of Sociology*, XXVIII (1922), 257-282.

Parodi, Dominique. *Le Problème moral et la pensée contemporaine*. Paris: Félix Alcan, 1910.

Pareto, Vilfredo. *Sociological Writings*. New York: Frederick A. Praeger, 1966.

Parsons, Talcott. *Essays in Sociological Theory*. Glencoe, Ill.: Free Press, 1954.

_____ *Social Structure and Personality*. Glencoe, Ill.: Free Press, 1964.

_____ *Societies: Evolutionary and Comparative Perspectives*. Englewood Cliffs, N.J.: Prentice-Hall, 1966.

_____ *Sociological Theory and Modern Society*. New York: Free Press, 1967.

_____ *The Social System*. New York: Free Press, 1951.

_____ *The Structure of Social Action*. Glencoe, Ill.: Free Press, 1949.

_____ and Edward A. Shils, eds. *Toward a General Theory of Action*. New York: Harper and Row, 1951.

_____ and Neil J. Smelser. *Economy and Society*. New York: Free Press, 1965.

_____ Edward Shils, Kaspar D. Naegele, and Jesse R. Pitts. *Theories of Society*, Vols. I and II. Glencoe, Ill.: Free Press, 1961.

Passmore, John. *A Hundred Years of Philosophy*. London: Gerald Duckworth & Co., Ltd., 1957.

Paulsen, Friedrich. *Introduction to Philosophy*. Translated by Frank Thilly. New York: Henry Holt and Company, 1930.

Perry, Ralph Barton. *General Theory of Value*. Cambridge, Mass.: Harvard University Press, 1954.

Piaget, Jean. *Judgment and Reasoning in the Child*. Translated by Marjorie Warden. Totona, N.J.: Littlefield, Adams and Co., 1966.

_____ *The Moral Judgment of the Child*. Translated by Marjorie Gabian. New York: Free Press, 1965.

Picard, Roger. *La Philosophie sociale de Renouvier*. Paris: Librairie Marcel Rivière, 1908.

Popper, Karl R. *The Open Society and Its Enemies*. London: Routledge and Kegan Paul, Ltd., 1945.

_____ *The Poverty of Historicism*. London: Routledge and Kegan Paul, Ltd., 1961.

Prichard, H. A. *Moral Obligation*. London: Oxford University Press, 1949.

Prosch, Harry. *The Genesis of Twentieth Century Philosophy*. Garden City, N.Y.: Doubleday and Company, Inc., 1964.

Quillian, William F. *The Moral Theory of Evolutionary Naturalism*. New Haven, Conn.: Yale University Press, 1945.

Radcliffe-Brown, A. R. *Structure and Function in Primitive Society*. Glencoe, Ill.: Free Press, 1952.

Rader, Melvin. *Ethics and Society*. New York: Henry Holt and Company, 1950.

Radin, Paul. *Primitive Man as Philosopher*. New York: Dover Publications, Inc., 1957.

Randall, John Herman, Jr. *The Career of Philosophy*, Vols. I and II. New York: Columbia University Press, 1962.

_____ *Nature and Historical Experience*. New York: Columbia University Press, 1958.

Rapoport, Anatol. *Operational Philosophy*. New York: Harper and Brothers, 1953.

Redfield, Robert. *The Little Community* and *Peasant Society and Culture*. Chicago: University of Chicago Press, 1960.

_____ *The Primitive World and Its Transformations*. Ithaca, N.Y.: Cornell University Press, 1953.

Renouvier, Charles. *Science de la morale*. Paris: Librairie Philosophique de Ladrange, 1869.

Rex, John. *Key Problems of Sociological Theory*. London: Routledge and Kegan Paul, 1961.

Ross, Ralph. *Symbols and Civilization*. New York: Harcourt, Brace and World, Inc., 1957.

Ross, Sir W. David. *Foundations of Ethics*. Oxford, Eng.: Clarendon Press, 1939.

_____ *The Right and the Good.* Oxford, Eng.: Clarendon Press, 1930.

Rossi, Peter H. "Emile Durkheim and Georg Simmel." *American Journal of Sociology,* LXII (1958), 579.

Rousseau, Jean Jacques. *Emile.* Woodbury: Barron's Educational Series, Inc., 1964.

_____ *The First and Second Discourses.* New York: St. Martin's Press, 1964.

_____ *The Social Contract and Discourses.* New York: E. P. Dutton and Company, Inc., 1950.

Royce, Josiah. *Herbert Spencer: An Estimate and Review.* New York: Fox, Duffield and Co., 1904.

_____ *The Spirit of Modern Philosophy.* New York: W. W. Norton and Company, 1967.

Ruggiero, Guido de. *The History of European Liberalism.* Boston: Beacon Press, 1959.

_____ "Positivism," in *Encyclopedia of the Social Sciences,* Vol. XII, ed. Edwin R. A. Seligman and Alvin Johnson. New York: Macmillan Company, 1934.

Rumney, Jay. *Herbert Spencer's Sociology.* New York: Atherton Press, 1966.

Sabine, George H. *A History of Political Theory.* New York: Holt, Rinehart and Winston, 1961.

Sahlius, Marshall D., and Elman R. Service, eds. *Evolution and Culture.* Ann Arbor: University of Michigan Press, 1960.

Saint-Simon, Comte Henri de. *Selected Writings.* Oxford, Eng.: Basil Blackwell, 1952.

Salomon, Albert. *In Praise of Enlightenment.* Meridan Books. Cleveland, Ohio: World Publishing Company, 1962.

Schaub, Edward. "A Sociological Theory of Knowledge." *Philosophical Review,* XXIX (1920), 319-339.

Schlick, Moritz. *Problems of Ethics.* Translated by David Rynin. New York: Dover Publications, Inc., 1939.

Schneider, Louis, ed. *Religion, Culture and Society.* New York: John Wiley and Sons, Inc., 1964.

Schnore, Leo F. "Social Morphology and Human Ecology." *American Journal of Sociology,* LXII (1958), 620-634.

Scott, John A. *Republican Ideas and the Liberal Tradition in France: 1870-1914.* New York: Octagon Books, Inc., 1966.

Seger, Imogen. "Durkheim and His Critics on the Sociology of Religion." Monograph Series. Bureau of Applied Social Research. Columbia University. September 1957.

Selby-Bigge, L. A., ed. *British Moralists.* Vols. I and II. Indianapolis, Ind.: Bobbs-Merrill Company, Inc., 1964.

Sidgwick, Henry. *Outlines of the History of Ethics.* Boston: Beacon Press, 1960.

_____ *The Methods of Ethics.* Chicago: University of Chicago Press, 1962.

Simmel, Georg. *Conflict and the Web of Group-Affiliations.* Glencoe, Ill.: Free Press, 1955.

Simpson, George. *Emile Durkheim.* New York: Thomas Y. Crowell Company, 1963.

Slater, Philip E. *Microcosm.* New York: John Wiley and Sons, Inc., 1966.

Small, Albion W. *General Sociology.* Chicago: University of Chicago Press, 1905.

————*Origins of Sociology.* Chicago: University of Chicago Press, 1924.

———— "Some Contributions to the History of Sociology." *American Journal of Sociology,* XXVIII (1923), 385-418, 711-734.

Smith, T. V., and William Debbins. *Constructive Ethics.* Englewood Cliffs, N.J.: Prentice-Hall, Inc., 1948.

Soltau, Roger H. *French Parties and Politics 1871-1921.* New York: Russell and Russell, Inc., 1965.

Sorokin, Pitirim. *Contemporary Sociological Theories.* New York: Harper and Brothers, 1928.

Sparshott, F. E. *An Enquiry into Goodness.* Toronto: University of Toronto Press, 1958.

Spencer, Herbert. *The Data of Ethics,* 2nd ed. London and Edinburgh· Williams and Norgate, 1879.

———— *The Study of Sociology.* Ann Arbor: University of Michigan Press, 1961.

Spencer, Robert F., ed. *Method and Perspective in Anthropology: Papers in Honor of Wilson D. Wallis.* Minneapolis: University of Minnesota Press, 1954.

Stace, W. T. *The Concept of Morals.* New York: Macmillan Company, 1962.

Stark, Werner. *The Fundamental Forms of Social Thought.* New York: Fordham University Press, 1963.

————*Social Theory and Christian Thought.* London: Routledge and Kegan Paul, Ltd., 1958.

Stein, Maurice R. *The Eclipse of Community.* Princeton, N.J.: Princeton University Press, 1960.

————and Arthur Vidich, eds. *Sociology on Trial.* Englewood Cliffs, N.J.: Prentice-Hall, Inc., 1963.

Stephen, Leslie. *The Science of Ethics.* London: Smith, Elder, & Co., 1882.

Stevenson, Charles L. *Ethics and Language.* New Haven, Conn.: Yale University Press, 1944.

Stone, Julius. *Human Law and Human Justice.* Stanford, Calif.: Stanford University Press, 1965.

———— *The Province and Function of Law.* Cambridge, Mass.. Harvard University Press, 1950.

Storing, Herbert J., ed. *Essays on the Scientific Study of Politics.* New York: Holt, Rinehart and Winston, Inc., 1962.

Strauss, Leo. *Natural Right and History.* Chicago: University of Chicago Press, 1953.

Stromberg, Roland N., ed. *Realism, Naturalism, and Symbolism.* New York: Harper and Row, 1968.

Tannery, Paul. "La Théorie de la matière d'après Kant." *RP,* XIX (1885), 26-27.

Tarde, Gabriel. "Criminalité et santé sociale." *RP,* XXXIX (1895), 148-162.

Taylor, Paul W. *The Moral Judgment.* Englewood Cliffs, N.J.: Prentice-Hall, Inc., 1963.

Timasheff, N. S. *An Introduction to the Sociology of Law.* Cambridge, Mass.: Harvard University Committee on Research in the Social Sciences, 1939.

Tiryakian, Edward A. "Le Premier message d'Emile Durkheim." *Cahiers internationaux de sociologie,* XLIII (1967), 21-23.

_____ ed. *Sociological Theory, Values and Sociocultural Change.* New York: Harper and Row, 1967.

_____ *Sociologism and Existentialism.* Englewood Cliffs, N.J.: Prentice-Hall, Inc., 1962.

Tönnies, Ferdinand. *Community and Association.* Translated by Charles P. Loomis. London: Routledge and Kegan Paul, 1955.

Tocqueville, Alexis de. *The Old Régime and the French Revolution.* Garden City, N.Y.: Doubleday and Company, Inc., 1955.

_____ *Democracy in America,* Vols. I and II. New York: Random House, 1945.

Warnock, Mary. *Ethics Since 1900.* London: Oxford University Press, 1960.

Webb, Clement C. J. *Group Theories of Religion and the Individual.* London: George Allen & Unwin, Ltd.; New York: Macmillan Company, 1916.

Weber, Max. *The Sociology of Religion.* Boston: Beacon Press, 1963.

_____ *The Theory of Social and Economic Organization.* Glencoe, Ill.: Free Press, 1947.

Westermarck, E. *Ethical Relativity.* Paterson, N.J.: Littlefield, Adams and Company, 1960.

Whitehead, Alfred North. *The Aims of Education and Other Essays.* New York: Free Press, 1967.

Wilson, Ethel M. "Durkheim's Sociological Method." *Sociology and Social Research,* XVIII (1934), 511-518.

Windelband, Wilhelm. *A History of Philosophy,* Vols. I and II. Harper Torchbooks. New York: Harper and Row, 1958. Translated by James H. Tufts. New York: Macmillan Company, 1901.

Wolff, Kurt H., ed. *Emile Durkheim, 1858-1917.* Columbus: Ohio State University Press, 1960.

Wolin, Sheldon S. *Politics and Vision.* Boston: Little, Brown and Company, 1960.

Worms, René. "Emile Durkheim." *Revue internationale de sociologie,* XXV (1917), 561-568.

Worsley, P. M. "Emile Durkheim's Theory of Knowledge." *Sociological Review,* New Series, IV (1956), 47-62.

Wundt, Wilhelm. *Ethics.* Vol. I, *The Facts of the Moral Life.* Translated by Julia Gulliver and Edward B. Titchener. London: Swan Sonnenschein and Co., Ltd., 1908.

———— *Ethics.* Vol. II, *Ethical Systems.* Translated by Margaret F. Washburn. London: Swan Sonnenschein and Co., Ltd., 1906.

———— *Ethics.* Vol. III, *The Principles of Morality and the Departments of the Moral Life.* Translated by Margaret F. Washburn. London: Swan Sonnenschein and Co., Ltd., 1901.

———— *Outlines of Psychology.* Translated by Charles H. Judd. New York: Gustav E. Stechert, 1897.

Zilboorg, Gregory. "Sociology and the Psychoanalytic Method." *American Journal of Sociology,* XLV (1939), 341-355.

Index